The Re-inherited Mind

*Recovering the Judaeo-Christian
inheritance in Western Christendom*

The Re-inherited Mind

Recovering the Judaeo-Christian inheritance in Western Christendom

The Revd Dr Kevin F. Scott

ISBN: 9781549528019

To
Rosamund & Colin
Gregory & Imogen
Richard & Victoria

CONTENTS

CHAPTER 1
INTRODUCTION

This book is about a cure for dementia. Not the kind of dementia that afflicts an individual in old age, destroying memory and intellectual processing, neutralising powers and reducing the person to uncomprehending vacancy and helplessness. But the kind of dementia which does all that to an entire civilisation. It begins with an inability to recall truths with which it has been familiar for centuries and upon which it has built a great edifice of learning, of intellectual achievement, of scientific discovery, of technological invention, of industrial manufacturing, of commercial and financial independence and success, all of which has commanded world-wide recognition and respect. When this great civilisation begins to dement, it cannot remember the foundational principles upon which its greatness was forged. Its glory lasts for a while, but it finds that it cannot go back to repeat those foundational calculations upon which its success was built - simply because it has forgotten them. So it resorts to 'getting by' as best it can on the resources that it has accumulated, but failing to husband or augment those resources, it finds the assets that it once had in abundance becoming thin and sparse in places and lacking altogether in others. In the words of G. K. Chesterton, it finds *its food won't feed, its cures won't cure and its blessings refuse to bless* (1). It is in decline.

In the early stages, this civilisation tries to adapt to its weaknesses and conceal them; it expects less of itself, it becomes more dependent, but it does so in such a way as to shield itself and the outside world, from the realities of its plight. It tells itself all is well, but its self-reassurance tends to sound shrill and unconvincing. It strategises to make it appear that it is much more healthy than it really is, like a confidence trickster who spends ostentatiously to give an impression of wealth that he does not have. The persistent efforts of its ministers of state to 'talk it up' are increasingly contradicted by a general feeling that it is run down, falling into disrepair and dysfunction. It tries lavish building plans to produce spectacular landmarks, but these only increase the contrast with the surrounding decrepitude.

As it avoids exposure so it becomes more reluctant to gain ground, content only to hold what it can, and hide its loss of the rest. It thus becomes anxious and fearful and likely to exhibit poor judgement when demands are made upon it. It begins to exhibit spasms of panic, over-reacting to crises and failing to act wisely in the face of them. Its officers resort to hoping nothing bad will happen on their watch and that they will be able to demit their offices before the next crisis breaks. This is understandable because, as the civilisation declines, the instinct for scapegoating and punishing those seen as responsible for mishaps increases. It becomes harder to find worthy occupants of the public offices as a consequence.

To cope with its memory loss and the decline of its powers of creativity and imagination, the dementing civilisation resorts to acronyms and slogans which are repeated continually to remind it of its own intentions. Its diminished capacities mean that it is less able to cope with alternative notions which it excludes by declaring them 'off-message'. The dogma becomes ever more trite and increasingly unrelated to the actual circumstances on the ground. But still it ploughs on. It can do nothing else - there is no care home for a dementing civilisation.

The Church, to a very great extent the custodian of the civilisation's spiritual memory, is itself dementing. In the last hundred years or so, the Western Protestant Church has exercised a ministry rather like that of a mad physician who believes that if he contracts all the diseases of his patients, he will be in an infinitely better position to help them. The exercise of this deluded quackery has meant that together with the patient, the Church has abandoned its powers of recall and has no counsel to give and no medicine to prescribe.

This might by now be sounding a little pessimistic! But unlike individual elderly patients, forgetful civilisations can remember again and find new life. It is possible that the Greek civilisation actually forgot how to read and write around the beginning of the first millennium BC, forgetting its alphabet, grammar and script, and reinventing their written language some three hundred years later. Old Greek has been identified as the Mycenaean language tagged Linear B which went out of use quite suddenly and was not replaced by what we know as ancient Greek for several centuries. The point is that civilisations do not lose their memories, they just stop remembering. This means that they can start remembering again, with some encouragement from a Church which can do the same. It may have been thoroughly pathological for the Church to abandon its recollections of its own Gospel, but it will be transformatively health-giving for it to start recalling these things again.

That is what this book is about. The idea of a re-inherited mind comes from H. Richard Niebuhr who describes the problem of western civilisation as a *Christendom which under the influence of repeated industrial, economic, scientific and political revolutions was in imminent danger of forgetting those fundamental principles, learned in its past and effective in its present, which had made those revolutions possible. Christendom faced - as it still does - the prospect of what has been called the "disinherited mind," that is, of a mind without capital with which to work, without fundamental, established axioms on which to rely, a mind so impoverished that it must justify itself in each present moment by its works, in constant activity* (2). Niebuhr's point is that the Church failed to keep ransacking the library of its own inheritance, and more importantly, failed to keep returning to its Lord, in faith and penitence, to learn again its truth, to hear again the word of the Good Shepherd without which it can only stray and become lost and thus disqualify itself from the public office to which it was appointed. When it does this, it merely buries itself in good works which, however laudable, are no substitute for its prophetic office. And as it does this, the Church's mind becomes progressively disinherited from its treasury of Apostolic witness, forgetful of the counsel of its forefathers and disengaged from the philosophical methodology by which it was able to forge a genuine Christian worldview.

In order to recover this treasury, the Church must be restored to the holiness proper to it. The holy ones, the saints, the Christians, are those who, when they are true to their calling, come when they are summoned by God. They attend to his word and obey his voice. Refusal or failure to do this is a particular form of unholiness or profanity. It is the real meaning of sloth. Karl Barth defines intellectual sloth, in which the mind refuses to come to God, as *stupidity*. He says: *[Stupidity] is disobedience, unbelief, and ingratitude to God, who gives himself to be known by man in order that he may be wise and live. It is thus a culpable relapse into self-contradiction; into incoherent, confused and corrupt thought and speech and action. We have to realise this if we are to estimate its power; the strange but mighty and tumultuous and dreadful force of its role - the leading role - which it plays in world history, in every sphere of human life, and whether secretly or flagrantly in each individual life. Whether great or small, every confidence or trust or self-reliance on what we can, and think we should, say to ourselves when we reason apart from the Word of God is stupid. Every attitude in which we think we can authoritatively tell ourselves what is true and good and beautiful, what is right and necessary and salutary, is stupid. All thought and speech and action which we think we can and should base on this information is stupid. And this whole frame of mind is self-evidently and even more acutely stupid in the form in which we think we have so heard the Word of God, and so appropriated its direction and wisdom in the guise of a principle or system, that we have no need to hear or practise it afresh; in the form, therefore in which we regard ourselves as so enlightened by the Word of God that we think we can throw off our open-ness to further and continuous instruction. Where an uncontrolled truth or rule, however clear, possesses man or men in the way in which they ought to be governed only in the knowledge of God Himself and by His living word, we certainly have to do with a revelation, and in principle with the whole economy, of stupidity (3).*

The urgent task of the Church is to return from a great excursion into this field of stupidity, to a place of holiness, to a sanctified mind. And let us not think this return to a sanctified mind is to the vague and confused disposition of the studiously muddled clergyman. No, the sanctified mind will bring its best powers, its greatest energies, its sharpest perceptions to the task of understanding the realities in which we live and the nature of our being before God. It will be able to dispel that impression that has enjoyed so much general reception in our current age, that Christianity is empty of intellectual or philosophical power, that it is all but defunct.

If this book contributes in the slightest degree towards this return to a sanctified mind and its recollection of holy truth, and the restoring of the reputation of Christianity as profoundly dependable, both intellectually and morally, then it will have fulfilled its task. We will first consider the nature of *knowledge*, *faith* and *memory*. The first of these is important because the Judaeo-Christian tradition brought a unique and powerful understanding of what knowledge is and how it is acquired over both Greek and Kantian and post-Kantian perceptions. We cover this ground in chapter 2. To recover a sound understanding of the meaning of faith as the acceptance of evidence is vitally important in face of the rising public presupposition that *faith* means merely credulity, the believing of something without any evidence. This false definition has been widely promulgated by the new atheists who wish to project the idea that Christians are indeed demented, stupid and hold to unwarranted and groundless superstitions. In repudiation of this position, chapter 3 offers a sound definition of faith and explains the way in which evidence of different kinds is heard and examined and either accepted or rejected. Chapter 4 investigates the role of memory and its function in bringing the meaning and significance of past events to bear on a present situation. It is an approach which seeks to reinstate *recollection* as the proper mode both of understanding of truths which have a long temporal meaning and of the evaluation of evidence from history. Memory can be used to challenge reductionist readings of reality and the obsession with the present and with the individual which we find in Expressionist and Post-modern thought.

In all the subsequent chapters, our understanding of knowledge from chapter 2, of faith from chapter 3 and memory from chapter 4, is applied to various aspects of what it is to be a human being. For each aspect, we compare and contrast the current socially constructed understanding of human beings with conclusions reached from the perspective of purely physical causality (i.e. understanding we might reach without recourse to evidence from the Judaeo-Christian tradition) and from metaphysical causality (which admits such evidence). The idea is to build up an intellectually defensible reading of what we are as human beings, the nature of our human lives and the scope and potential of our possibilities. Once we admit the well-scrutinised testimony of several millennia of our history and especially of its specific historical influences on European civilisation we can arrive at a self-understanding which challenges many of the contemporary assumptions of our age.

In chapter 5 we begin our enquiry proper into the nature of the human being. We consider social, biological and naturalist definitions, before recalling the Judaeo-Christian witness as to the uniqueness and high office accorded to man. At this point it may be useful to speak of the use of language in this book. The word 'man' as used has four significances. The first is to denote the species *homo sapiens*. This includes every member of the species without differentiation. This is a major use of the term within these pages. Grammatically, it is a masculine noun and pronouns which refer to it agree in gender and case. The second usage is in the context of the phrase "God and man". Again, this includes every member of the species, but the emphasis is on the theological understanding of human beings. 'Man' in this context means the aeviternal vicegerent creature of God, appointed to his right hand. 'Human' and 'human being' connote the natural origins of the primate species, while 'man' connotes his divine origin and appointment of which there is much to be said in this book. Thirdly, the word 'man' is essential to the language of the Incarnation of Jesus Christ. In the Incarnation, God did not merely become 'a human being,' just a single individual, nor merely 'human', a generalised representation of human qualities. Rather he became Man - a single individual man and, a Representative of the entire race. It is the property of the word 'man' to capture this individual singularity and the representation of the plurality, which makes the word entirely indispensable for theological discussion. The fourth meaning of the word 'man' is, of course, the male of the species and its use in this sense in the subsequent chapters is confined only to discussion of marriage and sex.

The author thus makes no apology for using the 'man' as defined in the various categories above, for it surely would be absurd to write a book about geese, without ever mentioning the word 'goose' for fear of upsetting all the ganders in the flock. Would it not be patronising and insulting to all the ganders to assume that they had no understanding of the use of language and, in particular, the different meanings attached to a single word? Would it not be, in itself, 'ganderist'? Heaven forfend! We will, accordingly, agree that the sauce for the goose is equally applicable to all members of the species without discrimination.

When it comes to human dignity, the modern world gives a confused message: on the one hand for example, there seems to be a continual expansion of 'rights' which might be thought to dignify us in some way. But, at the same time, there is a marked diminution of trust, which is considerably degrading. Chapter 6, attempts to found human dignity of more secure basis and align it with a high view of the office of the human being. Related to this is the matter of human interiority: the inner life which drives our true nature and gives it stature and distinction. In common with other attributes of humanity, there is a detectable instinct away from the powers of the human interior, an effort to live deliberately superficially, to live in the external world of party-going and imbibed stimuli, rather than commune inwardly. We will enquire into this in chapter 7.

In chapter 8, we consider human liberty, the various movements and principles which curtail it and the powers that authorise and sustain it. Here again we find the Judaeo-Christian inheritance providing a high view of human freedom - which we often find it hard to live up to. With freedom comes responsibility and a full-orbed human authority which we shy away from because we think it asks too much of us.

Chapter 9 recalls the impact of the Judaeo-Christian tradition on human endeavour both empowering it intellectually via the derivation from it of a new definition and understanding of science, and impelling it by creating an atmosphere of possibility from its contingent world view. In this chapter we aim to lay to rest the common mistaken impression that Christianity and science are in some way opposed to one another, and restore the recollected truth that modern science is a product of Christianity and the reasoning which has arisen from it. The idea that Christianity is anti-intellectual, and its obverse, that science has in some way 'disproved' Christianity, are both dislodged by the careful review of some of the vast amount of historical evidence available. In particular, the work of John Philoponus, a little known Christian physicist from the 6th and 7th centuries is honoured as one of the key thinkers in the establishment of modern science from Christian principles.

When it comes to the discussion of human error in chapter 10, we recall an ancient principle from the Judaeo-Christian tradition, the idea of holiness and sanctity. Because the concept is in part metaphysical it has been neglected ever since the Enlightenment, because the latter tended only to admit concepts that it could fully explain. Sanctity is not such a concept, but it is intelligible enough to be a powerful measure of human conduct and attitudes and has a long history of inspiring principled living. Chapter 11 plots the dysfunction of modern human relationships in terms of narcissism using the ancient parable of the Prodigal Son. The experience and life of the Prodigal in the far country is thus charted in modern terms and answered by the Judaeo-Christian concept of the presence and reality of God moderating and governing all human relationships. Finally, chapter 12 considers human time and destiny, and particularly the impact of the Incarnation and Resurrection of Christ upon ancient and modern philosophies of time.

REFERENCES FOR CHAPTER 1

(1) G. K. Chesterton, *The Everlasting Man*, p114

(2) H. Richard Niebuhr, *Theology, History, and Culture*, p7

(3) Karl Barth, *Church Dogmatics, Volume 4:2*, p412

CHAPTER 2
KNOWLEDGE

2.1. Socially constructed knowledge

We begin this enquiry at an everyday level. The most immediate answer to the question, *how do we know something*, is that it is something everybody knows. We know what everyone else knows. This is the basis of what Peter Berger speaks of as the social construction of reality (1). We estimate everything against a 'philosophical wallpaper' - the array of truths and assumptions which form the reality upon which general corporate agreement has been reached. If we are given some new idea or thought to examine we hold it up and assess it against the backdrop of this wallpaper. We use this to make factual, moral and even scientific estimates of things and we do it automatically usually without much analysis.

Every community has a shared set of generally accepted 'truths' by which judgements are made, conversation becomes possible, words and deeds are appraised and by which a corporate conscience is informed. This is the socially constructed reality in which consists the basic form of human knowledge. It operates as a network into which all the participants are in some way connected. Even in the ancient world, the socially constructed reality was maintained and circulated by a surprisingly rapid flow of rumour and news. The Roman postal service was remarkably efficient and the habit of disseminating information on notice boards erected wherever three roads met gave access to all kinds of news items which came, as a consequence, to be called *trivia*. This, coupled with a huge volume of commercial traffic by road and sea, innumerable wandering prophets, soothsayers and diviners, and the oracles from temples, serviced the socially constructed reality of the Roman world. A similar supply of information informed mediaeval Europe and this was immeasurably enhanced by the invention of printing which added the ubiquitous instrument of the *pamphlet* to the burgeoning availability of data and opinion. Then came radio and TV, the Internet and social media, the engagement with which has reached a degree of mania with its clientele.

Never before has a socially constructed reality proved so responsive and dynamic as it has in recent years. Everyone can 'log on' to this infinite array of knowledge, hints, rumours and scandal, comment on what he reads and add his insights. And inevitably we come to evaluate things presented to us in terms of what we have read and heard. Much of the material fed in to the socially constructed reality may be of quite poor quality, information may be faulty, news items may be fake, advice may be poor, but the average quality may be raised by the circulation of material from learned journals, quality newspapers and published books. The sheer number of participants and the breadth of the network mean that there is a widespread habit of review, which has the effect of refining the content.

Nonetheless, it is, to a great extent, freewheeling. It lacks any agreed reference points and would tend to drift perhaps arbitrarily, but for the fact that it is powerfully driven by politicians, governments and parties who have a definite interest in urging it in a particular direction. Politicians want to shape the socially constructed reality in a direction which will attract votes; advertisers have their understandable commercial motive; special-interest groups want to recruit to their cause.

If there is a rigorous commitment to free speech, all this lobbying is relatively benign because all shades of opinion can be voiced within it. But if it become more coercive and various kinds of pressure are applied to constrain the socially constructed reality towards a particular pole, if certain ideas be acceptable, but others be deemed illegal or unutterable, the socially constructed reality may become less socially-constructed - more power-constructed.

2.2. Power-Constructed Reality

A power-constructed reality can be a frightening and oppressive force. Czeslaw Milosz has written a penetrating description of life and thought under the power-constructed reality of Stalinist controlled Poland (2). He says people who flee from these regimes describe them as 'psychically unbearable'. It was not so much the bad housing, poor standard of living, and intense tedium, but the psychological suffocation that the power-constructed reality brings about. Not being able to think, speak, discuss anything with anybody is worse than not being able to breathe, to be looking over one's shoulder before one speaks, to be glancing anxiously at those who may, from malevolent intent, seek to overhear and then make their report, strikes down on the soul as an unbearable weight.

Milosz describes the consequences of these pressures. People who live under them are often hollowed-out by the experience: there is a deep and intense sorrow for the loss of humanity that the constraints engender. These are relieved or restrained in perhaps three ways: by suicide, by defection or by dissimulation, you die, you flee or you pretend. The dissimulation, Milosz points out, is the kind of internal psychological procedure used by Muslims, who don't really believe in Islam, in order to stay alive and endure in low-tolerance Islamic cultures. This dissimulation is called *taqiya* or *ketman*. The one who practices *ketman* cultivates an inner mental life which is kept as completely separate as possible from the outer life of conformity. He relieves the tension of living under the oppression of groupthink, by entertaining himself by his practice of dissimulation. He is a loud conformer in public, he reads the right books, the right newspapers and declaims on occasion for that which he opposes and against that which he embraces. The practitioner of aesthetic *ketman*, applauds approved art and literature in public, but has a collection of proscribed books at home. Professional *ketman* involves following the approved line in professional work while secretly harbouring a contrary and non-approved opinion about the matter in question. Milosz points out that the heart of *ketman* is self-realisation against the power-constructed reality, it is an internal self-affirmation in the face of an overwhelming dehumanising force. It becomes a vital asset for survival, but its exercise is brave and can be exhilarating.

The rise of political correctness in the West was the beginning of a transmutation of a socially-constructed reality into a power-constructed one. There was a time in Britain when you could think anything, believe anything, and *say* anything. But not so much now. Voicing an unacceptable thought, even using an unacceptable word, even being discovered to hold an unacceptable opinion can result in dismissal from employment and even arrest on a criminal charge. Already some people are feeling the psychic pressure, in speaking to a friend they may look over their shoulder first before leaning forward and speaking with a low voice. At the time of writing the coercion is light and mostly social. A conversation ensues in a dinner party and all the guests but one is of an 'orthodox' persuasion. The dissenter remains silent. It is not that he fears his views will not be accepted, but that he, personally, will be held in a contempt greatly disproportionate to the extremity of his opinion. It is not that there will be a socially-awkward moment which will pass as the conversation moves on. No, the dissenter will be shunned, socially obliterated from the group, 'defriended' from their Facebook accounts and generally reduced to pariah status. At one level, this is trivial and absurd, at a more serious and deeper level it is dangerous and deeply corrosive. This is because social obliteration may come to mean exclusion from a professional society, or from a trade union, the loss of employment, prosecution and ultimately incarceration. We have not moved along this line very far, but there are signs that the pace is accelerating.

Meanwhile, in this connection there has been a recent development in the sphere of sharply divided political opinion which has been referred to as 'post-truth'. This is a product of two opposing socially-constructed realities which have a very different reading of political statements, events and policies. Each side tends to dismiss the readings made by the other as 'post-truth' which really means false. This has arisen because a substantial proportion of the population, hitherto silenced by the dominant power-constructed reality, suddenly found its voice and it is offering its own reading of reality which profoundly challenges the previously dominant one.

2.3. The Necessary World of Greek Thought

In all but perhaps a few socially constructed realities there is an element of *necessity*. This is especially true of power-constructed realities. There tends to be a 'correct' opinion about things; some things are not open to question or challenge but are enshrined in what are practically *a priori* principles. Perhaps this an inheritance from the Enlightenment and the return to Platonic thinking which took place in the 17th and 18th centuries. If the idea of the socially-constructed reality being sustained and advanced by a network is added in, the result is something which looks like a modern transmogrification of some aspects of Platonism.

Of course, the idea of a socially-constructed reality is very different from the Greek thought of Plato and Aristotle. They do have certain parallels, however, and together, perhaps they represent the world of knowing which was confronted by the advent of Christianity upon gentile civilisation in the first century AD. Behind both Plato and Aristotle, there is the idea that everything has meaning derived from a common 'logos' or principle which informs the reality of all things. In the platonic realm of forms lay the perfect reality of everything, which was only imperfectly represented in the sensible phenomenal realm. Every object in the phenomenal realm had its perfect counterpart in the realm of forms. Thinking was done in the realm of forms and this, in principle, gave intellectual access to everything in its perfect representation. Therefore, according to Plato, all serious investigation of things ought to take place in the realm of thought where things were represented perfectly, rather than in the phenomenal realm where things were imperfect and unreliable.

Aristotle placed a little more confidence in the phenomenal realm and considered investigation of it worthwhile, but retained essentially the same worldview as Plato and his model of the regimes of form and phenomenon. Because the reality of all things was considered perfectly informed in the realm of ideas, they were all accessible to comprehension by intellectual activity. Here we encounter that foundational concept of Greek thought, that things were *necessarily* the way they were. In principle, everything could be understood perfectly through intellectual activity alone. Science could be conducted from an armchair because things had to be inevitably the way they are and that could be understood by careful reasoning alone. This was because everything was connected to the mind of the thinker through the intellectual plane of forms which Plato considered divine.

Aristotle's necessary thinking is clearly revealed by his mode of investigating the phenomenal realm. He devised a series of questions which could be asked about anything to elucidate what kind of thing it was, so that its precise nature could be classified. It was as if an imaginary rack of pigeon-holes was created each containing different types of thing and each representing one of a series of sub-types and sub-sub-types and so on. The questions Aristotle devised were to determine exactly into which pigeon-hole each item under consideration should be placed. It has to be said that this whole approach proved very useful - especially in botanical and zoological classification, but it did have one very great weakness: the nature of the contents of each pigeon-hole had to be specified beforehand, and therefore the method had a built-in principle of necessity at its core. So although Aristotle's powers of observation were impressive, and the precision and care with which he constructed his taxonomical method were beyond reproach, many of the details of his conclusions ultimately were shown to be wrong because of the presuppositions of his necessary thinking.

This intellectual gentile world into which Christianity made its debut had therefore a popular level, a socially constructed reality of generally agreed truths and mores on the one hand, and a more precise method of thinking which had a principle of necessity at its core. Putting aside, for the moment, the content of the Christian message, we can consider first, the impact of the Gospel on the understanding of the nature of knowledge. The Judaeo-Christian tradition has a very different understanding of how human beings come to know things. In the Graeco-Roman world of the first century, the popularly held body of knowledge and the intellectually analysed version both, in different ways, originated from the human mind, or maybe from the collective human mind. In the popular case everything was assessed against what a large number of other people thought, in the latter case, from careful inward reflection by an individual. In both cases the knowledge was, so to speak, home-grown.

2.3. Judaeo-Christian Understanding of Knowledge

When, through the preaching of the Apostle St Paul and his colleagues, the Judaeo-Christian story broke upon the world at large, it brought an entirely different perspective on the nature and origins of knowledge. For centuries, the Jews had sung Psalm 19:

The law of the Lord is perfect,
reviving the soul;
the testimony of the Lord is sure,
making wise the simple;
the precepts of the Lord are right,
rejoicing the heart;
the commandment of the Lord is pure,
enlightening the eyes;
the fear of the Lord is clean,
enduring forever;
the ordinances of the Lord are true,
and righteous altogether.
More to be desired are they than gold,
even much fine gold;
sweeter also than honey
and drippings of the honeycomb. (3)

The knowledge that makes the Israelite wise, enlightened, righteous and alive comes from the God of Israel. It is not surprising that he should understand the matter this way. To be an Israelite from beginning to end is to enjoy an identity which came about by a revelation of God which transformed a slave people who had little identity or status into a nation defined by divine choice. In a way everything Israel was, every good thing that Israel enjoyed, every asset accrued by Israel was super-natural - Israel came from a decision of God and Israelite knowledge and wisdom arose therefrom. The main point for our purposes at present, is that the people of Israel did not *generate* the knowledge, rather they *received* it, and, what is more, they received it *from a source over which they had no control.*

Any knowledge Aristotle had arose from his engagement with a world with which he was already necessarily connected. Any understanding he came to of anything was determined by the prior structure of knowledge which we represented above as a rack of pigeon-holes. For Israel there were no pigeon-holes and the processes of discovery for Israel were much less tidy and more turbulent that the organised discipline of Aristotle's method. For Aristotle, the pigeon-holes were labelled and the questions prescribed. These were *Quaestio* questions, asked when the range of possible answers is strictly circumscribed. Is something of the first kind, or the second, or the third? And so on. All very methodical, structured and controlled. The sort of question Israel asked was an *Interrogatio* question: "What on earth is this?" - the kind of question, the answer to which the questioner has absolutely no idea what it could be. And when the answer comes, it makes him puzzle, he reels and staggers, flounders about trying to make sense of what has been shown him. The answer he gets turns his world upside down.

Most importantly, the direction of travel of the information is to be noted in the two cases. In Aristotle's case the order created by the rack of pigeon-holes is impressed on the reality to which it is applied. The purpose of the *Quaestio* questions is to facilitate the passage of information from Aristotle's mind to effect an ordering of the observed reality. In Israel's case the information moves the other way, it comes from the observed independent reality and changes the mind of the observer as it impresses its truth upon it. Aristotle's approach is safe and conservative: it has already defined the range of acceptable answers to its questions, so it can ask them confidently. The restraint this introduces limits severely the advance of knowledge possible and tends towards tedium. Israel's approach is dangerous and radical: the answers occupy an infinite field of possibility, the conclusions may not be palatable or even fully intelligible, but clearly have much more power to enlighten the mind of the enquirer.

2.3.1. An example of the limitations of necessary thinking to the advance of knowledge.

Aristotle's world of knowledge was indeed safe and conservative, but it was also very limiting. An example of its limiting of science is to be found in the response of Greek science to the postulate of Aristarchus that the earth rotated around the sun. Aristarchus of Samos was a 4th - 3rd century BC astronomer and mathematician and it occurred to him that astronomical observations could equally be interpreted by a heliocentric model of the cosmos as by a geocentric model and evidently he went some distance to investigate the possibilities of the former. He realised that if the heliocentric model was correct, the observations of the stars might vary due to parallax, the absence of which variation, he did not think to be fatal to his theory if the stars were far enough away.

But as carefully worked out as his hypothesis was, it was rejected by the Greek scientific world. This was largely because of an Aristotelian assumption that objects tend to move to their 'natural' position: heavy objects move 'downwards', light ones, 'upwards'. This would mean that the earth would have to be located at the centre of gravity of the universe and be at its rest position there. Secondly, if the earth were moving at what would have to be a great speed, what effect would this have on objects flung into the air? Throwing something in an easterly direction should be impossible. These arguments appeared, in the second and third centuries BC, to be entirely reasonable, and more than enough to set Aristarchus' idea to one side, but they were all the more successful in this, because they were sustained by the idea that things could only be as they were thought to be in the necessary world of Greek thought. It would take the powerful Judaeo-Christian insight of contingence to enable Copernicus to change our minds about the cosmos (4).

The danger of this externally sourced knowledge is demonstrated by the hostility that Jeremiah receives in response to his unwelcome prophecies. His enemies oppose him on the ground that *the law shall not perish from the priest, nor counsel from the wise, nor the word from the prophet* (Jeremiah 18:18). Each of these vehicles of knowledge, the law, wise counsel and word of prophecy was not regarded as internally generated but inspired from the God of Israel, who himself was not integrated into the existence of his people, but was always separate from them, bound only to them by the Covenant of which he was the author. They were habituated to having the word of the prophet always within earshot. The only period which was an exception to this was the reign of Solomon who quite pointedly did not have a prophet in his retinue. The rise of the wise men during this time may have been an attempt to 'home-brew' knowledge, to organise and tame it, to regulate it and control it, but even then it was recognised to be a gift of God. However, as used as they were to knowledge being acquired from an independent, external source, early Israel was quite slow to translate this into a general theory of knowledge. Earlier, in the late Bronze Age, the period described by the book of Judges, the people of Israel was quite technologically backward, compared with their opponents. The Philistines had developed iron extraction, making wrought iron and pioneering blacksmithing which gave them a huge military advantage. The idea of knowledge being something received from an external source, was not extended into natural science or engineering or any other scientific discipline until the Christian era and it was here that the Israelite understanding of knowledge came as a direct challenge to the prevailing Aristotelian presuppositions of the Greek world.

2.4. Jesus Christ and the Nature of Knowledge

The advent of Jesus Christ marked a pivotal point in human understanding of the nature of knowledge for three reasons.

(i) The person of Jesus exhibited a uniqueness beyond that of any other individual. And this uniqueness lay not only in his personal character and attributes, but also much deeper in the nature of his being. He made an unforgettable impression on those who met him, not merely as an accomplished or exceptionally able person might do, but beyond that to a degree which forced observers to look for new categories with which to understand him.

(ii) Secondly, Jesus was not merely a passive object of his contemporaries' enquiry: he appeared to come with an express determination to be known and to be known rightly. He had a mission to reveal who he was and why he had come. He deliberately engaged his observers in such a way as their minds and hearts were transformed. Not only was his person and nature comprehended by those who met him, but his very character and purpose shaped their minds and re-oriented their wills.

(iii) Thirdly, by his coming Jesus expanded the constituency of the people of God from the compass of Israel and Judaism to include a new gentile constituency, which, in due course, would span the world. The unique perspectives of Israel were both sharpened and heightened by Jesus Christ, but also universalised to a worldwide currency of knowledge.

Consider, for example, the declaration of St Peter concerning Jesus at Caesarea Philippi:*Now when Jesus came into the district of Caesarea Philippi, he asked his disciples, "Who do people say that the Son of Man is?" And they said, "Some say John the Baptist, others say Elijah, and others Jeremiah or one of the prophets." He said to them, "But who do you say that I am?" Simon Peter replied, "You are the Christ, the Son of the living God." And Jesus answered him, "Blessed are you, Simon Bar-Jonah! For flesh and blood has not revealed this to you, but my Father who is in heaven. And I tell you, you are Peter, and on this rock I will build my church, and the gates of hell shall not prevail against it* (Matthew 16:13ff).

When Jesus asks what the general opinion is concerning himself, he is enquiring of the witness of the socially-constructed reality around him. Normally he did not seem very interested in what people thought of him, so it is not clear why he made this enquiry. Perhaps he wanted to draw a contrast between the common opinions of human beings and a revelation from God. The content of the socially-constructed reality of Jesus is, however, interesting to observe. When asked, they come up with several possibilities: maybe he's John the Baptist, or Elijah, or Jeremiah, or one of the prophets. They are looking in the Jewish equivalent of the Aristotelian pigeon holes. From Israelite history, there were a set of categories into which a preacher or prophet might fit, but clearly Jesus does not think any of them will satisfy Peter's estimation of him. In his response, Peter rejects all the Aristotelian type categories and the witness of the socially-constructed reality with which he is surrounded and goes out on limb. What he actually says is a wild statement: You are the Messiah, the Son of the living God. Of course "messiah" was an Israelite category, but Jesus, even accepting the title, radically redefines it in the course of his ministry, well away from the vision of a national leader who will throw off Roman domination. In fact, it is clear that the opinion in the market place did not include 'messiah' - his ministry, speech and demeanour evidently did not suggest a nationalistic leader with a political and military vision. This must mean that Peter was himself already understanding Jesus' messiahship as different from the popular image.

But then he goes on to a very remarkable and new category: Jesus is the Son of the Living God. What he saw in Jesus Christ pretty well excluded all the categories available to the crowd. They were not entirely on the wrong lines: Jesus did speak as a prophet and there were echoes of Elijah and John the Baptist in the character of his ministry. But these categories, Peter saw, were inadequate to describe and contain all that Jesus was. The way he spoke, the way he used words, not merely to describe, but to effect his will, the way he acted towards rich and poor, the politically powerful, and religious rulers, the way he exercised authority over the natural order and over unseen and ill-defined evils, all pointed to Jesus being far more than a prophet. Peter comes from a long Israelite tradition of regarding knowledge as that which is received - and here, like no other time in his life, he is certainly receiving knowledge. Moreover, we can see that the knowledge he was receiving was shaping his mind. He didn't force it into one of the pre-existing pigeon holes of Jewish thought. This new knowledge made a new place for itself in Peter's mind which needed a new descriptive vehicle to express.

When Jesus says, *flesh and blood have not revealed this to you, but my Father who is in heaven*, his meaning is not entirely clear. Did he mean that Peter's conclusions came from observing Jesus Christ, whom God the Father had sent, and thus the revelation was truly from God the Father, or did he mean that Peter was in some way inspired to say what he said? Whether or not Peter did receive some special insight from God, it clear from the rest of the New Testament, that it was Jesus' speech, actions, vision, mighty works, suffering, death and resurrection which forced the disciples into new categories of thinking. But it is useful to distinguish *insight* from *opinion*. Everyone has opinions and the socially-constructed reality is largely made up of them. But what is clearly of enormously greater value is an *insight* - something which is not generated within us, not borrowed from our fellows, but given to us from an external source, from God or from that which we are investigating.

The prologue to John's Gospel sums up the general conclusion reached by the Apostles concerning Jesus:- *And the Word became flesh and dwelt among us, and we have seen his glory, glory as of the only Son from the Father, full of grace and truth. ..... and from his fullness we have all received, grace upon grace.*

It represents a powerful instance where the brute manifestation of something, forces a conclusion by the observers which cuts across all their preconceived categories of reality. Especially in John's Gospel, it appears that they were most reluctant to reach the conclusion that they did concerning Jesus, but his reality compelled them to reach it. The idea that the Son of God meant there was a relatedness within God himself was substantially new: it was not clearly prefigured in the Old Testament, and the continual Jewish repetition, 'The Lord our God is One' (Deuteronomy 6:4) provided a powerful resistance to the conclusion to which the Apostles were forced. There evidently were three highly persuasive aspects to Jesus' self-manifestation: glory, grace and truth. The Apostles concluded that all three of these were only traceable to God himself and could only be exhibited by God in person. Glory has to do with God's reputation. All the great things that had been heard about God: his holiness, the power of his voice, his aseity, his implacable resolve to be for his people and for his people to be for him, his severity and his compassion which were not antithetical but collaborative, all these attributes of God's glory, they saw manifest and in unqualified operation in Jesus. In the Old Testament days, the Israelites learned that God had an unremitting will to have them as his own people, on his terms, to their infinite advantage. The operation of this unremitting will is called God's grace. And this grace is what the disciples saw controlling and issuing from everything Jesus did and everything he said. It was an unmistakeable divine mark. By 'truth' is not meant merely a factually accurate statement, although this is not excluded. To say that they perceived the truth in Jesus meant much more to the Apostles. What was involved in seeing Jesus, was a penetration into a realm of reality which might have been glimpsed here and there in the Old Testament, but now was fully disclosed to them. To be with Jesus, was like entering into the very life of God, where truth and genuineness were the air the Apostles breathed, where they were uniquely aware of their kinship with God himself. The Apostles' witness in this matter, teaches us that Jesus' manifestation of the truth was far more than a mere resolution of true statements from false, but had to do with the authenticity of the life of God, and life of a human being in God.

2.5. Jesus Christ and the Challenge to Greek Theories of Knowledge

But the reflections in the prologue to St John's Gospel were the result of relatively immediate reflections - years, maybe decades later, to be sure, but still betraying a fresh perception and discovery. Jesus sent the minds of all those who had to do with him, reeling - but the initial astonishment gave way to a much more enduring intellectual and moral seismic shift. This was especially true when the Gospel entered gentile territory and the world of Greek thought.

In the first place, what the Apostles observed exploded the basic presupposition of Plato. According to Plato, the world of the divine, the sphere of forms and intellect and perfection, cannot possibly have any contact with the fluctuating imperfections of the material, phenomenal realm, for which Plato had a certain contempt. In fact there was an insuperable barrier between the realm of forms and the phenomenal realm according to Plato. This famous *chorismos* kept everything in order, in the right places and particularly prevented the chaotic imperfections of the phenomenal realm from corrupting and contaminating the realm of forms. But the Incarnation of Jesus Christ did the fatal thing and bridged this *chorismos*. St Paul says that Jesus broke down the dividing wall between Jew and Gentile, which was certainly a seismic event, but at the same time the Incarnation broke down an invisible, intellectual barrier which really had prevented the Greek world from taking as seriously as it should have, the phenomenal, material realm.

Thus, contrary to Plato, and thanks to the Incarnation of Jesus Christ, we find that the material realm is just as much the province of divine presence and power as any other imaginable realm. The material world matters much more than it ever did under the Greeks. Knowledge which comes from the material world needs now to be taken much more seriously in the light of Christ's coming. It was St Athanasius, that champion of the Nicene settlement, who saw the implications of the Incarnation so clearly in this regard. He saw that, in repudiation of the Greek demoting of the material order, the Incarnation appropriates the whole of it to Christ. He saw that space and time were now to be regarded as properties of the Son of God. The material order thence became the sphere of divine action, and as St Paul so clearly saw, the whole of creation then has become the object of divine redemption. The grounds for Greek reserve about the phenomenal realm are thus addressed, not by screening God off from the imperfect material order, but by God's invasion of it with his power and will to restore it.

If God can be at home in the material order in the way that Jesus demonstrated, then so can man. The diffidence of the Greeks with respect to the phenomenal realm meant that they had difficulties taking it seriously and therefore did rather few experiments. They did do some, but even their treatment of the results betrays the fact that observations they made did not have a ruling place in their thinking.

An example of the disadvantage of this Greek presupposition of material inferiority is the investigation of refraction by Claudius Ptolemy and the way he treated his results. Claudius Ptolemy measured the angle of incidence and angle of refraction when light passed from air to water in order to determine the law which relates the two. The nearest function he could find to fit the data was a parabola. It would have been reasonable if Ptolemy had accepted that although the parabola does not quite fit the data, it is a useful approximation to them. But to him, the parabola, being a geometric function, belonged to the perfect world of forms, and the data he had measured belonged to the imperfect realm of phenomena, so the data would have to give way to the curve. So he edited his list of values to make his data fit the curve. He thus missed an opportunity to understand refraction much better. If he had believed his data and looked for a different geometric function, he might have found it, because Greek geometry would have been easily capable of it.

2.6. Knowledge and the Resurrection

There was a further profound change in world-view which was brought about by Jesus Christ, and specifically by his resurrection from the dead. In an exhaustive study, N. T. Wright has shown that the idea of bodily resurrection from the dead was entirely foreign to Greek thought and totally antithetical to it

(5). This meant that when the Apostles declared Jesus to have risen from the dead, their message was met by incomprehension and derision. The response recorded in Acts 17, when Paul visited the Areopagus, was typical. In the end, when the Christian Church insisted on the veracity of Jesus' resurrection, it was the singularity of the event, its uniqueness and unforeseeability, which changed entirely the scientific world-view prevailing in western civilisation. Even with his interest in phenomena, Aristotle, as we have seen, was a *necessary* thinker. He really did think that everything was the way it was because it could not be any other way. Believing as he did in the divinity of reason, there was, according to him, a world-logos which inevitably connected his reasoning with the nature of everything. This meant that if sufficiently careful thought was exercised about anything, any elucidation that came about must be inevitably correct. All science could be, in principle, conducted from an armchair. Actually, Aristotle made many accurate and perceptive observations of the natural world, but many of the conclusions he reached through cogitation and reflection turned out to be incorrect, and his wide-ranging studies, impressive as they were, probably marked something of a limit to the possible achievement of Greek science.

Greek science under Aristotle was both disciplined and plausible. Plausibility has to do with predictability: an idea is plausible if it can be generally seen as an extrapolation of other accepted ideas. The Greek philosophical landscape was a gently undulating series of curves, all related to one another, and all, at least in principle, derivable from one another. What the resurrection of Jesus Christ did, was to place in the middle of this smooth undulating, predictable landscape a great towering singularity, underivable from any existing knowledge, but stuck there as a brute fact, difficult to ignore and calling into question the validity of the gentle undulations with which it was surrounded.

It took several hundred years for science to respond to this crisis. It required a paradigm shift of the type Thomas Kuhn describes in the development of scientific understanding (6). But this shift took some time to make. What the Resurrection of Jesus Christ effected, first in the disciples of the time, and then in the wider Christian Church and civilisation, was a realisation that far from understanding the way things inevitably were, it was suddenly realised that they may not be that way at all, but some other way! The shift that took place arising from the Resurrection, was thus a shift from a *necessary* world-view to a *contingent* world-view. The Aristotelian thinker in his armchair was caused to consider whether his conclusions were after all inevitably correct. The Resurrection may have inspired faith in the disciples, but equally it raised a doubt in the mind of the Greek thinker. And of course, if things could not be relied to be as they were thought to be, it became necessary to find out how they really were. And this must mean a rise in experimentation. The place of discovery moved from the armchair to the laboratory bench.

The pre-science of Aristotle had a certitude about it, but it was essentially a bogus certitude. If you live in a necessary world, there is not much room for doubt, at least not profound doubt. There is only one way things could be and it has never occurred to you that they are not this way. So there is a kind of false certitude in this way of thinking. It is a certitude founded on the conviction that there is no other possibility. The modern rejection of the existence of God has this kind of false certitude about it. On the other hand, if your view of the world was derived from speculative conjecture only, as was that of the Greeks, there can be no real certitude either. You can never have any secure assurance that your understanding of things is accurate or properly related to the objective realities to which they refer. Both these difficulties are addressed by a contingent world-view and scientific enquiry based on experiment. It is not accidental that these both have arisen and flourished wherever the Christian Gospel has had long influence informing the thought processes of civilisations among which it has been proclaimed. The result has been a huge expansion of knowledge and this knowledge is of a very dependable kind - a coherent knowledge with sufficient load-bearing capacity to sustain a huge edifice of human endeavour.

Apart from this pivotal move from necessary to contingent thinking, Christianity brought two other critically important elements to rise of modern science. The first is one which is now taken completely for granted: that of the rational unity of the universe. The pantheon of Greece and Rome envisaged a multitude of deities each with their own particular interest and domain in the phenomenal realm. Events which took place in these various domains, in the sea, in woodland, in the field of human commerce, in the law courts, in marriage, in family life, were attributed to the spheres of operation and responsibility of the appropriate god or goddess. This inevitably introduced into Greek thought a polymorphism in which an event or phenomenon in one sphere might not have any relation to an event in any other. The Judaeo-Christian understanding that all of the natural order was created by one God and thus by a single Intelligence, meant that the whole of reality was held together by a single informing rationality.

This important foundation of scientific research has now passed into our thinking at such a level that it is never questioned. Experiments are assumed to be repeatable and scientific publications and patents now must contain sufficient information to enable other researchers to repeat them and build further research upon them. The enormous volume of such experiments and the repetition of them and development from them has verified to a high degree the presupposition upon which they rest.

2.7. Judaeo-Christian Knowledge and the Natural Order

The second vital principle of Judaeo-Christian thinking in this connection is the relationship between God and the natural order. Plato integrated the two, he divinised the intellectual sphere and that effectively inserted God as a factor inside the natural realm. This monism was a completely unquantifiable factor in any serious investigation and limited the usefulness and exportability of any results. In the Judaeo-Christian tradition, God is absolutely differentiated from the created order, and specifically that order is a human province, delegated to man. There is an interesting hint of this in the Genesis story, in which a helper is sought for man, first among the animals. Genesis 2:19 reads: *So out of the ground the Lord God formed every beast of the field and every bird of the heavens and brought them to the man to see what he would call them. And whatever the man called every living creature, that was its name. The man gave names to all livestock and to the birds of the heavens and to every beast of the field.* Each of the animals was named by the man: that is, he characterised them, identified, described and defined them, and his decisions on these matters stood. The man did not make suggestions which were approved or disapproved by God, rather, God gave the man the responsibility and left it to him. This establishes that in the Judaeo-Christian tradition, science is a conversation between man and the created order with which God does not interfere. Again this is a very basic presupposition of scientific research.

2.7.1. The Liberating Power of the Jewish Torah for the Human Intellect

David Novak makes the point that the Jewish Torah is not merely prescriptive, but frees the human mind to use its own powers for (in his case) moral reasoning. He quotes the great Rabbinic exegete, Israel Lipschuetz as saying, *The Torah permits human reason to soar by its own strength, to analyse, enquire, and determine by its own sights.... to weigh and judge according to its own reason....*

human reason has the ability to be quite precise in its intention of the final truth in any matter, over and above the fact that he has been obligated [by the Torah], to do so (7). This coincides with a high view of the human being expressed by the Judaeo-Christian tradition referred to in many places in this book. This tradition, sets the scene for being a man and confides that he will rise to his great office and achieve what is divinely expected of him.

2.7.2. Muslim reintegration of God and the natural order
One of the difficulties with Islamic theology, in contrast, is its tendency, as it seeks to magnify the sovereignty and invincible will of Allah, to absorb all will to the divine and make every occurrence subject to that will and a consequence of it. This inevitably inhibits the potential for human endeavour and makes us keep looking over our shoulder to check for divine approval instead of confidently stepping forward to achieve our objective in our own right (see section 8.3. below).

It is to John Philoponus' great credit that, as a Christian physicist in the 6th and 7th Century, he was able to marshal all these Judaeo-Christian insights and present a coherent understanding of science based on them which challenged Aristotle at multiple points and at a profound level. Philoponus' famous definition of science as *the knowledge I come to of something under the compulsion of its independent reality* stands sure today as the foundation of all that is known about everything, and he deserves to be recognised and honoured much more that he is. Here, we will review some of his insights and conclusions in physics which had profound consequences on the development of science.

Aristotle had not been able to explain why a javelin continued to move forward after leaving the thrower's hand. He attempted an explanation in which pockets of

41

air supplied the necessary continuing force. Philoponus suggested that a force could be implanted by the thrower directly into the javelin. This force came to be known as an *impetus*. Thomas Kuhn has called the switch to impetus theory a paradigm shift, or a scientific revolution (although he spoke of it as a fourteenth century development, writing before it was generally appreciated to be due to Philoponus) (8).

Aristotle had thought that the celestial sphere was divine and alive and constituted differently from the sublunary sphere. According to Aristotle, rocks fell downwards and fire moved upwards because of an inner nature which controlled each. These disparate explanations of things were examples of Greek polymorphic thinking, and it was Philoponus who sought to unify dynamics. Philoponus argues from Genesis for a rational unity grounded in the fact that God made the world. It is God who implanted the motive force into the sun, moon and stars at creation and is thus of a piece with the impetus implanted in the javelin.

Philoponus' conviction that the universe was created causes him to assert the perishability of the heavens. Aristotle held that the celestial sphere was divine and composed of a fifth element *aether*, which did not share the changeable properties of air, fire, water and earth. Aristotle's thinking on this is strange and rather unsatisfactory: because the sun is in the celestial region, it cannot really be hot, so it must generate its heat by a friction with the sublunary sphere. Philoponus does away with this contortion by asserting the created nature of the whole cosmos and thus an intrinsic unity between the celestial region and sublunary. Finally, the world is a contingent, non-necessary entity, created out of nothing. From this Philoponus deduced that nothing in this material world is inherently evil. In conformity with Judaeo-Christian eschatology, he supposed that the heavens and earth would be created afresh *ex nihilo*, while present human bodies will be replaced by new, superior vehicles for the soul. There was thus a clear intention by John Philoponus to express an integratedness of the natural order in space and time and the Judaeo-Christian worldview. Much of this nascent perception has been retained and developed in the subsequent rise of the natural science, and has proved to be essential to that rise.

One of the reasons that John Philoponus has not received the credit due him was that the hold that Aristotle exercised even upon the Church was so great that Philoponus' contributions were rejected at the Synod of Constantinople in 680 AD. He was nicknamed Philoponus, Mataioponos, 'the man whose labour is lost'. This was a tragedy which delayed the advance of science, for perhaps a thousand years. According to Simplicius, Philoponus' rejection of the fifth element, and his rejection of Aristotle's contention that the universe is eternal, are both only a passing fancy. The whole edifice of modern science shows how erroneous that estimation was. It is noteworthy that Galileo, nearly a thousand years later is impressed by Philoponus' rejection of Aristotelian dynamics. Wolff points out that in his *de Motu* of 1590, Galileo mentions Philoponus as one of those who, forced by the 'power of truth' realised the falsity of Aristotle's views regarding the relation of quantities which play a role in the motion of falling bodies (9). But he notes that Philoponus arrived at his views 'by belief' rather than by real proof. Wolff suggests that Galileo blamed Philoponus for merely believing the truth without having any real insight into it. However, Philoponus himself seems not merely to believe what is, in Galileo's view, true, but also to have what Galileo would take to be a real understanding of the truth. In fact, *insight* is exactly what Philoponus had concerning the truth.

What we have observed is the profound redefinition of what knowledge actually is. The overall impact of the Judaeo-Christian tradition is to move the centre of gravity of knowledge from the human mind to the object to which it refers. To use Thomas Kuhn's language, this is the greatest of all paradigm shifts and has provided the platform not only for seemingly limitless scientific research and achievement, but also for an entire rational edifice of understanding of the human being.

REFERENCES FOR CHAPTER 2

(1) Peter Berger, *The Social Construction of Reality*
(2) Czeslaw Milosz, *The Captive Mind*
(3) Psalm 19, *Revised Standard Version*
(4) G. E. R. Lloyd, *Greek Science after Aristotle*, p57ff
(5) N. T. Wright, *The Resurrection of the Son of God*
(6) Thomas S. Kuhn, *The Structure of Scientific Revolutions,* 3rd Ed.
(7) Israel Lipschuetz, quoted by David Novak, *The Sanctity of Human Life*, p26
(8) Thomas S. Kuhn, *Ibid,* p124
(9) see Richard Sorabji, *John Philoponus,* p9-11

CHAPTER 3
FAITH

Wolff's suggestion that Galileo criticised Philoponus for *believing* the concept of impetus rather than from proof introduces us to the relationship between faith, evidence and knowledge. This is of considerable importance at the present time because "faith" is deprecated and held in contempt in many quarters. Recently, the media editor of the BBC, Amol Rajan in a tweet, declared, 'Faith is belief without evidence' and this is a common bogus definition of faith, intended to disparage it as the benighted and groundless convictions of the foolish and deluded.

Even dictionaries suggest the same: The Oxford Dictionary defines faith as *complete trust or confidence in someone or something,* or *strong belief in the doctrines of a religion, based on spiritual conviction rather than proof.* Richard Dawkins describes faith as *the great cop-out, the great excuse to evade the need to think and evaluate evidence. Faith is belief in spite of, even perhaps because of, the lack of evidence.* What all these definitions have in common is the complete separation of faith from the concept of evidence.

But contrary to this evaluation faith is basic and ubiquitous, being in the most general sense, the *acceptance* of evidence. Correspondingly, *unbelief* is the rejection of evidence, and *doubt*, a reserve about evidence. Insight is the understanding of the significance of evidence. If evidence is well-accepted it becomes knowledge, the recognition of its truth is cognition and if knowledge is securely comprehended its holder can become a witness to its content (1). This means, of course, that everyone exercises faith at one level or another. It is not the exclusive domain of the religious or other-worldly not to mention the deluded or ignorant. Virtually everything we know we take on faith: we derive nothing from absolute first principles. We exercise faith when we believe the results of other researchers, who have done the same with the results obtained by still others. Even in our every-day lives we believe and act on results of a vast edifice of human enquiry going back over thousands of years. Many of these results are beyond contention and our appropriation of them as the founding basis of our thought and actions we would hardly even regard as an act of faith. In fact, however, the exercise of faith is so commonplace we hardly notice or recognise it as such. It is only when the evidence can be taken more than one way, or that different pieces of evidence conflict, that we might decide to reject certain evidence altogether or exercise a reserve in our acceptance of it. We often carry out this calculation and we may be persuaded one way or the other depending on our estimate of the weight of evidence on either side. This process is most clearly carried out in law courts on a daily basis. Businesses and governments have to make frequent estimates of the outcomes of their decisions, and we make similar judgements in our personal lives.

3.1. Categories of Truth

Imagine a set B containing all truth. (See figure 3.1.) Contained within set B, is a subset A containing all explicable truth. That is all truth which can be fully explained. Subset A is therefore the confines of Enlightenment thought which has for its premise the principle that only that which can be explained can be believed.

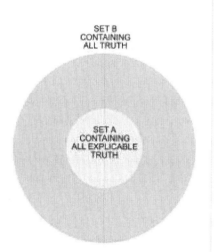

Figure 3.1. Truth: explicable and non-explicable

Within set A, there is clearly evidence of different types - some easier to explain than others, some self evident, and others the support for which is more difficult and complex to derive. What Thomas Kuhn describes as 'normal science' takes place within this subset A (2). Research takes place, in part, at the boundary of subset A. There must be exploratory probes beyond the edges of subset A, and from time to time discoveries will be made which result in paradigms shifts causing the envelope of the subset A to advance.

In subset (B - A), the outer shaded annulus of Figure 3.1. there are truths of various types: truths supported by evidence, but nonetheless not entirely explicable. In this case the evidence available may avail itself of several different explanations each of which may be defensible to different degrees. In each case the enquirer must come to a decision as to which explanation he considers fits the available evidence best. Again in this subset, the quality and type of evidence available will vary.

In subset (B - A), there will be truth which is inaccessible to enquiry because of a lack of evidence. This category of truth is in principle comprehensible or incomprehensible. It may be comprehensible in the sense that it is theoretically possible for the mind of man to grasp it fully and many things about the far reaches of the universe, for example, will fall into this category. Evidence may in the future be forthcoming which opens up an ever increasing scope of understanding with at least a theoretical possibility that the truth in question can be fully comprehended.? n the other hand there also will be truth in this subset that may be in principle incomprehensible - truth which theoretically cannot be fully embraced by the mind of man. According to Origen, writing in the third century, there is only one incomprehensible truth and that is the truth of God. The universe is comprehensible in principle because it is finite. God is the only true infinitude and therefore he is incomprehensible in the strict sense of the term.

The Enlightenment mind, as it has developed in our own age, is confined largely to subset A and often regards excursions into the uncharted territory of subset (B - A) as ill-advised or unfruitful. This in our modern-day tends to give rise to a particular form of dogmatic atheism. The Enlightenment mind is constrained by the principle, *Intellego ut credam*, I understand so that I may believe, and so operates comfortably only within subset A (3). The Christian on the other hand, although always concerned with evidential truth, has the entire field of set B as the range of his enquiries, and that, of course, includes set A. Anselm's *Credo ut intellegam,* I believe so that I may understand, applies to the Christian enquiry of the contents of set B. His faith allows him to move beyond the safe confines of subset A, and explore both the evidence and the internal coherence of the truth that he discovers in subset (B - A).

There is of course, an element of risk in straying from the safety of subset A, into the sometimes uncharted and sometimes mysterious territory of subset (B - A). Not everything found there will be attested to with the same bolted-down, downright certainty of the evidence for the truth in subset A. But there is infinitely more to explore, more to understand and more to discover about ourselves, the universe we live in and the God to whom we belong than we could ever begin to access if we are unwilling to leave subset A.

Even within subset A, we can encounter issues in which a judgement needs to be made between two or more reasonable possibilities, perhaps between theories which explain the same set of facts. Perhaps these will be resolved by further experimentation, but perhaps not. The exercise of faith in reaching the best judgement we can on such a matter is the best we can do, and we may well reach a different conclusion from our colleagues. The different schools of thought within the scientific community in certain areas, underscore that the principle of faith is operative in the scientific sphere as elsewhere.

However, the idea of faith is not usually applied to conversations entirely within the realm of the physical sciences, even if it is present to some extent. The term is much more frequently used in a more contentious area of thought. If questions are asked about cause and effect, starting in the sphere of science, they start by being concerned with *physical causality*. How is the energy released from the oxidation of glucose turned into muscle contraction? Why do Chromium salts exhibit their characteristic range of bright colours? Why is the whole of matter constructed using the 100 or so elements of the Periodic Table? These are all questions which have answers within the realm of physical causality. Huge efforts in biochemistry producing the metabolic pathways describing mitochondrial processes were an answer to the first. Pioneering work in spectroscopy answered the second and cosmological research on the Big Bang Theory answered the third. These are all answers strictly from within the realm of physical causality. But if the questions are pressed further and further back eventually the limits of the possibilities of physical causality are reached and the question becomes of a different type, questions of *metaphysical causality*. We might now be asking about the possibility of an Intelligence behind the creation of the universe, or what was before the Big Bang, or what brought it about, or what made the events of the first 10^{-19} seconds after the Big Bang yield the potential for all the elements of Periodic Table? Or we might be asking about life itself - what makes life, life? These are questions raised in the sphere of metaphysical causality, because they raise the possibility of answers lying outside the realm of physical causality (i.e. outside subset A above). The word *faith* is often used to describe answers given to these sorts of questions.

3.1.1. Enquiries on the Edge of Knowledge: The Wise Men.
There is, indubitably, a certain risk attached to exploring the outer edge of Subset A and the content of Subset (B-A). This is similar to the challenge presented to a judge or a jury when they are required to arrive at a verdict and the evidence might be ambiguous. They have to rise to the challenge and exercise courage in giving a judgement in which they accept they might be wrong, and yet are prepared to act on as the best available reading of the evidence.

Criminal cases have criteria for carrying this out which protect the accused from conviction if the evidence is too finely balanced. The famous wise men, described in Matthew's Gospel, very far away from the action of the Incarnation, and equally far away from the Israelite storyline which might give some historical basis for it, were presented with a tiny fragment of evidence - the appearance of some star, or perhaps a comet - and on this tiny fragment of evidence they embark upon, perhaps a two-year journey to visit the Christ child. Putting aside all analysis as to the historicity of this event, the Wise Men have been hailed as heroes by the Christian Church for taking the risk and acting on such slender evidence. The point for our purposes is that, slender as it might have been, it was on *evidence* that the Wise Men acted and they were vindicated, and given more evidence. If faith was not a matter of the acceptance of evidence, and just a blind credulity, they could have stayed at home, not bothered to attend to their astronomical observations, and declared themselves champions of faith nonetheless. Faith as mere credulity dissolves into nothing. But faith is not blind credulity, it is a response to evidence and involves action and exertion to give it substance.

3.1.2. The Limits of Atheism

The boundary between physical and metaphysical causality is generally acknowledged, but does not have to be interpreted by insisting there is a God. It does take us to an open question about ultimate causes, but really no further. In an article in the *Spectator* (4), reporting an interview with Henry Marsh the celebrated neurosurgeon, Mary Wakefield writes, *Henry Marsh is an atheist. No surprise, you might say, after all the horrific deaths he's seen. But it's not the suffering that makes him an unbeliever so much as his understanding that the human personality - humour, character - is identical with grey matter. There's nothing transcendent about a self. 'and that is just a fact with a capital F,' he says. 'Everything we think and feel is electrochemical.' Nonetheless, life is still a mystery for Marsh, which is reassuring. 'I don't want to be all reductionist about it, saying it's all just chemicals. The thing is, we still don't know what elevates matter in this way. We can't explain the single most interesting thing in the world, which is our own consciousness, and I find that quite consoling.'*

53

3.2. Jesus Christ and Physical and Metaphysical Causality

The same distinction between answers constrained by the realm of physical causality, and those raised by the realm of metaphysical reality can be made in the case of the person of Jesus Christ. The main evidence concerning Jesus Christ has been collected together, and the resultant material constitute the canonical Scriptures of the New Testament supported by the Old. In these documents the evidence of many individuals is presented and the enquirer can review them rather as a jury hears the evidence from a series of witnesses. One by one they give their testimony and the jury have to assess it and make a decision on its veracity and draw conclusions accordingly. The New Testament contains much evidence which could be considered essentially belonging to the realm of physical causality: it has dates and places, and cultural, political, architectural and social details all of which testify to the authenticity of the witnesses statements. The evidence of this type offered by the New Testament has been subjected to intense scrutiny and compared to the other available evidence from archaeological and literary sources. But it also contains evidence of the type belonging to the realm of metaphysical causality. So while it gives details of some of the genealogy of Jesus Christ, details of his home life, the family trade, and his place of birth and town of residence, as we have seen, it also testifies that when the disciples, who had spent three years of public ministry with Jesus, were asked about him, they said things like *He is the Christ, the Son of the Living God*, and *he is the only-begotten Son of the Father*. These are clearly answers from the realm of metaphysical causality. Of course, there is a relationship between the evidence from the two spheres. Particularly, if it could be shown that the evidence from the realm of physical causality was seriously flawed, this would inevitably cast doubt on the metaphysical witness, but as the review in Appendix 1 shows, the evidence appropriate to the physical realm is of a very high quality.

3.2.1. A Cautionary Word about the Use of Scripture

We must keep in mind that the Bible is evidence. It is not identical with the divine utterance to which it testifies. H. Richard Niebuhr has issued a salutary warning against this confusion: *As a preliminary device for establishing a basis for communication, as in the case of young children, or in the case of our own learning of a foreign language, or a new science, the dogmatic method doubtless has a place in communication among men and between them and their common world. But when it is used primarily, it is no longer a way of communicating but simply of proclaiming. And its persistent use leads to loss of meaningfulness. Neither the symbol nor that which is to be understood by it can retain their meaning, since meaning is a function of relation; and what is identical is no longer related. It is significant, meaningful to say that the Bible is the word of God, when I and my hearer understand that "Word of God" is a symbol with the aid of which the Bible can be apprehended and understood. But when the two are identified so that the word of God means Bible and Bible means word of God, nothing meaningful is being said anymore about the symbolised reality or about the symbol. When we say that the word of God is the Bible and the Bible is the word of God, we no longer communicate meanings to each other or communicate with the Bible. We simply affirm that we have decided to use two names for the same thing.*

This illustration leads us then to the problem of the loss of vitality in the religious and specifically Christian symbolism in our time. The question arises for us whether we are not, in our Protestantism,

55

at something like the point at which the Medieval church found itself in the days before Luther and the Reformation. We also have used our formulae and our symbols to an unheard-of degree. Evangelistic and missionary preaching for hundreds of years now, sermons in millions of Protestant churches, avalanches of printed paper, Sunday school lessons, Church papers, tracts, brochures, pamphlets, commentaries, popular and academic theological treatises- every minister's wastebasket and study table bears witness- have repeated and repeated and repeated the words and the symbols of our evangelical faith. The language is familiar. The symbols are worn. Are they worn out? The words slide from our tongues and enter our eyes and ears without ever causing a shock, a shock of recognition of ourselves, a shock of encountering with a reality that is different from all our imaginings. They bring us no surprises, whether by joy or sudden pain, whether by discovery of the unknown or by revelation of a long sought secret (5).

The word *faith* is used sometimes, therefore, in a narrower sense, to describe conclusions which are reached by the acceptance of evidence from the realm of metaphysical causality. Although the Greeks were relatively at home with metaphysical causality (Aristotle did not think it unreasonable to trace all motion back to an Unmoved Mover, i.e. God) nevertheless the 18th Century Enlightenment, in recovering Greek thought, also appropriated a rationalism which tended to reject everything which could not be explained. This had a powerfully cathartic effect on scientific thought and enabled the world of physical causality to be investigated with much needed clarity, but also deprecated enquiries into the realm of metaphysical causality, reducing the status of faith accordingly. Evangelicalism was a response to this emergency and represented a Christianity which maximised the Church's dependence upon physical causality in, for example, the development of a doctrine of mechanistic atonement which could be reasonably easily explained, and minimised its dependence on, for example, Sacraments which were more difficult to sustain on purely physical grounds. But overall, confidence in faith diminished and even if deference was still paid to ecclesiastical institutions for a time, the integrated nature of mediaeval Christian society gave way to an increasingly secular culture with a Christian presence within it. This has continued to the present day in the western world, with the opposition to apprehension of the realm of metaphysical causality now reaching a level of public hostility.

3.3. The Church and Opposition to Metaphysical Causality

Further responses of the Church to this hostility, even if misguided, were nevertheless deft and sometimes ingenious. First, perhaps the volume of material in the New Testament which was redolent of metaphysical causality could be minimised. This was the motivation behind the famous "Search for the Historical Jesus", a massive effort which has pre-occupied scholars and the Church for more than 200 years. It took two main forms: that due to Albert Schweitzer yielding a pathway called the Schweitzerstrasse, and that due to Wrede yielding the Wredestrasse. Both of these, although very different approaches, aimed at removing the metaphysical causality from the evidence concerning Jesus. These approaches have been very thoroughly documented, so a brief outline will be sufficient for the present purposes (6). Schweitzer's approach was to strip away what he regarded as magical accretions which the original person Jesus had attracted through the fanciful additions of subsequent writers, to reach the essential character of a wandering preacher, soothsayer or prophet. Evidently a charismatic personality with a gift for the memorable *bon-mot* emerged from this process which involved going through the Gospel narratives with a red pen and crossing out all the material which could not be attributed to such a person, leaving a residual personality entirely explicable in terms of physical causality. It is to Albert Schweitzer's great credit, that having reduced Jesus to such plausible ordinariness, he went on to heroic sacrifice in his African medical mission in the service of that same ordinary itinerant preacher. Wrede's plan was very different. He regarded the story of Jesus as a complex collection of material penned by various factions in the ancient Near East which were in theological or political conflict. The identity of these groups has been lost but, according to Wrede, they stood behind various names in the New Testament with various axes to grind. Effectively, the person of Jesus disappears altogether in this analysis, and the New Testament becomes merely a product of endless theological wrangling and debate. Thus everything which could possibly be attributed to metaphysical causality can now be regarded as devices used by the competing parties in their attempts to gain ascendency over the others. Wrede's line of argument was so successful and so many scholars joined the throng on the Wredestrasse, that it soon became known as the Wredebahn and its heavy traffic has been well documented by N. T. Wright (7).

Rudolf Bultmann offered yet another approach to the 'problem' of metaphysical causality. Again this has been exhaustively treated so the briefest of sketches will be given here (8). Bultmann used the idea of the myth. A myth is a story set in space and time which has a timeless and universal meaning. According to this model, the story of Jesus is such a myth: the details of time and place, what Jesus is said to have taught and done, his death on the Cross and his rising again are clothing for the timeless and universal meaning, the conveying of which is the real purpose of the stories. In order to comprehend that timeless meaning, we need to "demythologise" the gospel stories and re-mythologise them using appropriate elements from our own time and place. This removes the embarrassment of history from the real meaning of the stories and re-presents them as intelligible to a modern world. There is no doubt that was a very clever idea and it became popular among scholars and liberal exegetes. It effectively removed all the points in the narrative concerning Jesus where metaphysical causality is indicated. Thus specific statements about Jesus Christ, became general statements about human beings. This meant that the realm of metaphysical causality was transmuted into a realm of psychological causality in which the whole story of Jesus was really about timeless and universal ideas rather than any event in space and time.

There has, therefore, been a colossal effort to avoid the realm of metaphysical causality for the past 300 years and while it has marginalised traditional Christian faith to a marked degree, it has by no means been wholly successful. During this period there have been millions of Christians who have readily accepted that the person of Jesus Christ can only be understood, as the Apostles testify in the Scriptures, as God's only begotten Son. But the exercise of faith as the acceptance of evidence from the realm of metaphysical causality has had to be exerted against secular presuppositions of increasing strength and confidence.

The Early Church, the Church of the first millennium and the mediaeval Church had no difficulty with accepting evidence from the realm of metaphysical causality. The evidence must come from this realm if Christianity is about God at all. How could it be otherwise? For St Irenaeus, for example, the Incarnation meant that man could participate in God. The whole life of Jesus was a manifestation of God himself and therefore none of it could be excluded from the realm of metaphysical causality. The life of faith, as it was a participation in God through Jesus, was itself supernatural. This is about as far as it is possible to get from the efforts of post-Enlightenment Christianity to distance itself from the metaphysical. The life of God is the daily reality of the Christian, according to Irenaeus and there is no reason to think his perspective to be exceptional.

3.4. Accepting Evidence from the Sphere of Metaphysical Causality

If we are to recover our confidence in accepting evidence from the sphere of metaphysical causality, or more shortly, to recover faith in God as he is revealed in genuine Christianity, we need to understand the terms under which this acceptance takes place, as they are not the same as those prevailing in our enquiries in the realm of physical causality. First, as Torrance has so clearly shown, God is not an 'Aristotelian' object which can be examined by asking a series of *Quaestio* questions (see section 2.3.) to elucidate the type of object he is. Torrance explains:

The Object is given to us in a unique sense of given. It is given to us as all other objects are given to our knowledge in the whole field of science, within the subject-object relationship, but in accordance with the unique nature of this object, it is given in grace. Natural objects, when we know them, have to be objects of our cognition–that is part of their determinate nature. This is not to deny that knowledge of them requires effort on our part, and indeed the discovery. Even though we must engage in intuitive and discursive thought, we do not discover God by our own efforts, and when we know him he does not have to be an object of our cognition in the same way as in natural knowledge. He gives himself to our thinking; he objectifies himself for us, in an act of pure freedom and grace, and therefore in such a way that he does not resign that freedom and grace, but remains free to give himself to us as he pleases, or even to withdraw himself (9).

It is clear from this that the evidence afforded by the self-revelation of God is not something over which we have control. He reveals himself as he wills. But there are many examples of evidence from the realm of physical causality which exhibit similar restrictions.

Many astronomical and geophysical observations are single events which we cannot control or repeat. We do not think less of the evidence because this is so, and it may have a powerful impact on our understanding of the reality in which we exist. The self-revelation of God in Jesus Christ similarly takes place at a time and a place not of our choosing but it affords a great deal to observe and presents a large amount of evidence for us to consider.

But the person of Jesus addresses us at a level far beyond that which astronomical or geophysical observations do. Acceptance of evidence in the realm of metaphysical causality takes place at the deepest level in the human soul. It does involve intellect - there are facts to be known and information to be digested - but it is much more than that. It has the power to redirect our whole life, to arrest us from activities, dispositions and perspectives and re-orient us along new lines, with new endeavours, new motivations and new instincts. Again Torrance expresses the transformation implicit in the reception of this kind of evidence:

Such is our vocation in Christian theology: it is a kind of ecstatic passion, in which - under the sheer impact of God's own Being in Word and Act - we are called to think of and know him, not from a centre in ourselves, but from a centre in God, in such a way that it cuts across the grain of our natural desires and mental habits and creatively reorients them. In it we have to do with the eloquent and dynamic Being of God himself, whom we may know only in accordance with the steps

*he has taken in reconciling us to himself, through the
incarnation of his Son within the ontological structures
of our human existence in this world, in such a way that
he sets up within it the laws of his own internal relations
and our rational understanding takes on the imprint of
what it is given to know, the triune reality of God himself*
(10).

Merely because this is unlike the observations in the
physical realm and contains a depth which exceeds
them, does not warrant its dismissal by a straitened
perspective of narrow materialism. Rather the converse:
the very depth of it, the mystery of it, invites the best
endeavours of the enquirer. The Church in almost all of
its history has understood that its reception of evidence
of this kind has taken it to much greater depths of
understanding of the world, of human nature and of
God, than any arbitrary limit of enquiry imposed by a
rationalistic outlook.

3.5. Metaphysical Causality and Mystery

But it takes us into a mystery. A mystery is the revelation
of an incomprehensible truth. A truth is
incomprehensible, not because it cannot be understood,
but because it cannot be fully contained by the human
mind. A mystery is a disclosure which cannot be fully
mastered by those to whom it is made known. Despite
their reception of it, their understanding of it, they are
always out of their depth. This is perhaps why it is
despised by Enlightenment man who is made anxious
by being out of his depth and so needs the pool to be
shallow enough so that his feet are securely planted on

the bottom. In order to do this he has to drain the pool so most of the meaning runs out of it.

At all the points where Jesus reveals a metaphysical truth, we encounter a mystery. There is much we can know and say about the Incarnation and we can draw a great deal from its significance, but God becoming man is not something we can ever fully master. Many of the Church Fathers thought about it deeply and concluded that it profoundly changed the status of the human race and opened a new being and destiny for it. Irenaeus understood it as a recapitulation of humanity in the man Jesus Christ which had the effect of requisitioning our humanity and bringing it into the life of God. For Origen, the Incarnation mediated the grace of God to the human race and revealed the nature of God through the acts, speech and sacrifice of the Saviour. Athanasius saw it as the means by which God restored man from a lostness into which he had fallen, granting him a new humanity (11).

These all represent but a small part of the full meaning and purpose of the Word of God becoming flesh but they, nevertheless, inform us very well of ourselves, of the God who made and restored us, and the office we have in Jesus Christ as the appointed vicegerents of his reign. When we have understood all that there is to understand, the Incarnation remains a deep mystery - incomprehensible, yet presented as evidence of the nature, will and action of God through Jesus Christ.

The death and resurrection of Jesus Christ are mysteries of a piece with this, and it may suffice for this discussion to quote St Athanasius on the significance to Christians of these Easter mysteries:

The way that Christians despise death and take the aggressive against it and no longer fear it is ample proof that death is actually destroyed and the Cross has become the victory over it, and that it has no more power but is actually dead. By the sign of the Cross and by faith in Christ, they tread death down as dead itself. For of old, before the divine sojourn of the Saviour took place, even to the saints death was terrible, and all wept for the dead as though they perished. But now that the Saviour has raised his body, death is no longer terrible; for all who believe in Christ tread death down as nothing, and choose rather to die than to deny their faith in Christ. For they verily know that when they die they are not destroyed but actually begin to live, and become incorruptible through the resurrection. And the devil that once maliciously exulted in death, now that its pains were loosed, remained the only one truly dead. And proof of this is, that before men believe in Christ, they see in death an object of terror, and play the coward before him. But when they are gone over to Christ's faith and teaching, their contempt for death is so great that they eagerly rush upon it and become witnesses for the resurrection the Saviour has accomplished against it. So weak has death become, that they who were formerly deceived by it, mock death as dead and paralysed. For as when a tyrant has been defeated by a real king and bound hand and foot, then all that pass by laugh him to scorn, buffeting and reviling him, no longer fearing his fury and barbarity because of the king who has conquered him, so also death having been conquered and exposed by the Saviour on the Cross, bound hand and foot, all they who are in Christ, as they pass by, trample on death, and witnessing to Christ scoff at him, jesting at death, and saying what has been written of him of old: 'O death, where is thy victory? O grave, where is thy sting?' (12)

What this demonstrates is the seriousness with which Christians of the fourth century took the resurrection of Jesus Christ which they allowed to shape their attitudes and their actions. Evidently, metaphysical causality did not meet the same reserve and diffidence as it does now: it was regarded as hard-edged and as solid as any evidence from physical causality if not more so. This goes a long way to explaining why Christianity was so persuasive in that era, and why it lacks infectious power in our own day.

3.6. Christianity and Things Generally Regarded as Impossible

Not only did the ancient Church confidently declare that, in Jesus Christ, God did things which were generally regarded as impossible, far from being embarrassed that the world scorned it for this, rather it exulted in the differences between Christianity and all other positions. It is true that Justin Martyr and other apologists sought common ground between Christianity and Greek thought, but where differences arose, they did not give the Christian ground away. Christians were, in those days, quite content to be thoroughly differentiated from the world around them, both doctrinally and morally. Take, for example the three antitheses of Romans 4:5, 17. These are *creatio ex nihilo* (creation of the universe out of nothing), *justificatio impii* (justification of sinners), and *resurrectio mortuorum* (resurrection of the dead). These were, and probably still are, all considered by the world as intrinsically impossible. And yet all three of them are of vitally important constituents of Christian faith, and all of them belong to the sphere of metaphysical causality.

The doctrine of *creatio ex nihilo,* the creation of everything from nothing was important in Christianity because it asserted the primacy of God, that everything is in his hands, and nothing, even unformed matter, had any position of antecedent advantage over him. Only if everything was in his hands and exclusively so, could God not only redeem his own people, but also the very substance of an entire fallen world. The prologue to John's Gospel shows that the early Christians perceived this through Jesus Christ. Even in his ministry in Galilee and Jerusalem, Jesus behaved as if all things were in his hands and exerted authority over all things on that basic assumption.

The *justificatio impii,* the justification of the unrighteous has an impossibility about it which is surmounted by God in Jesus Christ and practically the whole letter of St Paul to the Romans is an examination of how this has been done, without impugning the justice of God. It has been generally accepted in the

67

world that guilt can be punished but not effaced. A secular understanding of forgiveness is an overlooking, the turning of blind eye, a neglecting of liability, 'all things considered.' What the Cross of Jesus Christ achieved, according to Christianity is, an absolute change of status of the sinner from utter reprobate to unimpeachable righteousness and holiness. This is so thorough-going that Karl Barth can say, *[The Christian Church] is constituted in the right, even though it sets itself a thousand times in the wrong against that right* (13). St Paul declares, *Who shall bring an accusation against God's elect?* (Romans 8) This is the daily miracle of Christian life. The forgiveness of sins, makes every Christian begin each day from position of moral completeness.

The *resurrectio mortuorum*, the resurrection of the dead, as we have considered in Chapter 2, was absolutely impossible in the eyes of the ancient Greek world as it is in our own. It is so inconceivable that the suggestion is met by mirth and derision. The Pharisees predicted it on the grounds that the promises of God could not be inherited by the dead, and since the promise of God could not go unfulfilled, inheritors of God's promise would have to be raised to life to receive it, if they had died in the meantime. But this was an entirely theoretical idea. The resurrection of Jesus Christ was recognised by Paul as the first practical instance of what pharisaic reflection had anticipated, and their basic reasoning still informed it. If God was going to be true to his promise, in the Old Testament and the New, he would have to summon forth from the dead all those who were to be recipients. This third 'impossibility' thus becomes the mainstay of Christian hope and, as St Paul sets out in 1 Corinthians 15 the great motivation for Christian service and endeavour.

Any review of the early Church, especially before the Peace of Constantine at the beginning of the fourth century, could not fail to recognise a faith securely confident of the evidence from metaphysical causality upon which Christianity rests, and a defiance in the face of pagan opinion, criticism and opposition. We know from ancient cartoons, that Christianity was widely lampooned and dismissed as a superstition as Pliny wrote to Trajan (14). But we also know that it grew like wildfire but that no compromise was made to secular reasoning or reservation. The Church was obstinately insistent on maintaining Apostolic witness to Christ and living a holy life in conformity with it. It was also oblivious of the opinions of the world, indifferent to its own reputation and not in the least committed to maximising its numbers. It remembered that Jesus did nothing to increase his own following - if anything he discouraged it. He would give no quarter to anyone who wanted to follow him, but who would only do so with a reservation or after fulfilling a prior commitment (see Matthew 8:18ff). He would only accept those whom he chose, who followed him without reservation. The early Church had largely the same perspective. In the third century there were long waiting lists for those wishing to be baptised. For them a two-year learning and preparation period was required, and there was a long list of jobs which were forbidden to Christians because they involved swearing to pagan gods: working in the Roman civil service, or serving a licentious object such as working in the theatre. But these constraints did not prevent very large numbers of people seeking to be counted among the followers of Jesus Christ.

3.7. The Impact of the Peace of Constantine

The Church in the modern west is certainly not in the same situation. She is not oblivious to public opinion, in fact quite the converse and at least in part, this is due to the long toll that the Peace of Constantine has exacted. In some ways, it was a boon to the Church - relieving the burden of persecution and giving it an opportunity for unopposed public witness, but it also seduced the Church into a dependence on the state. It was able to build impressive cathedrals and fine parish churches but these same buildings are now proving to be burdensome. They have vast capacities which inspires a need for large memberships; they cost a great deal to maintain so a considerable constituency of donors is needed. So the Church becomes self-conscious about its reputation and inevitably feels the pressure to modify its message to please those upon whom it is dependent. It is no longer joyfully oblivious to the world or courageously facing it, but rather seeks to charm it. It is much more committed to enlarging its membership, but from mixed motives. It needs the validation of populous Sunday congregations, the money to pay the clergy and fix the buildings, and the cultural approval to which it has become accustomed.

It is not surprising that it has toned-down the mystery and tended to explain itself and its message in the conceptual currency of its surroundings; in fact in some sections of the Church, becoming "culturally-relevant" has become a prized ambition. In others, the whole mission has been transmuted to a progressive social agenda. It is busy finding its own *raison d'être* in all these self-redefinitions, and it feels, at present no imperative to find its way back. It could never do so on its own. If St Cyprian were consulted on this matter, he would say that persecution will come and cleanse the Church of these infidelities and restore it to the faith and godliness proper to its true nature(15).

REFERENCES FOR CHAPTER 3

(1) Karl Barth, *Church Dogmatics, Volume 1:1*, p188

(2) Thomas S. Kuhn, *The Structure of Scientific Revolutions,* 3rd Edition

(3) James Hannam, *God's Philosophers,* p56

(4) Mary Wakefield, in *The Spectator,* 6th May 2017

(5) H. Richard Niebuhr, *Theology, History and Culture*, p27

(6) William Sanday, *The Life of Christ in Recent Research,* Oxford, 1907

(7) N. T. Wright, *Jesus and the Victory of God*

(8) *see for example*, Ralph P Martin, *New Testament Foundations, Volume 1*, p41ff

(9) Thomas Torrance, *Theological Science*, p37

(10) Thomas Torrance, *The Ground and Grammar of Theology*, p155

(11) St Athanasius, *De Incarnatione Verbi Dei* 4, 5

(12) St Athanasius, *De Incarnatione Verbi Dei, 27*

(13) Karl Barth, *Church Dogmatics, Volume 4:2*, p702

(14) Pliny the Younger, *Letter to Trajan*, in H. Bettenson (Ed), *Documents of the Christian Church,* 2nd Edition, p3.

(15) St Cyprian, *Ante-Nicene Church Fathers Volume 5, Treatise on the Lapsed*, I

CHAPTER 4
MEMORY

4.1. The Vector of Recollection

The recollection of the past meets with mixed responses in the modern world. In the brave effort to usher in a new utopian civilisation, the past is often either ignored or rejected as that bad regime from which our enlightened leaders are progressively rescuing us. On the other hand many people hanker after trophies and reminders of bygone times; there is a significant market for 'retro' merchandise. But much of the bad press that the past receives is grounded in the conviction that recalling it might encourage us to attempt to retrace our steps to recover things we have lost, a movement which is deprecated as retrogressive. The braver, sounder way to proceed is to advance into the future creating a new order of civilisation which will outpace the lingering recollections of the past and flourish in a new morality of acceptance and diversity and a new prosperity in equality.

The Judaeo-Christian understanding of memory challenges the vectors in this argument. In the Old Testament and in the New, memory did not take the mind from the present back to a past event which is the modern conception of what we might call the vector of recollection. Rather, memory brought a past event forward for consideration, judgement and action in the present. The direction is reversed. Memory does not hanker to return to a supposed golden era, but it summons forth things from the past for present examination. So, for example, in 1 Kings 17:18, in her distress at the death of her son, the widow of Zarephath, exclaimed to Elijah, *What have you against me, O man of God? You have come to me to bring my sin to remembrance and to cause the death of my son!* What she thought was happening was that her sins were being remembered, that is brought to the present for judgement, and that her penalty was being exacted.

In Isaiah 43:25 God says, *I, I am he who blots out your transgressions for my own sake, and I will not remember your sins. Put me in remembrance; let us argue together; set forth your case, that you may be proved right.* When God says he will not remember the sins of the people, he means that he will no longer bring them in recollection for a present judgement. When he invites the people to put him in remembrance, he is inviting a conversation in the present not some kind of recourse to antiquity.

In the Eucharist, when Jesus says, *Do this in remembrance of me*, it is not a invitation for the participants merely to cast their minds back to the ministry of Jesus and his passion. Rather it is, in the celebration of the Sacrament of the Eucharist, the ministry and passion of Jesus is brought forward and applied to the participating company in the present. When the thief on the cross asks Jesus to remember him when he comes in his kingly power, he is asking that Jesus summon him forth on that day to be with him when his Kingdom is revealed.

This forward movement associated with recollection is principally revealed by the resurrection of Jesus and the future resurrection of those that belong to him. Torrance has described the forward movement of resurrection time in which the redeemed are recollected and brought to God who is the Source of their life. In this recollection they become younger and younger as does the Lady in the Shepherd of Hermas who, beginning as an aged and wizened woman, during the conversation between the two, becomes ever more youthful and finally is presented as a beautiful young bride to her heavenly Spouse. The recollection of God achieves this forward movement for the sake of those he redeems, and its direction is quite the opposite of forgetfulness which slips back into oblivion and lostness.

4.2. Covenant Recollection and Hope

Thus recollection gives rise to hope. When God remembered Noah in the Ark, he brought him forth to a new life and new future. Genesis 6 describes a tragic descent into violent ruin of a civilisation which, forgetting God, and thus losing its entire *raison d'être* faces only the prospect of extinction. God's remembering of Noah contradicts this catastrophe and re-engenders in the human race a destiny of life and fulfilment under divine promise.

This, of course, is counter-intuitive according to the secular tenets of our age in which so often, we renounce and dismiss the past and believe we can create and embrace our own self-made, glorious future. We enjoy ourselves in this delusion. We continually elect and appoint leaders who promise to bring it about, and when they take office they become desperate to make us happy, to make us live for ever, to fulfil our every aspiration. But what they are really doing is attempting to extend and burnish the present: trying to make us a little bit more affluent, a little bit healthier and a little more equal. Hope has contracted from the long-range prospect of God's eternal glory, to the myopic aim of a short term postponement of discomfort. That is not hope, but rather a masked despair in which we stretch an elastic present just a bit more each year until the inevitable cataclysmic fracture takes place.

The recollection of God re-establishes a genuine hope, an anticipation of a new heaven and a new earth, redeemed from all wrong, and established in all fruitfulness and prosperity. Moreover, in the present order, the characteristics of this future glory are manifested within the Christian community just as they were within the occupants of the Ark, who despite the discomforts of their present circumstances, became aware that they were the objects of God's recollection by his promise and thus destined for a life the glory of which they could only glimpse.

The recollection of God abolishes shame and reproach, the emptiness, futility and redundancy of disqualified humanity. In Genesis 30, Rachel's barrenness, a signal representation of human disfunction was totally reversed when *God remembered Rachel, and God listened to her and opened her womb. She conceived and bore a son and said, "God has taken away my reproach." And she called his name Joseph,? saying, "May the Lord add to me another son!"* This was not simply a kindness to Rachel, to remedy her personal sadness. It was that, but much more. It was the opening up of the whole promise of God for the future of his people. Joseph, Rachel's son was the saviour of Israel, when through the cruelty and ill-treatment from his brothers, he was sold into slavery in Egypt. He rose to prominence as Pharaoh's right hand man from which office he was able to offer shelter and protection to his whole family in a famine. In this way, he too prefigured the Christ.

4.3. Memory and Prophecy

The history of Israel as set out in the Old Testament displays a contest between the forces which engender forgetfulness of the special covenant office of the people of God and the continual divine inspiration to remember it. At many points the forgetfulness seems to have the upper hand and the nation finds itself deprecating its exceptionalism and seeking to imitate the surrounding empires in their autonomy and vainglory. Walter Brueggemann has so well portrayed this as it took place particularly in the reign of Solomon, Israel embracing, as he describes it, *the world of briefcases and limousines* (1). It was the prophets' task to assault this spiritual amnesia and call Israelites back to their remembered covenant with God which alone could inform their true nature and office.

But this was no easy task. It was not merely a question of giving Israel a reminder to which the people would immediately recognise and assent to; it could not be done, so to speak, with a post-it note on the Israelite fridge. To challenge the amnesia of Israel and to call the people back to the recollection of God and his Covenant was a fight to the death for those called to it. For human forgetfulness of God is no minor matter, no neutral oversight, but rather a determined, sustained and cultivated obliviousness exercised by a bold and bitter mutineer.

Moreover, the life of forgetfulness of God somehow works quite well, at least in the short term. The 'empire' into which Solomon transmuted Israel, was outwardly very successful and impressive. Even if small, it was wealthy, and equipped with all the trappings of national success and prestige and it took significant measures to place itself beyond criticism. And in successive reigns following Solomon, these innovations became embedded institutions. But for the prophets, this cultivated and institutionalised amnesia would have become seamless and unassailable. As it was, it presented to them a seemingly unscalable height, a massive worldly self-confidence and unshakeable conviction that the nation could manage God or manage well without him. Brueggemann has listed the weaponry which the prophets utilised to tackle this edifice:

Grief is offered against establishment denial and cover-up..... Holiness is proclaimed against conventional theology that never quite faces the otherness and always hopes for and forms a utilitarianism that links God's holiness to some historical purpose. Memory is asserted against amnesia in which nothing is noticed or critiqued and everything is absolutised in its present form. Thus I take denial, utilitarianism, and amnesia to be the context in which the gospel is now to be proclaimed and practised. (2)

It is striking how similar forgetful Israel was to the modern post-Christian world. The Church, when it recovers its prophetic office, will need those same three tools of grief, holiness and memory, if it is to impinge in any significant way upon the adamantine monolith of worldly forgetfulness. As Brueggemann says, it needs a counter-imagination which arises from the recollection of God and his covenant. But it needs to address itself with this before laying it before the world. He writes:

When the church conducts its liturgy, when the church reads the Bible, when the church declares the gospel, it engages in a counteract, counteracting the world so long dominant among us. The most important resistance to this evangelical counter-imagination does not come from militant secularists. It comes from well-intentioned believers who are infected with modernity. It comes from the pastor's own sinking sense that none of this is true. So we worship and proclaim: a memory in a community which aggressively forgets, a covenant in a community deeply enmeshed in commodity, and a hope in a community that believes very little is promised or possible (3).

It is clear that this recollection of how things really stand between the people of God and their Creator and Redeemer and the corresponding displacement of spiritual amnesia is an immense event which calls into question all the so-called absolutes of the old order and ushers in a completely new way of thinking, understanding and being for all who come under its transformative power. Exercising this ministry in their own day, the prophets of the Old Testament understood and experienced the consequences of being agents of such an enormous shift. They found it compulsive but intensely weighty, joyous, but profoundly serious and thus they were themselves types of the One who was to come after them who was himself the embodiment of the Kingdom he proclaimed. Brueggemann captures both the depth of the transformation that recollecting the Covenant engenders and the danger that such a recollection involves:

....It is announced that God's faithful people may expect to receive from God a new mode of public existence. Life can begin again in a new community that is trustfully obedient to the norms of covenant. Such a theological reading of reality, one which envisions the destruction of idols and the emergence of a new community, will inevitably evoke resistance. These poetic traditions [of Jeremiah, Ezekiel and 2nd Isaiah]

do indeed subvert conventional readings of reality and conventional arrangements of power. These traditions evidence the process in ancient Israel of presenting and making available an alternative world that often seems unwelcome and unreal. Its welcome and its reality are based only on the conviction that God's resolution of Israel's history is one to embrace in obedience and celebrate in praise. Such obedience and praise are a practice of a dangerous alternative and a rejection of a world designed apart from and against the rule of God (4).

It is worth underscoring at this point that we find our true nature under God, our fulfilment as his people, our destiny as his inheritors by *remembering*. We do not seize it from our present world, nor do we reach in to the future to grasp it, nor enquire into our own souls to find it, but, repudiating all these adventures, we simply remember it, as that which was from the beginning, that which has Almighty God for its author, that which becomes the Christian's life's work to recollect.

4.4. Memory and Sacraments

Just as Christian faith is a correlate of God's faithfulness, so also Christian recollection of God's salvific acts is a correlate of God's recollection of his people and his drawing of them forward to the inheritance he has purposed for them. Thus recollection has both a godward and manward side. To a great extent the faith of the Christian and the faithfulness of God both rest on the capacity each has for exercising memory. When we recite the Apostles' Creed we are exercising our memory of the acts of God by which he remembers us and brings us into his present. But this concerted exercise of recollection is no better exhibited and revealed than by the Sacraments.

The Church has had a hard time understanding the Sacraments, especially in the West. In the first place, it could not easily decide how many Sacraments there were. Irenaeus thought there were two in the most general sense: Jesus Christ and the Created Order. Mediaeval Christianity recognised seven: Baptism, Eucharist, Absolution, Confirmation, Ordination, Marriage, and Extreme Unction. The reformed Church recognised two "gospel" sacraments, Baptism and Eucharist, while in the New Testament the only sacrament spelt out using sacramental language is Marriage in Ephesians chapter 5. What, however, is generally agreed is that a sacrament has two parts: (i) an outward visible sign, of (ii) an inward spiritual grace. That is, behind the obvious human actions, there is a work of God which is to some extent hidden, but which gives meaning and significance to the outward act.

But in each of the sacraments there is a dual recollection: on God's side, he remembers his people for good and brings them forward to encounter his grace afresh. On the human side, the great acts of God for our redemption are recalled, and by the working of the Holy Spirit are made a present reality which is applied to the participants. The Western Church has found this difficult to explain, particularly with its post-Enlightenment mindset. But even before that, attempts to to use Aristotelian categories to interpret sacramental action failed and were rejected at the Reformation. Subsequently, the Enlightenment made things more difficult for a large fraction of the Church was persuaded by the Enlightenment principle that only things which could be proved and which could be explained could be believed. Since a complete explanation of the action of God in a sacrament cannot be made, the sacraments became a problem for the Church and in some quarters were sidelined or even were a source of embarrassment to it. This in itself is a form of forgetfulness by the Church in which its confidence to recall all it has been taught falters and is replaced by a misguided adherence to a principle or movement inherently foreign to it.

The idea of recollection is a useful key to grasping the meaning and significance of the Sacraments. In Baptism, the new birth of which Jesus spoke and which his Incarnation represented for humanity is recollected and brought forward and applied to the baptismal candidate. In providing a new past in Jesus Christ's own human beginnings, a new future for the candidate is opened up. His whole life is thus framed in a God-given newness, but only because of the recollection of acts of God for him in history. The Eucharist has always been hard to explain, but the Eastern Church has a profound understanding of it. The basic idea is that the celebration of the Eucharist bears the same relation to the Cross of Jesus as does the Last Supper just before it. What the

Last Supper did was to identify the disciples with Jesus, that they might participate in his life, so that when he is sacrificed on the Cross, their lives too are surrendered to God with the same perfection as that of Jesus Himself. Subsequent celebrations of the Eucharist recollect that same identification of the participants with Jesus thereby enacting their self-offering with Jesus to the Father.

The remaining sacraments, if we allow them so to be described, are illustrative of the same principle of recollection. In the case of Absolution, the recollection of the Cross and its present application to the penitent is obvious. Confirmation and Ordination which both correspond to the Holy Spirit's setting apart of certain individuals for particular tasks, both involve the recollection of the ministry of Jesus and its application to the candidates in the present. Marriage can be viewed in two ways: It can be a recollection of God's creation ordinance in that his resolve that man should not be alone but should have a helper and companion suitable for him, and the application of that gift to the couple who present themselves for marriage. But it can also be a recollection of the union of Christ and his Church, achieved by his sacrificial grace and answered by the devotion of the redeemed. As this recollection is applied to husband and wife they become living exponents of the past victory achieved by Jesus Christ and, through their love, exhibit it in their lives. Extreme Unction, the anointing of the dying, recollects the saving messiahship of Jesus and applies it to the present exigency of the dying, thus asserting once again the identification of the mortal recipient of grace with the eternal life of the Christ.

4.5. Memory and Education

Hear, O Israel: The Lord our God, the Lord is one. You shall love the Lord your God with all your heart and with all your soul and with all your might. And these words that I command you today shall be on your heart. You shall teach them diligently to your children, and shall talk of them when you sit in your house, and when you walk by the way, and when you lie down, and when you rise. You shall bind them as a sign on your hand, and they shall be as frontlets between your eyes. You shall write them on the doorposts of your house and on your gates (Deuteronomy 6:4ff).

Among the many strengths of Jewish civilisation, two are prominent: (i) the concern for education of children and (ii) the integrity of family life founded on the institution of marriage. The principal responsibility for the education of children lies with parents, but the task of remembering the truth, rehearsing it, and discussing it was an occupation which engaged the whole family on a daily basis. The presupposition was that knowledge was to be received by recollection, comprehended by discourse, and reinforced by repetition. The commandments of God were not merely to be held to be true or respected ceremonially, but they were to be the warp and weft of the Israelite's mind and soul; they were to reside in his bones and govern his every instinct.

All this, of course, predates the Kantian invention of *a priori* knowledge (see section 4.8, below). This Israelite knowledge was that which, according to the simplest model, entered the Israelite mind by instruction and by the recollection of commandments which came through revelation to Moses from God. The text from Deuteronomy clearly suggests that this knowledge was processed in the conversation and reflections to which it gave rise. It was not vainly memorised and recited with no understanding or analysis. Its implications were examined to an enormously fine degree, and although Rabbinic argument may not always appeal to the Christian mind, it nevertheless demonstrates the seriousness and exactness with which the commandments were treated and the respect they commanded.

The Christian instinct for education has inherited much from this Israelite foundation. The principle is the same: The Christian educational tradition is to learn from what is taught, that knowledge comes from outside of the learner, who is also taught to cogitate, process and manipulate what has been learned. The definition of science we encountered from John Philoponus (see section 2.7.) essentially controls education under this conception.

Education in the post-Christian West has not escaped the influence of Kant. In terms of the Judaeo-Christian inheritance of education founded on recollection, Kant's conviction that individuals originate knowledge represents a sophisticated form of forgetfulness. In the light of it, education doctrine and practice became muddled: even the origin of the word was confused. In a supposed conformity with Kant, 'education' was taken to be derived from *educere*, to lead out, rather than from *educare* to rear. The aphorism *obstetrix educit sed nutrix educat,* the midwife brings forth, but the wet-nurse rears, was forgotten, and a generation of teachers embarked on a programme which centred on the concept that that children could generate knowledge rather than merely receive it.

This movement has disinherited at least some people from the assets of a genuine education founded on real learning. The old principle of education through recollection has diminished only slowly, and has been most clearly reduced in the context of early and primary school learning. But it is in the perception of the purpose and meaning of education that the loss is more noticeable. For the Israelite, education had to do with his ontology: what it was for him to be an Israelite. He learned many things but what he really learned was his beginning and end in God. He learned that he was the chosen companion of the Creator and Redeemer of the world. This discovery shaped his whole existence and meaning in the world. The Christian inherits all this and learns it again in the context of discovering his sonship of God in Jesus Christ. He discovers that he is Christ's agent in the world with material, moral and spiritual powers and responsibilities. His whole education is subservient to this vision.

4.6. The Hermeneutic of Recollection

The serpent said to the woman, "Did God actually say, 'You? shall not eat of any tree in the garden'?" So runs the fatal question which stands as the source of what becomes a very wide river of bad theology. Implicit in the question are three ideas. The first is that the speaker believes he knows better than God, in fact he knows God better than God. Secondly, the serpent suggests, and this is brought out clearly in the subsequent story, that God has some ulterior, and unworthy reason for making his commandment. Moreover, it is suggested that the command derives from a sense of weakness in God, a sense that he is threatened by the potential superiority of human intellect, so he is protecting himself from that risk and accordingly acting defensively. And thirdly, the serpent is inciting the woman to live and act on the basis of this false reading of God.

It is striking that at the very start of the biblical story, within three chapters, we are introduced to the essence of all bad theology, all false understandings of God and that this falsification of the nature of God stands at the head of all human wrong-doing. At its heart, this bad theology rests on *suspicion*. Suspicion that God is not levelling with us, or that he cannot be trusted because he has an ulterior motive by which he covers his weakness. A suspicion that, when all is said and done, human beings know better how things stand than the God who made them, are better equipped to evaluate truth than he, and have good reason not to take his advice, not to heed his word and not to render him obedience.

Throughout the biblical narrative this suspicion is an ever present opponent of God and of his creature. It is implicit in all human struggles, both internally within the conscience, and externally in human strife and competition. It is that against which the prophets campaign and battle, the wise men counsel and instruct, the priests sacrifice and implore. It makes its appearance in the cynical laughter of Sarai when the three divinely appointed visitors announce that she is to bear an heir for Abraham and in the false prophecies of the the 400 prophets advising Ahab according to 1 Kings 22:

For three years Syria and Israel continued without war. But in the third year Jehoshaphat the king of Judah came down to the king of Israel. And the king of Israel said to his servants, "Do you know that Ramoth-gilead belongs to us, and we keep quiet and do not take it out of the hand of the king of Syria?" And he said to Jehoshaphat, "Will you go with me to battle at Ramoth-gilead?" And Jehoshaphat said to the king of Israel, "I am as you are, my people as your people, my horses as your horses."
And Jehoshaphat said to the king of Israel, "Inquire first for the word of the Lord." Then the king of Israel gathered the prophets together, about four hundred men, and said to them, "Shall I go to battle against Ramoth-gilead, or shall I refrain?" And they said, "Go up, for the Lord will give it into the hand of the king." But Jehoshaphat said, "Is there not here another prophet of the Lord of whom we may inquire?" And the king of Israel said to Jehoshaphat, "There is yet one man by whom we may inquire of the Lord, Micaiah the son of Imlah, but I hate him, for he never prophesies good concerning me, but evil." And Jehoshaphat said, "Let not the king say so." Then the king of Israel summoned an officer and said, "Bring quickly Micaiah the son of Imlah." Now the king of Israel and Jehoshaphat the king of Judah were sitting

on their thrones, arrayed in their robes, at the threshing floor at the entrance of the gate of Samaria, and all the prophets were prophesying before them. And Zedekiah the son of Chenaanah made for himself horns of iron and said, "Thus says the Lord, 'With these you shall push the Syrians until they are destroyed.'" And all the prophets prophesied so and said, "Go up to Ramoth-gilead and triumph; the Lord will give it into the hand of the king."

And the messenger who went to summon Micaiah said to him, "Behold, the words of the prophets with one accord are favourable to the king. Let your word be like the word of one of them, and speak favourably." But Micaiah said, "As the Lord lives, ?hat the Lord says to me, that I will speak." And when he had come to the king, the king said to him, "Micaiah, shall we go to Ramoth-gilead to battle, or shall we refrain?" And he answered him, "Go up and triumph; the Lord will give it into the hand of the king." But the king said to him, "How many times shall I make you swear that you speak to me nothing but the truth in the name of the Lord?" And he said, "I saw all Israel scattered on the mountains, ?s sheep that have no shepherd. And the Lord said, 'These have no master; let each return to his home in peace.'" And the king of Israel said to Jehoshaphat, "Did I not tell you that he would not prophesy good concerning me, but evil?" And Micaiah said, "Therefore hear the word of the Lord: I saw the Lord sitting on his throne, And all the host of heaven standing beside him on his right hand and on his left; and the Lord said, 'Who will entice Ahab, that he may go up and fall at Ramoth-gilead?' And one said one thing, and another said another. Then a spirit came forward and stood before the Lord, saying, 'I will entice him.' And the Lord said to him, 'By what means?' And he said, 'I will go out, and will be ? lying spirit in the mouth of all his prophets.' And he said, 'You are to entice him, and you shall succeed; go out and do so.' Now therefore behold, the Lord has put a lying spirit in the mouth of all these your prophets; the Lord has declared disaster for you."

Then Zedekiah the son of Chenaanah came near and struck Micaiah on the cheek and said, "How did the Spirit of the Lord go from me to speak to you?" And Micaiah said, "Behold, you shall see on that day when you go into an inner chamber to hide yourself." And the king of Israel said, "Seize Micaiah, and take him back to Amon the governor of the city and to Joash the king's son, and say, 'Thus says the king, "Put this fellow in prison and feed him meagre rations of bread and water, until I come in peace." ' " And Micaiah said, "If you return in peace, the Lord has not spoken by me." And he said, "Hear, all you peoples!"

So the king of Israel and Jehoshaphat the king of Judah went up to Ramoth-gilead. And the king of Israel said to Jehoshaphat, "I will disguise myself and go into battle, but you wear your robes." And the king of Israel disguised himself and went into battle. Now the king of Syria had commanded the thirty-two captains of his chariots, "Fight with neither small nor great, but only with the king of Israel." And when the captains of the chariots saw Jehoshaphat, they said, "It is surely the king of Israel." So they turned to fight against him. And Jehoshaphat cried out. And when the captains of the chariots saw that it was not the king of Israel, they turned back from pursuing him. But a certain man drew his bow at random and struck the king of Israel between the scale armour and the breastplate. Therefore he said to the driver of his chariot, "Turn around and carry me out of the battle, ? or I am wounded." And the battle continued that day, and the king was propped up in his chariot facing the Syrians, until at evening he died. And the blood of the wound flowed into the bottom of the chariot. And about sunset a cry went through the army, "Every man to his city, and every man to his country!"
So the king died, and was brought to Samaria. And they buried the king in Samaria. And they washed the chariot by the pool of Samaria, and the dogs licked up his blood, and the prostitutes washed themselves in it, according to the word of the Lord that he had spoken. Now the rest of the acts of Ahab and all that he did, and the ivory house that he built and all the cities that he built, are they not written in the Book of the Chronicles of the Kings of Israel? So Ahab slept with his fathers, and Ahaziah his son reigned in his place.

This passage is worthy of careful study because it betrays the anatomy of the human falsification of the word of God and demonstrates how prevalent it is even among his own people. Both Ahab and Jehoshaphat know very well that the 400 prophets are not true to the word of God. Jehoshaphat asks if there is not another prophet of whom they can enquire and Ahab knows very well when Micaiah fails to level with him. Ahab thinks he can get a better word from the false prophets than he can from the true, a word that suits him better, authorising his escapade and indicating a better result from it. He is suspicious of the true word from Micaiah because it seems to him to be always adverse to his, Ahab's interests. He prefers a false endorsement to a true criticism.

It is noteworthy that the false word is delivered very much more impressively that the true, that agents of the false word are much more numerous, more confident, more accepted, and more secure in their appointments than the true. The agents of the false word despise and are violently disposed towards the agent of the true word, who is treated with contempt and cruelty by the king. And finally it is to be noted that the false word proves fatal to Ahab, who loses his life in following it, while the true word would have been a saving word if he had heeded it.

It sometimes remains, however, a subtle matter to distinguish a true word of prophecy from the false. The test supplied by Deuteronomy 18:22 is that if the word spoken by a prophet does not come true, he is not henceforth to be heeded. But clearly the test must be applied after the fact. It is more difficult without the benefit of such hindsight. The test given in

Deuteronomy 13:1ff is one of consistency with the knowledge Israel has already received. The prophecy may be fulfilled, but should the prophet urge convictions and actions foreign to received faith, that prophet faces a capital charge. The diagnostic in the case of Micaiah ben Imlah, is more subtle. In that case, the initiative came from Ahab's instinct for vainglory and he had decided what he was going to do before consulting any prophet. He wanted to recruit divine support for his mission and he thought that the prophet's declaration of his success would cause him actually to succeed. He was using the prophets' words in the same way as Israel tried to use the Ark of the Covenant to succeed in battle against the Philistines as described in 1 Samuel 5. Even before the battle, there are signs that both kings knew the 400 prophets were false and the witness of Micaiah was correct. But they thought they knew better, and could estimate the outcome accurately with or without the word of God.

The reluctance of the people of God to recollect what they had learned from the foundational encounters with God in their past and attempt to reason afresh from some other reference point in order to address some contemporary situation, was often exhibited in Israel's history and only occasionally, perhaps in response to their prophets' prompting, do they repair to the ancient premises upon which their faith was founded. By the time we get to the New Testament, the problem is endemic. Jesus warns the disciples several times of the dangers of false prophets, and St Paul has a running battle with the so-called super-apostles afflicting the

Corinthian Church. Almost all the doctrinal instruction that is given to the Church in the Epistles is to counter a false idea propagated among the Christian community often with compelling persuasiveness. And the battle continued beyond the New Testament throughout the succeeding centuries. Early opponents included the so-called Gnostics who substituted speculation and imagination for recollection, and soon the Arian controversy arose which took more that 200 years to put to rest. The Arian contest was between Greek reasoning about God and the recollection of the person of Jesus Christ. It is not surprising that the Nicene Creed which resulted from this conflict was founded principally on the recollection of the revelation of God in Jesus even if it was expressed to some extent in Greek terms.

4.6.1 St Irenaeus' engagement with the Gnostics.

St Irenaeus' main argument with the Gnostics was that they failed to receive their learning as the Judaeo-Christian tradition prescribes. Instead, they took the words of the Christian Gospel and attached speculative Greek meanings to all of them. This meant, at a superficial level, they could sound vaguely Christian while meaning and believing things that were far from true to genuine Christianity. It is striking to note that this trick has scarcely died out in the supervening years between the Gnostic high-noon of the 2nd and 3rd centuries and the modern era. But St Irenaeus uses humour very effectively to inhibit any possible seriousness being attached to Gnostic delusions. He writes, concerning the Valentinian account of creation: *And what comes from all this? It is no trivial tragedy, indeed, which each of these men pompously expounds, each in a different way, from which passion and from which element, each essence derived its origin.... For who will not spend his entire fortune to learn that from the tears of the aeon involving passion, the seas, springs, rivers and all liquid substances derived their origin, that the light came from her smile, and a corporeal elements of the world came from her perplexity and anguish? However I want to make my contribution to their fructification..... For, since all tears have the same property, it is unlikely that from them come both salt and fresh waters. It is more probable that some are from her tears and some from her perspiration. Furthermore since then exist also in the world waters which are hot and acrid, it is for you to understand what she did it to produce them and from what part of her they came. Such are some consequences of their hypothesis* (5).

4.7. The rise of so-called Theological Liberalism in Post-Mediaeval Western Europe

This general tendency towards spiritual amnesia and the reluctance to return to the vantage points in history of Judaeo-Christian revelation, substituting instead some speculative idea from contemporary imagination, formed the backdrop to the rise of so-called theological liberalism in post-mediaeval Western Europe. Even in the face of the fact that the Reformation was founded on a recovery of biblical authority and the recollection of its message, it was also part of a movement which assaulted Catholic intellectual hegemony and opened up possibilities of thought which hitherto could not be embraced. In Germany, particularly, from whence the Reformation principally sprang, Catholic intellectual governance gave way to an enthusiasm for Greek thought which became a dominant principle of German philosophy for 300 years. E. M. Butler writes, *Greece has profoundly modified the whole trend of modern civilisation, imposing her thought, her standards, her literary forms, her imagery, her visions and dreams wherever she is known. But Germany is the supreme example of her triumphant spiritual tyranny. The*

Germans have imitated the Greeks more slavishly: they have been obsessed by them more utterly.... only among a people at heart tragically dissatisfied with themselves could this grim struggle with a foreign ideal have continued for so long (6).

The scene is thus set in post-mediaeval Europe for a re-run of the battle between Christian revelation and Greek thought, which had dominated the first 500 years of the Church's life in Asia Minor and was now set to dominate 500 years of her life in Western Europe. The return to dominance of Greek thought was heralded by the archaeology and scholarship in ancient literature by Winckelmann and Wolf who both shared the propensity of prodigious hard work: Winckelmann read Greek from 4am to midnight and Wolf read long into the night with his feet in a bowl of cold water to keep himself awake! The capacity of Greek literature to grasp and direct even the daily habits of a human life made it a formidable opponent of Christian orthodoxy, sustaining its power long into the second millennium AD (7).

The return of the dominance of Greek thought in the eighteenth century in Europe challenged the Christian understanding of knowledge which, as we have seen (see Chapter 2) was epitomised by John Philoponos' definition of science. The centre of gravity shifted in philosophical perspective from 'out there' to 'in here', from the world-view of knowledge received from externals to an internal world of self-authenticating cogitation and speculative reflection.

4.7.1. Post-Mediaeval Philosophical Developments in Europe reflected in Music

It is possible to trace the change in mindset in Europe following the close of the mediaeval period via its music. In J. S. Bach, does one not find the mellifluous sound emanating from the heavenly portals where all is light and happiness? Then comes Mozart with light-hearted melodies of life, if not within the portals of heaven, then most certainly under heaven. But in the music of Beethoven, do we not find the troubled and restless spirit of man at some distance from his heavenly home? Then finally, in Schoenberg, man is altogether off the leash, the key signatures are abandoned and a Kantian-derived musical expressionism fills the world with dissonance.

4.8. Kant's Great Idea

The real turning point in this process was accomplished by Immanuel Kant. Peter Watson writes, *Kant's great contribution.......was to grasp that it is the mind that shapes knowledge, that there is such a process as intuition, which is instinctive, and that the phenomena in the world that we can be most certain of is the difference between I and not-I. On this account he said, reason as 'a light that illuminates nature's secrets' is inadequate and misplaced as an explanation. Instead, Kant said, the process of birth is better metaphor implying that human reason creates a knowledge. To find out what I should do in a given situation, I must listen to an inner voice. The mind does not grasp knowledge, it creates it.* (8) This proved a huge resource with which to assault Christianity because Christianity is founded on the grasping of knowledge and had been fighting for 1700 years against the idea that the mind generates it. It was the intellectual authority of Immanuel Kant which gave such momentum to the movement which has now given rise to post-modernism and the post-truth mentality.

4.8.1. Kant's *a priori* knowledge

In the preface to his *Critique of Pure Reason* in its second edition, Kant refers to the reversal he undertook in his earlier dissertation: *until now it was assumed that all our knowledge must conform or be adjusted towards objects. But upon this assumption all attempts to figure out* a priori *by concepts anything regarding such objects, that is, anything which would enlarge our knowledge, were failures. Therefore let us try to see whether we can get ahead better with the tasks of metaphysics if we assume that the objects should conform or be adjusted to our knowledge. This would harmonise better with the desired possibility of* a priori *knowledge of objects which should determine something regarding objects prior to their being given to us. It is like the first thought of Copernicus who, when he could not get ahead with explaining the motions of the heavenly bodies as long as he assumed that the stars revolve around the observer, tried whether he might not be more successful if he let the observer revolve and allow the stars to remain stationary* (9).

This takes us right back to Aristotle and the Greek preference for the realm of forms over the phenomenal realm. Once again we are imposing our thought on the object, instead of letting the object inform our minds. It is noteworthy that Kant's great idea never managed to control natural sciences, where Philoponus has ruled the day at least up to recent decades. It was in philosophy, the arts, music and, lamentably, in theology, that Kantian thought had the greatest impact. Finally it is irksome to the scientist, that Kant tries to recruit Copernicus to his *a priori* scheme, when, as we shall see, it was the celestial objects themselves that impressed their reality upon Copernicus' mind.

This idea that we do not receive knowledge but we create it was used by Feuerbach to construct a formidable argument against religion in general and Christianity in particular (10). If knowledge can be generated within the mind, then anything can be generated together with the faith to believe it. It was a short step for Feuerbach to take that makes God and the whole of religion, especially Christianity, to be a creation of the mind. Christianity was a psychological phenomenon in which the idea of a perfect human being, and the qualities of moral perfection are projected by the mind into heaven and the idea of God thus created. Feuerbach was an ardent and determined opponent of Christianity, but that has not restrained the Church from coming under his spell.

In our own day, lyricist Tim Rice has commented, *No one in charge of Christianity seems to be that convinced about the product.* We have been half-convinced by Feuerbach. We hear bishops speaking of the 'idea of God', or 'the idea which we call God', Feuerbachian constructions which suggest that we have swallowed his whole analysis. Even if we have not done so, it sounds sophisticated and learned to use his formulae. In the period of the great reign of psychology, in the Freudian years and those of his successors, Feuerbach's explanation of Christianity was so persuasive that the Western Church found it difficult to answer so, instead of confronting it, the Church extended a qualified welcome to it. Christianity started to be seen more widely as a phenomenon of the mind, rather than an act of God in history. It became about how people think and feel, instead of what God has done.

This was a sophisticated form of spiritual amnesia, in which even if the acts of God were remembered, they were not really acts of God at all, but merely the expressions of a vision of human perfection or the promise of a human fulfilment. It was an amnesia in which even if the Christian remembered the words, the deeds were not there to be remembered. They did not matter much. The whole centre of gravity of Christianity was moved from the great salvific events of history, principally of the Incarnation, Passion, Resurrection and Exaltation of Christ, to the present world of the Christian's mind. Although this was not completely successful, it was a predominant shift which occupied the Church for a good deal of the twentieth century. It was remarkable how readily the Western Protestant Church embraced this. In the 1970s the Bishop of Durham espoused the widely held position that the central Christian events in history, if they were events at all, did not matter much. The Resurrection of Jesus was much more than a mere 'conjuring trick with bones' - it was the timeless truth that it represented which really mattered (11). The concept of the "timeless truth" was slipped in without explanation, defence or challenge. This movement of Christian forgetfulness, in which the stories were remembered but the deeds forgotten, received widespread support and was considered a great asset by sections of the Church because it was considered to make believing in Christianity much easier for the modern mind or much more possible. It performed much better than even its advocates expected. You could now be a Christian and not believe at all. You could recite the Creed in all good conscience and not believe a word of it! It was a stroke of genius to gut the Church of faith but keep the outward appearance of liturgy and piety untouched. On an individual level it licensed unbelief as a form of faith, and required no sacrifice to be made by the adherent - no difficult faith to believe or defend, and a doctrine which proved flexible enough to endorse practically any conviction or behaviour.

4.9. A Shifting Understanding of Scripture

Specifically, this atmosphere was conducive to a shifting understanding of Scripture. Instead of being a recollection of God's actions in history, Scripture became regarded as a vehicle for generalised spiritual expression. The whole structure which flowed from Feuerbach's reductionism, taught that whatever Scripture said, it really meant something else. This led to an institutionalisation of doubt concerning the worthiness, reliability and meaning of the Bible. The authority of Scripture was thus impaired and qualified, and in many parts of the Church has been lost altogether. The witnesses to which the Church has listened in every generation, are not now called to the stand to give their evidence. Once the Church detached from the Scriptures its witness to the historical events of salvation, it made those Scriptures redundant and extraneous to its life. Having done that, the Church can no longer know accurately the One who calls it to himself, who gave his life for it, who was raised to life for it, and who ever-lives to make intercession for it.

4.9.1. The Word and Deed of God

The Church should have rejected the whole scheme of Feuerbach, if for no other reason than the fact that there is an intimate relationship between the word of God and his deed. Feuerbach treated Christianity as a matter of words only - words that man could say every bit as well as God. In fact, they were really only man's words as far as Feuerbach was concerned.

But are the words of God and the words of man so interchangeable? Consider Jesus Christ's own use of words: *And getting into a boat he crossed over and came to his own city. And behold, they brought to him a paralytic, lying on his bed; and when Jesus saw their faith he said to the paralytic. "Take heart my son: your sins are forgiven." And behold some of the scribes said to themselves, "This man is blaspheming.." But Jesus, knowing their thoughts, said, "Why do you think evil in your hearts? For which is easier, to say, 'Your sins are forgiven,' or to say. 'Rise and walk'? But that you may know that the Son of man has authority on earth to forgive sins" -- he then said to the paralytic -- "Rise take up your bed and go home." And he rose and went home* (Matthew 9:1-7).

To pronounce the forgiveness of sins was not strictly blasphemy. Blasphemy is the slandering of God, but the term was appropriated (as it was by the church in the middle ages) by those in religious authority to signify anything which might undermine their exclusive right to administer spiritual benefits. The real objection of the scribes was that, although there was a system in place to provide the forgiveness of sins (through sacrifices in the Temple, the officiating priests and the whole apparatus of Levitical law), Jesus was dispensing with it, and doing it all himself. The real offence of Jesus in the eyes of the representatives of the religious establishment was that he short-circuited all their procedures and replaced them with himself. If Jesus could forgive sins, you did not need the Temple sacrifices nor the order of priests - instead you needed only one thing, that Jesus would say the word.

The forgiveness of sins and the healing of a paralytic are both hard things to do - in fact impossible for anyone but God. But the contrast is not in the doing but in the saying. God's speech is different from man's speech. Man's speech is essentially descriptive: we can use language to tell ourselves all about say, light, in a textbook on optics. But God did not write a textbook on optics - when he said, *let there be light*, there was light. His word does not merely describe: his word creates and also redeems. Jesus used words in the same way God his Father used them. He does not describe the illness, he speaks a word which heals it. He does not merely list the offences, he speaks a word which forgives the sin. His word is his deed, and his deed his word. It only becomes easy to say this or that when the word is separated from the deed. It is easy to say *your sins are forgiven you*, if you are only responsible for the words and not for the deed. (The Cross shows us how hard it was for Jesus to say these words as he took responsibility for the deed). Religious officials can only say the words - they are unable to take responsibility for the deed - but they get away with it because the separation between word and deed in their case is not obvious because forgiveness is, for the present, a hidden thing. But in an instantaneous act of healing, it is clear at once whether the deed accompanies the word or not. In healing the paralytic Jesus clearly demonstrates that, like God his Father, his word is his deed. So Feuerbach's scheme to transfer the word from God to man, could not also transfer the deed.

There was, of course, no great scheme or plan to shift the ground in this way, it just happened. Once the shift in the intellectual centre of gravity from knowledge being external to the human mind and acquired by it, to knowledge being created by the human mind had taken place, profound changes could be expected in the manner in which the Church viewed the Scriptures. And the new view it took exhibited high degrees of scholarly sophistication. The tools of biblical criticism were applied with great enthusiasm and new tools were continually added to the armoury. It is not easy to come to a confident assessment of their value. On the one hand, the Church should study the Scriptures with diligence and apply all available tools to the elucidation of their meaning and message. This will most certainly mean that questions will need to be asked and answered about the meaning of words, date and authorship, composition and character of the texts concerned. Much of great value can be discerned from Scripture in these ways. On the other hand, there was a considerable detraction from the authority of Scripture during the critical process and this made the faith of the Church waver, even if only temporarily. Looking back, the whole critical project rather got out of hand. A low point was perhaps the so-called "Jesus Seminar" founded by an American professor who invited his colleagues from all over the United States to discuss the sayings of Jesus one by one and vote on their authenticity (12). Numerous works were included in addition to the Canonical Gospels and coloured beads were used for the voting, their colours signifying different levels of probable authenticity: red = authentic, pink = probably authentic, grey = probably inauthentic, black = definitely inauthentic. Certain ribaldry accompanied the publication of the results which predictably showed that the participants doubted pretty well all the significant sayings of Jesus concerning his own person and ministry, his Sonship of the Father and much else besides.

Despite this type of excess, for most of the twentieth century there was a strong impression that the scholars had the high ground: it was thought they really did know better, but their thraldom is passing and the Church is retracing its steps and finding its memory again. Even at the start of the critical adventure, there were those who were, without rejecting it altogether, evaluating it with restraint. P. T. Forsyth wrote *The essential thing in a New Testament Christianity is that it came to settle in a final way the issue between a holy God and the guilt of man. All else is secondary. All criticism is a minor matter if that be secure. The only deadly criticism is what makes that incredible; the only mischievous criticism is what makes that less credible* (13). On this reading, there most certainly was some deadly criticism and a lot of mischief in the undistinguished twentieth century of the Western Church.

As the tide of twentieth century scepticism has receded, it has left a jetsam of presuppositions in the Church most of which are false and destructive. There is, first, the lingering notion that in some way the Bible has been debunked and is no longer to be regarded as a dependable guide to Christian belief and practice. Actually, there is every reason to reject this notion. Practically all the sceptical conclusions of the adventure into biblical criticism, those things we were repeatedly told were the 'assured results of historical-critical scholarship,' have been since proved false. The Bible has well survived the mauling it received and, as we have seen, its reliability and authority have been strengthened by both archaeology and literary research in the mean time.

However, the instinct to set aside the Bible altogether remains, and it is now widely believed that its interpretation is an arcane matter and can come up with widely conflicting results. The perspicuity and simplicity of the Biblical message, which we have already considered, needs to be recovered. It is now common to find that when people wish to hold to a conviction not supported by Biblical witness and they are challenged on this, they often respond by suggesting it is all a matter of interpretation. The remedy for this particular form of post-critical jetsam it to start reading the Bible again.

It is of a piece with the general doubt about the Bible, that it is now thought that it is possible to have a Christianity without it altogether, or at least without its controlling reference. Already we are seeing in the western Church the chaos and dissolution which this idea engenders. But even in church traditions which have placed great emphasis on the importance and centrality of the Bible, there is a tendency not even to read it in the course of public worship.

We have seen that this complex manifestation of spiritual amnesia was a serious opponent of the people of God in the Old Testament but it did not prevail because even if Israel forgot God, God did not forget Israel. The same principle applies to the Christian Church to an even greater degree. Jesus himself says to his disciples, *These things I have spoken to you while I am still with you. But the Helper, the Holy Spirit, whom the Father will send in my name, he will teach you all things and bring to your remembrance all that I have said to you.*

4.10. Christianity Unforgettable

What this means is that despite the considerable efforts of the Church to adopt and devise sophisticated forms of spiritual forgetfulness, they are all doomed to failure. As Karl Barth so tellingly maintains, Jesus Christ is unforgettable. Not because he simply was a striking person who did memorable things, but because he was unforgettable as no other man was unforgettable. *Jesus was also there - and this, too, is a common assertion of the whole tradition - in a way which could not be forgotten. In this respect, of course, the emphasis and interpretation given by his resurrection and ascension exercise a particular influence. In his appearances his own had seen him come from the place from which no man has ever come and go to the place where no man had ever gone. What was revealed by these appearances? They revealed that this man - a man in his time like all others - did not come and go again like all other men in their time. It is a tribute to the power of this self revelation that it could shape the recollection of his life and death as it undoubtedly did, and to such an extent that we cannot separate in practice between a pre-Easter and a post-Easter picture of this man in the new Testament* (14).

Notice that: he did not come and go like all other men in their time. And therefore his Church does not come and go like all other human institutions in their time. And this despite the fact that the Church does often seem perversely dedicated to its own extinction and oblivion.

It would make Christianity a grim business indeed, if it was up to the Church to summon up its own memory, to strain its powers of recollection to regain but a tiny fragment of the deposit of faith that it has received. But that is not the way it works: buried in their forgetfulness, his people are constantly confronted with their unforgettable Lord who awakens them to a recollection not their own, but a recollection that is his, and only then, theirs.

REFERENCES FOR CHAPTER 4

(1) Walter Brueggemann, *The Prophetic Imagination*, p42

(2) Walter Brueggemann, *Hopeful Imagination*, p131

(3) Walter Brueggemann, *The Bible and Post-modern Imagination*, p55

(4) Walter Brueggemann, *Hopeful Imagination*, p5

(5) St Irenaeus, *Against Heresies*, 1, 4, 3, 4

(6) E. M. Butler, *The Tyranny of Greece over Germany*, p6

(7) Peter Watson, *The German Genius*, p95

(8) Peter Watson, *Ibid*, p194

(9) David Appelbaum, *The Vision of Immanuel Kant* p6.

(10) Van A. Harvey, *Feuerbach and the Interpretation of Religion*

(11) David Jenkins, in *Poles Apart*, BBC Radio, 4th October 1984

(12) N.T. Wright, *Jesus and the Victory of God*, p29

(13) P.T. Forsyth, *The Person and Place of Jesus Christ*, p5

(14) Karl Barth, *Church Dogmatics, Volume 4:2* p159

CHAPTER 5
HUMAN BEING

In this and subsequent chapters we will ask what we can know, what we can believe and what we can remember about humanity as we are informed about various aspects of human life from our socially constructed reality, from the realm of physical causality, from the realm of metaphysical causality, and from the recollections of the past. We will thus be using the various concepts and tools which we have considered in the last three chapters and apply them to an understanding of the human being. This is, of course, a vast subject and we will only be able to consider some general aspects, but the principles used will be applicable to any more detailed study which might be undertaken with more tightly circumscribed parameters.

5.1. The Socially Constructed Human Being

For the most part, we get on with being human without thinking too much about it. But the closest reference we have to understanding our own being, is the crowd of beings with which we share our lives. At the most basic level we conceive of ourselves in the context of our families, our working colleagues, friends and associates and, more recently, in the vast, somewhat anonymous community which is accessed through social media. We therefore unconsciously consider ourselves as the children of our parents, the parents of our children, the husbands of our wives and the wives of our husbands. We also find our identification in our trade or profession, in our employment or in our occupation of a public office. Various businesses and institutions further define us in relation to themselves. They write to us: "Dear consumer, customer, client, tax-payer, voter, complainant, claimant, tenant...."

Increasingly, we are defined by our circumstances as victims, patients, students, applicants, and as much as we might want to resist these classifications and claim some humanity or identity which transcends them, inevitably, we give some level of acquiescence to them, even if unwillingly. We are defined by our ages as children, teenagers, millennials, baby-boomers, pensioners, and by our economic status, JAMs (Just About Managing) being the latest designation at the time of writing. Add the ever more numerous sexual categories (of which Facebook identifies some 71 types), marital status, race, degrees of social and economic mobility, our purchasing power and our buying inclinations and there is enough information for marketing organisations, epidemiologists, pollsters and social science research students to generate an infinite array of correlations to prove just about anything about us. All this is like a huge Aristotelian classificatory system with an ever-growing number of subdivisions.

As complex as this array of definitions is, it does not actually describe human beings at all. It defines them all in relation to their function as objects of commercial, political, or social systems. It is similar to the Marxist understanding of human beings as units of labour, and it shares with the Marxist perspective the treatment of human beings in the mass, as a bulk resource, rather than as individual persons. Instead of elucidating the nature of individual human beings, it obliterates them, reducing them to statistical data from which certain performance can be calculated and anticipated. They do not have names, merely quantified spending habits, typical levels of consumption, and they exert a measurable demand upon public services.

The socially constructed human beings might occasionally be congratulated because they have increased productivity, or have adopted a healthy life-style, or have reduced their impact on the environment. On the other hand, they are frequently rebuked for low productivity, for becoming obese and therefore stressing the health service, or for failing to give up smoking and thereby poisoning their children, and reducing their own effectiveness in the workplace. Hillary Clinton summed up the utilitarian vision for human beings when she said, in October 1997: *The lack of good quality, affordable child care is a silent crisis. We want American parents to succeed at the most important task they have: caring for the next generation and being good workers* (1). At one level her aspiration for affordable child-care was quite reasonable, but she was possibly unaware of the low view of human beings implied by that statement. Whatever happened to the pursuit of life, liberty and happiness? What Hillary

Clinton seems to be advocating is the transformation of America into a giant slave farm.

There is, undoubtedly, something cruel about this bulk understanding of humanity. In his book, *The Making of a Counter Culture*, Theodore Roszak says: *We may only have to wait until our fellow humans have converted themselves into purely impersonal automatons capable of total objectivity in all their tasks. At that point when the mechanistic imperative has been successfully internalised as the prevailing lifestyle of our society, we shall find ourselves moving through a world of perfected bureaucrats, managers, operations analysts, and social engineers who will be indistinguishable from the cybernated systems they assist. Already we find these images of internally deadened human beings appearing in our contemporary novels and films. . . Each 'in here' confronts the other's 'out there' with indifference, callousness, exploitive intention.* (2)

In 1947, Leonard Lyons in *The Washington Post* reported a famous dictum of Stalin: *If only one man dies of hunger, that is a tragedy. If millions die, that's only statistics.* When a pregnant woman loses her unborn child through a miscarriage there is sorrow and mourning, but since 1980, 1.4 billion unborn children have been killed by abortion across the world, and Stalin is right, it is just a statistic, no one even winces.

This is really a problem of scale. It is possible for individuals to love millions of people if they are in a position to act for their good, for that is what love really is. But it is not possible to experience empathy for millions of people, or grieve for them in the same direct way deceased family members and close friends are mourned. This is one of the great assets of the family: it limits the range over which kindness can sensibly be exerted and experienced. Combining small institutions into a single large one, might make sense to accountants, and offer more diverse services to the clientele, but there are losses in the process. Cottage hospitals are often greatly missed when they are closed and the bright, new, cure-it-all megalith which replaces them hardly redresses the loss.

While, on the one hand we may rile against this bulk understanding of humanity, we also find resistance to the idea of our exceptionalism. The idea of extra-terrestrial life seems to prompt this notion: *It's arrogant for human beings to think they're the only thing in the universe. I mean the Earth is probably like Inverness. Inverness is in Britain so Earth probably has the same relationship to the rest of the universe.* (3). We seem to want to mediocritise ourselves, to be ordinary, to merge into the warp and weft of the natural order - to be like all the other species. We are embarrassed by our own success and suspect that we have gained it in some way unethically with respect to the other species, and in our more extreme moments we might propose drastic solutions to this perceived wrong.

The founder of *Planned Parenthood*, Margaret Sanger said, *The most merciful thing that a family does to one of its infant members is to kill it* (4). The Princeton professor, Peter Singer wants to have abortions after the baby is born. He would allow parents 28 days to decide whether to keep it. He suggested that no newborn should be considered a person until 30 days after birth and that the attending physician should kill some disabled babies immediately after delivery. In 1979 he wrote, *Human babies are not born self-aware, or capable of grasping that they exist over time. They are not persons; therefore, the life of a newborn is of less value than the life of a pig, a dog, or a chimpanzee* (5). According to Singer, *Christianity is our foe; if animal rights is to succeed, we must destroy the Judaeo-Christian religious tradition.* Alan Gregg, of the Rockefeller Foundation, said, *the world has cancer and the cancer is man* (6).

This is not yet a majority position but it shows that our opinion of ourselves is deteriorating, and because a low view of human beings reduces our sense of responsibility and obligation, we are inclined to go along with it. But the proponents of this doctrine of human beings as toxic to the earth are right to recognise that the Judaeo-Christian tradition is their enemy. As we shall see in this chapter, evidence from metaphysical causality integral to the Christian perspective indicates that the human being is infinitely more valuable than their estimate and has an implicit sanctity beyond their imagining.

5.2. The human Being from Knowledge

The Oxford Dictionary definition of a human being runs: *A man, woman, or child of the species* Homo sapiens, *distinguished from other animals by superior mental development, power of articulate speech, and upright stance.* The Encyclopaedia Britannica's definition is similar: *Human being (Homo sapiens), a culture-bearing primate that is anatomically similar and related to the other great apes but is distinguished by a more highly developed brain and a resultant capacity for articulate speech and abstract reasoning. In addition, human beings display a marked erectness of body carriage that frees the hands for use as manipulative members. Some of these characteristics, however, are not entirely unique to humans. The gap in cognition, as in anatomy, between humans and the other great apes (orangutans, gorillas, and chimpanzees) is much less than was once thought, as they have been shown to possess a variety of advanced cognitive abilities formerly believed to be restricted to humans. Traditionally, humans were considered the sole recent representatives of the family Hominidae, but recent findings indicate that chimpanzees (and bonobos) are more closely related to humans than are gorillas and orangutans and that the chimpanzee and human lines separated only about five million years ago. Therefore, all great apes are now gathered with humans into Hominidae, and within this family humans and their extinct ancestors are considered to make up the "tribe" Hominini.*

These definitions are, of course, grounded in the realm of physical causality and are of an Aristotelian type. What is interesting is that the Encyclopaedia Britannica entry discloses a recent re-allocation of the contents of neighbouring pigeon-holes. Traditionally, humans were

116

the only occupants of the Hominidae family pigeon hole, but now the great apes have been added to it. There will be some classificatory justification for this - the closeness of the DNA from respective species, perhaps, but the decision sounds at least partly political. The uniqueness of humans and their position of pre-eminence in the animal kingdom is being generally questioned as well it might, if only evidence from physical causality is taken into account. Superior mental development, power of articulate speech, and upright stance may be distinguishing features, but, it may be argued, they do not justify the absolute distinction of human beings as ontologically differentiable from other species. This is part of the philosophical justification of the animal rights movement and the sweeping vision of the Agenda 21 project, which above all, seeks to put the human race back in its perceived place to give land area and advantages to all the other species (7). This is meant to be a plan for sustainable development but it rests on a conviction that human beings are merely one species amongst many. Within the constrains of physical causality, the only argument against this plan is that may be anti-Darwinian. In its modern form Darwinian evolutionary theory is founded on the basis of the survival of the fittest which, left to itself, would apply ruthlessly in every circumstance in the natural order. If human beings are merely members of the family Hominidae, worthy of co-equal consideration with all other members, and as animals, co-equal with all other animals, and if they are so successful they take over the whole world, this is a predictable result of their status as the fittest. Should this exalted position not, therefore, stand? What then drives this instinct to disadvantage themselves with respect to the other competitors, which an examination of the plan certainly suggests? Perhaps behind the Agenda 21 vision, there rests a faulty understanding of human beings which contains more than could be derived from merely physical causality. Theorists argue that Agenda 21 is the linchpin in a plot to subjugate humanity under an eco-totalitarian regime. One of its most outspoken critics, American Policy Center president Tom DeWeese, has described the resolution as *a new kind of tyranny that, if not stopped, will surely lead us to a new Dark Age of pain and misery yet unknown to mankind* (8).

On the other hand, our traditional care of animals is entirely consistent with our survival. We look after animals for our own benefit, we farm them, attempt to optimise them for aesthetic or useful purposes, we control their numbers to gain best advantage for ourselves from the countryside and we use animals for transport, as a source of motive power and for entertainment. All of these uses render to us, in one way or another, an advantage with which we advance ourselves. Cruelty to animals might give us a short-term advantage, but it is, in the long-term destructive to ourselves. Of all the animals, human beings are the most able to exploit, for their own advantage, other species and control their environment for the same purpose. These activities, unlike Agenda 21 priorities, can be fully explained within the boundaries of physical causality.

5.3. The human Being from the Perspective of Faith

Here we ask different kinds of questions about human beings from the realm of metaphysical causality. What if, we ask, human beings are distinguished from the animals by divine intention. After all, upright stature, superior intellect and articulate speech are not the only uniquenesses exhibited by humans. Human beings pray, they have an awareness of God, their lives have a moral and spiritual imperative which prompts them to live in ways which are not readily calculable from a purely physical causality.

In Genesis 1:24ff we find a description of the creation of man by God:

And God said, 'Let the earth bring forth living creatures according to their kinds—livestock and creeping things and beasts of the earth according to their kinds.' And it was so. And God made the beasts of the earth according to their kinds and the livestock according to their kinds, and everything that creeps on the ground according to its kind. And God saw that it was good.

Then God said, 'Let us make man? in our image, after our likeness. And let them have dominion over the fish of the sea and over the birds of the heavens and over the livestock and over all the earth and over every creeping thing that creeps on the earth.'

So God created man in his own image, in the image of God he created him; male and female he created them.

119

And God blessed them. And God said to them, 'Be fruitful and multiply and fill the earth and subdue it and have dominion over the fish of the sea and over the birds of the heavens and over every living thing that moves on the earth.' And God said, 'Behold, I have given you every plant yielding seed that is on the face of all the earth, and every tree with seed in its fruit. You shall have them for food. And to every beast of the earth and to every bird of the heavens and to everything that creeps on the earth, everything that has the breath of life, I have given every green plant for food.' And it was so. And God saw everything that he had made, and behold, it was very good. And there was evening and there was morning, the sixth day.

If we allow this passage to reflect the metaphysical causality behind human existence, what does it tell us about the nature of that humanity? We notice, first, that humanity is unique in the animal kingdom, for while all the animals were made by God, only human beings were made in God's image after his likeness. In his masterly work, *A Theology of the Body*, (9) Pope John Paul II, proceeds to define some of the respects in which man can be said to have been made in the image of God. He notes that man was not made in accordance with natural succession, but there is a halt before the Creator brings him into being...*as if He entered back into Himself to make a decision. 'Let us make man in our likeness'* (10). John Paul notes that when all the animals were brought before man, not one was found suitable to be his helper. None of them were akin to man. Thus man is on his own in the creation, as God is on his own.

Let us consider the significance of that halt in the sequence of creation, before the creation of man. It is a very small feature of the text, but when the jury is listening to a witness, a pause, a change in inflexion can be very significant. The most immediate conclusion we might reach is that it was a much bigger step to create man, than it was to create any of the other species. And that conclusion is borne out by the kind of creature man proved to be. Man belongs to a different order of creation and is a different kind of being from all the other creatures. Positively, this man was to be a creature but also like God himself, someone after God's own heart, one with whom God could commune at a level of common mind and goal, of personal affinity and familiarity, a partnership in holiness. Psalm 8 captures something of the high rank and office of the human creature:? O Lord, our Lord,

how majestic is your name in all the earth!
You have set your glory above the heavens.
Out of the mouth of babes and infants,
 you have established strength because of your foes,
 to still the enemy and the avenger.
When I look at your heavens, the work of your fingers,
 the moon and the stars, which you have set in place,
what is man that you are mindful of him,
 and the son of man that you care for him?
Yet you have made him a little lower than the heavenly beings
 and crowned him with glory and honour.

You have given him dominion over the works of your
hands;
you have put all things under his feet,
all sheep and oxen,
and also the beasts of the field,
the birds of the heavens, and the fish of the sea,
whatever passes along the paths of the seas.
O Lord, our Lord,
how majestic is your name in all the earth!

Nonetheless, there was a risk involved. This man was to be a creature so closely ranked with God as to make him liable to the temptation of usurpation. He was made for fellowship with God, with a liberty not dissimilar to that of his Creator, with a mind and heart like his, with a will and powers of resolve and an instinct to accomplish. He was to be a moral and spiritual being, a being capable of deification, that is, capable of taking his place within the very life of God. The rank was so high, the position so exalted, the liberties so far-ranging that there was always the risk that things could go badly wrong, and, of course, they did. The rest of the story is that of the divine remedy for the catastrophe that followed, but let it suffice at this stage to envisage the calculation which took place in the divine mind, in that pause before the momentous act of creating man in God's own image. Evidently that decision was a close-run matter. In Genesis 6:5, when the outcome was looking so very bad, God reconsiders: *The Lord saw that the wickedness of man was great in the earth, and that every intention of the thoughts of his heart was only evil continually. And the Lord was sorry that he had made man on the earth, and it grieved him to his heart.* The divine answer to this problem was a combination of judgement and redemption and the history of the world is full of both of them. But together, they represent a single principle in the mind of God: that he will have this man as his companion, soul-mate and vicegerent, but he will have him the way he, God, intended him to be, not, in any way less than that. A fallen man will not do, only a perfected man will fill the office. So judgement marks the end of the man of sin, redemption, the beginning of the man of righteousness.

5.4 The Human Being: a Unique Creature

It is clear that God treats man, subject as he is to the powers of divine redemption, as the creature that he intends him to be; God's appointment of him to high office is not dissolved by man's attempts to contradict it. Man finds he cannot efface the imprint of the divine image, nor expunge the divine likeness that he bears. He remains, therefore, the unique creature of God with his high office from which he is not dismissed, and in fact in which he is actively endorsed and sustained by the will and resolve of God.

The biblical witnesses we have quoted and many others besides have given this kind of evidence from the realm of metaphysical causality: that of the human being comprehended in the light of God's creative intention, and millions of 'jurymen' down the ages have accepted their testimony as authentic that man is a creature not only qualitatively differentiable from animals but ontologically different from them. That he is a creature alone among creatures, a creature with an inner life unlike others, capable of inward cogitation, wrangling with conscience, with opposing inclinations for good or ill. Man is the creature with a ruling will, and a will to rule, a drive to know and a capacity to understand, an eye to exploit, and the imagination to create.

A reductionist like Feuerbach (see section 4.8.) will assert that these properties, in a perfected form are simply projected into the heavens to conceptualise God as one who exhibits them. But if this is so, it does not lead us to the origin of these properties and why man is uniquely what he is. The point of reductionism is to *reduce* man to what he is conceived really to be, a creature ontologically like any other creature, with a purely physical causality. But he is not like any other creature in all these manifold ways. So reductionism simply relocates the metaphysical cause of man from within God to within man himself - the mystery is still there and an account of it must still be found. The location of metaphysical cause within the psyche of man is traceable to Plato and Aristotle, so the argument down the ages is not whether there is or is not a metaphysical cause lying behind reality, but its location - whether it is integral with the world in the realm of thought as the Greeks conceived it, or whether it resides in the mind and purpose and being of a creator God external to, and entirely separate from, his creation as the Judaeo-Christian tradition would have it.

124

5.5. The Human Being from History

Recourse to history, and in particular to the history of Jesus Christ, achieves two things in this connection: (i) it puts reductionism into obsolescence and (ii) it resolves between the Judaeo-Christian and Platonic/Aristotelian views of the location of the metaphysical cause of the human being.

Projection of an imagined human perfection into the heavens, as Feuerbach portrayed religion, is rendered meaningless and redundant, if after doing so, we look down and find that same perfection embodied in a human being standing on the earth. In order to resume our heavenly projection experiment, we would have to deny the Incarnation of the Word in the person of Jesus Christ. As we have seen (section 3.3.) the manifold and ingenious efforts to do this have been largely discredited and set aside and the genuineness of the biblical witness concerning Jesus is recognised with increasing seriousness.

But when the Word became flesh, what kind of humanity did he take? A great deal of Christian thought has gone into this because several truths need to be held in tension. First there is a genuine perfection in the humanity of Jesus Christ. This is attested to in the witness of the Apostles who affirmed, not only his sinlessness, but that he was like God himself in his human life. *We have beheld his glory, as the only-begotten of the Father*, they said. Secondly, there was nothing absent in his humanity - all the components of a human life were there, without sin: however the make up of a human life is expressed, whether it be with body and soul, or body mind and spirit, or body, mind, soul and spirit, Jesus' humanity had all those necessary components. All attempts to create a model for the Incarnation involving substitution of human spirit or soul with the logos or the Spirit of God, were rejected by the church on the grounds that the whole of the human being must be taken by the Son, if the whole human being is to be redeemed. *What is not taken, is not redeemed*, is the principle expressed by the Cappadocian Fathers (11). So Jesus' humanity must have been entirely genuine, but was it fallen, or unfallen? The Apostles testify that he was without sin, yet, says the author to the Hebrews, *He was tempted as we are*. The generally held view is that Jesus exhibited a perfection and a sinlessness himself, he did not commit sin, but he was not immune from it and was content to be associated with it, even identified with it. Karl Barth puts it this way:

'God with us' in the sense of the Christian message means God with us men who have forfeited their predetermined salvation, forfeited it with a supreme and final jeopardising even of our creaturely existence. As the way from that beginning in God to the end of man with God is revealed in this particular event, its line is not a straight one, but one which is radically and - if God Himself were not there as hope - hopelessly broken.

126

The situation of man in this event is this. He occupies a position quite different from that which he ought to occupy according to the divine intention. He does not conduct himself as the partner God has given Himself to receive His redemptive grace. He has opposed his ordination to salvation. He has turned his back on the salvation which actually comes to him. He does not find the fulfilment of his being in participation in the being of God by the gift of God. Instead, he aims at another salvation which is to be found in the sphere of his creaturely being and attained by his own effort. His belief is that he can and should find self-fulfilment. He has himself become an eschaton. *This is the man with whom God is dealing in this particular redemptive history: the man who has made himself quite impossible in relation to the redemptive grace of God; and in so doing, the man who has made himself quite impossible in his created being as man, who has cut the ground from under his feet, who has lost his whole* raison d'être. *What place has he before God when he has shown himself to be so utterly unworthy of that for which he was created by God, so utterly inept, so utterly unsuitable? When he has eliminated himself ? What place is there for his being, his being as man, when he has denied his goal, and therefore his beginning and meaning, and when he confronts God in this negation? Despising the dignity with which God invested him, he has obviously forfeited the right which God gave and ascribed to him as the creature of God. But it is with this lost son in a far country, with man as he has fallen and now exists in this sorry plight, that God has to do in this redeeming event. And this is what reveals the gulf. This is what shows us how it stands between God and man* (12).

It is of a piece with this that we notice that, as Jesus' ministry continues from the shores of lake Galilee, through the towns and villages of his mission and up to Jerusalem to the final *denouement* of the Cross and Resurrection, his reputation grows in two directions. It grows positively, as he is increasingly regarded as heaven-sent, as an agent of God's mercy, as a wonderworker, as a prophet, and even as the promised Messiah, and he is hailed by the crowd as one who does all things well. At the same time, his reputation grows in a negative direction: first as a somewhat strange individual, then as a drunkard and a glutton, then as a sorcerer who casts out devils by the prince of devils, then as a blasphemer and a destroyer of the Temple, then an an insurrectionist worthy of death as a traitor. It is extra-ordinary that both these reputations grew apace during his ministry, and that Jesus makes little attempt to correct, direct, or repudiate either of them. He lets them grow, seemingly oblivious to them.

Jesus is content to have both reputations because as the Perfecter of the human race who makes the perfect offering of himself to God the Father, his perfection was a necessary property of the sacrifice. At the same time, he came to be the end of sin and so his growing reputation as a reprobate, as misguided as it was, was a prophetic affirmation of his ministry to carry sin to its judgement and finally to do away with it. Feuerbach may have thought Christianity was gazing into heaven to see a synthesised human perfection there, but the reality of the manifestation of that perfection on earth, proved to be an infinitely more subtle matter. There was no static perfection, but a dynamic one, which seized sin and carried it away for judgement to the infinite advantage of its perpetrators, and it did so right in the theatre of its commission not in some rarefied stratospheric plane of ideas.

5.6. Metaphysical Causality Located in Space and Time

This brings us to that second achievement of the Incarnation, the location of the seat of metaphysical causality, amongst us, in space and time, in history, in the human and physical realm. No longer is it an idea only, it is now an act of God in the sphere of man. That is why it has such immeasurable power to transform human beings, to direct the path of their history, to make them to be the exalted creature of God's intent and purpose. We cannot now understand ourselves without remembering Jesus Christ. Without him, we can only read a confused message from the mystery which is ourselves. Without him we can have at best, only a mutilated conception of what a human being is. There is some echo of glory, of our greatness, of our high office, of our powers, but in him, that glory, greatness, office and power are revealed. Without him, we have some notion of our fallenness, the degradation of that glory, the poverty of our weakness, but we can make no sense of it, nor of the evident ambiguity of our condition. But if we take Jesus as our starting point, and his life as the bearing for our travel, we can recall a consistent meaning of human life, a sure basis for its value, and a perspective on its future.

Of course, from outside, this perspective of the Christian understanding of the human being is apt to be misunderstood. St Paul's description of the human race in its depravity, for example, can easily be misread as a low view of human beings in general: *And since they did not see fit to acknowledge God, God gave them up to a debased mind to do what ought not to be done. They were filled with all manner of unrighteousness, evil, covetousness, malice. They are full of envy, murder, strife, deceit, maliciousness. They are gossips, slanderers, haters of God, insolent, haughty, boastful, inventors of evil, disobedient to parents, foolish, faithless, heartless, ruthless...* (Romans 1:28) Christian authors are sometimes thus accused of demeaning humanity. Richard Niebuhr defends Jonathan Edwards against this charge:

Now who demeans humanity? The one whose standard for man is small or the one whose standard is very great? The one who judges him as a domestic lover or as a citizen of a universal commonwealth? The one who looks upon him as faithful or unfaithful administrator of lawns and stores, stocks and bonds, or the one who sees in him the steward of eternal riches? What is greater, the neatly painted, well-constructed five or eight room house or the ruins of the Forum or the

130

Parthenon? What Edwards knew, what he believed in his heart and with his mind, was that man was made to stand in the presence of eternal, unending absolute glory, to participate in the celebration of cosmic deliverance from everything putrid, destructive, defiling, to rejoice in the service of the stupendous artist who flung universes of stars on his canvas, sculpted the forms of angelic powers, etched with loving care miniature worlds within worlds. In the light of that destiny, in view of that origin, because of the greatness of that calling, it depressed him, angered him that men should throw away their heritage and be content with the mediocrity of an existence without greater hope than the hope for comfort and for recognition by transient fellow men. Man who had been made to be great in the service of greatness, had made himself small by refusing the loving service of the only Great One; and in his smallness he had become very wicked, covetous of the pleasures that would soon be taken from him. But in the end, man could not make himself small, Edwards knew, for the way of man is not in himself (13).*

Thus the recollection of the witness of Jesus Christ renders a more nuanced understanding of the status of human beings. With a special, close and trusted relationship with God, a high office on earth and a deep-seated likeness to the Creator, with a visionary participation in glory, all brought into grave question and jeopardised by a catastrophic refusal of God by the man himself, a seemingly irreversible disaster using any ordinary means, is the state of things which brings God himself in human flesh to address the crisis personally. The historical witness in the person of Jesus testifies to his life, death and resurrection as the means that God employs to reverse the catastrophe, reinstate the man, and set his purposes once again on the path to fulfilment.

According to St Irenaeus, Jesus Christ is the exponent of God's active intellect and his dynamic economy. Jesus Christ is God setting things in order according to his wisdom and re-asserting his proper union with human beings. The result is a deepened union and a yet heightened station for man who is the object of divine redemption. The economy of God is the history of humanity but it is also the history of salvation, it is not only the undergirding purposes of God but also the action by which God accomplishes his restoring work. A second favourite concept of St Irenaeus is the *recapitulation* accomplished in Christ in which the beginning is joined to the end and everything between is set in order in so doing. Jesus Christ, in his representative capacity as the Second Adam gathers human history and fulfils it properly and presents it to the Father.

What this demonstrates is the profound impact that the life of Jesus Christ had on the evaluation of all history, time and space and future. And central to this panoply of divine purpose is the special office and place of the human being, whose existence is so absolutely authorised by God that even the radical imperilling of it by man's sin, could not deflect, but only deepen the divine resolve to accomplish his purpose, of a glorious union of heart and mind with the creature without whom God has not willed to be God.

It will also be clear that the overall effect of the catastrophe of man's fall and the towering divine act to redress it, did not merely restore the human condition to its original prelapsarian status, but it raised it immeasurably higher. The coming of Jesus meant opening the inner life of God to redeemed humanity. No longer is man merely a trusted, high ranking, beloved creature, given plenary authority over all that God has made, but he is now, through the sonship of Jesus Christ, grafted into the divine family. According to the letter to the Hebrews, when Jesus comes to the Father, he says, *"here am I and the children thou hast given me"*. Jesus speaks of his disciples as his brothers and taught them to address God as Father. The provisions of the New Covenant are thus infinitely superior to those of the Old.

5.7. The Status of the Redeemed Human Being

The intimacy which now stands between God the holy Creator and man is of such order that the Church Fathers had to take a few theological risks to express it properly. St Irenaeus, spoke of the union between God and man through the Son in terms of the *deification* of man. This, of course, was in the face of the absolute Judaeo-Christian conviction of the differentiation between Creator and creature. St Irenaeus knew this very well, and had no intention of challenging the principle, but he still felt constrained to speak of the union between

God and man in Jesus in very intimate terms. To be a Christian was to have a direct union with God through participation in God's grace and glory. St Irenaeus recognises that some considerable "habituation" or accustomisation will be necessary and this is the everyday substance of the Christian life. It is the practice of the presence of God, living in union with him, learning to think with him and cooperate with his purposes. This is illustrated in Scripture in many ways, but perhaps most powerfully in the description of Mary's consent to the Angel Gabriel, to bear God's Son. Urs von Balthasar expresses it this way: *At the beginning is God's Word that will become flesh. God's is the praxis, mine is the letting God's will be done in me, the agreement, the consent, down to my fingernails. And it really is someone who in perfect creaturely freedom becomes womb and bride and mother of the incarnating God. This fundamental act is neither in a Buddhist way: a surrender of the unfree being oneself into the abyss of the absolute, nor - in a Marxist way - a self-endowing with freedom so that the human being can become its own creator, but a being gifted - by the unconditionally self-giving God - with the freedom to receive God unconditionally. Thus Mary's consent marks the beginning of the catholic church: In this fundamental act in the room at Nazareth, in this alone the church of Christ is founded as catholic. Its catholicity is the unconditional character of the 'behold the handmaid' whose offer of infinite accommodation is the creaturely counterpart to the infinitely self-bestowed love of God* (14).

We are in urgent need of recollecting this intimacy between God and man, secured by Jesus Christ, which is actually the centre of gravity of all practical Christianity. We once knew it well. In the early days before the Peace of Constantine all Christianity was lived very close to the truth of the resurrection appearances of Jesus in the upper room. There was an immediate sense of the presence of Jesus Christ and the Christian was gripped by it and life was led under the direct impact of it. And Christians became very numerous because of this spiritual intimacy: people could see that Christians lived holy lives, they were restrained from vice, they were trustworthy and dependable. Christianity was virtually defined by the Christian living consciously and deliberately in the presence of Jesus Christ by his Spirit. It does not appear that this kind of life was only exhibited by a "spiritual" fringe, or exceptional holy people, or those who might be considered deranged. Living of one's life in the presence of Jesus Christ was what it was to be a Christian.

This immediate sense of the presence and reality of God persisted into the mediaeval period and, through the acceptance of Christianity as the prevailing faith and worldview, it was endorsed by public practice and observance. In mediaeval Europe, God was everywhere: a farm worker tilling the soil would hear the church bell ring thrice and he would know that God was doing a great and incomprehensible deed for him in that church. He would drop to his knees and cross himself. Maybe this was not quite the same as the first-hand spiritual reality of Jesus experienced by the early Christians but it was something like it. It meant that a consciousness of the presence of God still directed the Christian from hour to hour in his working day. It was entirely right that God should be part of living, prayed to, depended on, trusted in every part of life. Homes, marriages, education, child-birth, family life, working, earning, employment, service, infirmity and death were all sanctified and that sanctification was not merely private, but public, open and accepted.

But then the Reformers came. They stopped the daily mass, they stopped ringing the bell, they told the farm-worker not to kneel or cross himself, but to just get back to work. In the name of a new piety, they stopped an old one. The new piety might have been more accurate and it might have rediscovered what grace was, but that was the same grace as was experienced by the farm worker in the first place. Maybe he failed to understand it correctly, maybe he didn't understand it at all, but there God was, in all holiness, with all his power and with all his grace, and with him, the farmworker. It is hard to avoid the conclusion that the Reformation chased God out of the fields and streets and market places and began regulating how and when, and under what terms God could be known.

This changed, profoundly, how the human being was now understood. The highest definition of the human being which Christianity revealed was one who enjoyed the company and trust of the living God. There could be no higher office or greater rank than this. All other definitions fall away. The Reformation did not abolish that. It could not, but it did reduce its profile in the public sphere. In post reformation Europe, the recognition that life was lived publicly in the presence and power of the Spirit of Jesus Christ inexorably diminished over the centuries until we find that now we are practically back in an atheistic world.

5.7.1. The Nature and Status of the Reformation.

H. Richard Niebuhr give us a clue as to how to evaluate the Reformation. In section 3.2.1. above he is quoted as suggesting that as words and symbols take over as the substance of Christianity, we are left with a religion to which God is scarcely relevant save as a label for an idea. We use the words and the symbols, but we really do not know God at all. Since this is a ubiquitous problem that always threatens genuine faith, it may well be that because it afflicted the world of mediaeval Catholicism, the Reformation was simply a reaction to it. The story of Luther's life strongly suggests this. The losses implicit in the Reformation, seem a heavy price to pay for the remedy of this affliction, which was bound to arise again in any new Church. And as Niebuhr has pointed out it has certainly done so.

It makes the Reformation seem regrettable. G. K. Chesterton points this out in a parable: *Suppose that a great commotion arises in the street about something, let us say a lamp-post, which many influential persons desire to pull down. A grey-clad monk, who is the spirit of the Middle Ages, is approached upon the matter, and begins to say, in the arid manner of the Schoolmen, 'Let us first of all consider, my brethren, the value of Light. If Light be in itself good......' At this point he is somewhat excusably knocked down. All the people make a rush for the lamp-post, the lamp-post is down in ten minutes, and they go about congratulating each other on their unmediaeval practicality. But as things go on they do not work out so easily. Some people have pulled the lamp-post down because they wanted the electric light, some because they wanted old iron; some because they wanted darkness, because their deeds were evil. Some thought it not enough of a lamp-post, some too*

137

much; some acted because they wanted to smash municipal machinery; some because they wanted to smash something. And there is war in the night, no man knowing whom he strikes. So, gradually and inevitably, to-day, to-morrow, or the next day, there comes back the conviction that the monk was right after all, and that all depends on what is the philosophy of Light. Only what we might have discussed under the gas-lamp, we now must discuss in the dark.(15)

5.8. The Recollection of the Spiritual Union with God

So our recollection will necessitate remembering far more than mere doctrine. There needs to be a recollection of our spiritual union with Jesus Christ. We need to learn again to think with him, to engage with our tasks in collaboration with him, to make decisions with his mind and ours conjointly in agreement. We need to learn again to think his thoughts and live his life. In this connection we need to recall the great responsibility and authority we have been given to act in his name and represent him in the world. As St Paul says we are ambassadors for Christ and thus represent him in a plenipotentiary capacity with which he entrusts us. Many things are given to us to decide for ourselves. We can make plans, invent and design methods and tools, create beautiful art and build elegant buildings. We do not wait to be told to do this. We are not simply functionaries carrying out God's inexorable will, but we are his companions and fellow workers with Christ. This means that if we make a decision to carry out some plan which is in conformity with the principles we have shown by Christ in the Gospel, this is our decision and we can rely on his loyalty to it. We are his creative agents in the world and he trusts us and is loyal to our plans and assists their fulfilment. God does have a great and holy will, but it does not smother everything in its path. It does not exclude every other will with a jealous insistence that it be the only will. In Islam, the will of Allah has a suffocating ubiquity, neutralising all other will. The companions of God, the brothers and sisters of his Son do not exist - Allah only has slaves. They inevitably must carry out his single will which fills the whole world. Not so, in the reign of Christ Jesus in the Kingdom of God! In that Kingdom, all powers of intellect, all insights of imagination, all skills of creation, all visions of glory and the human will to use them all, are sanctified, elevated, empowered and honoured. As St Paul declares, *I can do all things through him who strengthens me.*

REFERENCES FOR CHAPTER 5

(1) *The Chicago Tribune,* 24th October, 1997

(2) Theodore Roszak, *Making of a Counter Culture,* p133

(3) Ex-Spice Girl Geri Halliwell, 5th July 1999

(4) Margaret Sanger (editor). *The Woman Rebel, Volume I, Number 1.* Reprinted in *Woman and the New Race,*1922

(5) Peter Singer, *Practical Ethics,* 1st ed., p122–23

(6) Alan Gregg, *A Medical Aspect of the Population Problem, Science* 121 (1955): 681-682, p682.

(7) Glenn Beck, *Agenda 21*

(8) Tom DeWeese, *Sustainable Development: the root of all our problems,* NewsWithViews.com, January 8, 2008

(9) John Paul II, *A Theology of the Body*

(10) John Paul II, *Ibid.* p135

(11) Gregory of Nazianzus, Epistle 101, *Early Church Fathers 3.7.2.2.1.1*

(12) Karl Barth *Church Dogmatics, Volume 4.1* p10

(13) H. Richard Niebuhr, *History Theology and Culture* p128

(14) Urs von Balthasar, *Das Katholische an der Kirche* quoted in *The Von Balthasar Reader,* p214

(15) G. K. Chesterton, *Heretics,* p6

CHAPTER 6
HUMAN DIGNITY

We begin with a definition of dignity. Anything which is an affront to our real nature is undignified and everything which is consistent with our true nature is dignified. We might add a further category: there is an absolute dignity associated with our real nature, but there is a *perceived* dignity which reflects our *perceived* nature. We are not shamed or embarrassed by what we perceive as consistent with how we regard ourselves, but we are ashamed of things which are inconsistent with such perceptions. So dignity has to do with the evaluation of how we conduct ourselves, whether our behaviour, speech, thought, appearance, conduct, attitudes are proper or improper reflections of what we are or how we see ourselves. In this chapter we will consider human dignity from the point of view of socially constructed reality, from our knowledge of the human being, from the insights of the Judaeo-Christian tradition and from the basis of our recollection of our human nature.

6.1. Socially Constructed Dignity

In modern western everyday thinking, dignity does not seem to have a very prominent place. Sometimes it is regarded negatively as a principle. 'Standing on one's dignity' may well be despised as a sign of hypocrisy and thus 'bad,' otherwise dignity is not something which appears to be very seriously guarded in our present

141

social climate. This is perhaps because we are uncertain as to our true nature so we are unclear what behaviour, attitudes, beliefs, are proper to it. We take our cue from everyone else. The effect of this is to base most our evaluations of dignity on appearance. How we seem to others, how we look, the impression we give, our profile, demeanour, stature are all things which pre-occupy us. This was exactly true of the ancient Graeco-Roman world, particularly of high-born members of society. Young men and women were schooled in deportment, in striking the right physical attitude, down to the line of jaw and tilt of the head. Today, the descendants of these celebrities practice walking down the red carpet looking as elegant as possible and sign up to the most politically correct set of opinions and political enthusiasms and their examples inform hosts of their disciples and imitators. Clothing becomes fashionable because the A-list trend-setters set the standard and create a huge market in the reproduction of their appearances. As in the Greek world, prized body image has been defined and established in the same way, and, now assisted by modern technology, has spawned a correspondingly large and profitable plastic surgery business. In scores of different ways, standards of appearance, behaviour, belief and conduct arise almost arbitrarily. As in chaos theory, where large numbers of random phenomena eventually exhibit patterns, so new habits, satisfaction of appetites, the practice of exhibitionism, craving for publicity, eventually gel into fashions. And these fashions summon a conformity, generate their own sense of propriety and dignity and set new standards against which non-conforming attitudes and behaviour become rated as undignified.

This shifting sand of habit and behaviour will always be part of a socially constructed human reality and is often entertaining and benign and, especially in hindsight, quite amusing. But if it become the principle basis upon which the virtue and value of human beings and human thought are derived and established, it is revealed as a feeble foundation for any civilisation and can result in degeneration of human life and a source of human emptiness and misery. We cease to know for certain, under these conditions, what is dignified and what is not. Because we have locked ourselves in to a shifting frame of human values which have no real source, or point of reference, we can easily find ourselves living in a world of anxiety, governed only by a socially validated hedonism, and thus led into vice or corruption. If we have no sound basis for knowing what we are, we have no secure basis for assessing what it is that dignifies or shames us.

Yet in our world of socially constructed reality, there are currently agreed dignities and indignities. Physical weakness is generally rated as undignified, especially among men. Prowess at sport is applauded. Intellectual capacity gets mixed press, sometimes applauded, sometimes derided. Pride and humility are similarly treated ambiguously. Wealth is treated variously according to its source: earned wealth is sometimes respected, inherited wealth less so, and wealth from a lotto win subjected to envious contempt. Huge efforts are made to avoid and cover the indignities of death, mainly because of the weakness exhibited by the dying, the unattractiveness of it, and because it reminds the observers of their own mortality. Nudity is not always considered undignified: celebrities wearing revealing clothing seem increasingly unashamed of the inevitable exposure which their garments permit. The public exhibition of rage does not attract the opprobrium that it once did, although newspaper readers enjoy deprecating it and the enraged are not generally as ashamed of it as they would have been a few decades ago. Divorce is not regarded as generally undignified, nor homosexuality, nor, so much, marital infidelity, but more extreme sexual proclivities may attract lifelong disgust and rejection.

What does this jumbled array of responses suggest? That socially constructed perceived human dignity rests on appearance, image and the impression an individual may have on others. What matters, it seems, is what we look like to other people, who estimate us, in the absence of any external reference, against an idealised view they may have of themselves. This constitutes a massive circular argument which drifts over the landscape of human living in a more or less random and arbitrary way, breaking new ground of acceptability on its leading edge and leaving a trail of newly disparaged attitudes and behaviour in its wake. There are some constraints to its movement, however. New law and new political correctness urge its movement in certain directions, and restrain it in others. On the other hand sudden shifts in public opinion and attitude rebellions can halt and reverse its progress even against these urges. The upshot of all this is that whatever is considered dignified for human beings varies over a wide range of possibilities and that which is condemned as unworthy is similarly changeable. What is more, none of it has any authority if socially-constructed reality is the only frame of reference.

6.2. Dignity and Knowledge

If we confine ourselves, in the first instance, to knowledge from the realm of physical causality and ask what conduct, thought, speech and attitude is proper to our nature and therefore dignified, we would perhaps have to start with our biology and biochemistry. We can, from these considerations, calculate certain factors which would contribute positively to what we might call our "bio-dignity". We would get the right amount of sleep and sex, eat and drink correct amounts of correct foods and beverages. We would take the correct amount of exercise and avoid damaging life-styles. We would avoid the absorption of poisons, refrain from the consumption of dangerous drugs. If we add psychological health into the mix, we would avoid stressful experiences, emotionally unpleasant encounters and we would seek harmonious living in a safe environment. A glance at the plethora of life-style and health magazines shows how prominent is the devotion to this bio-dignity around which a certain morality has been constructed. Greek physicians gave this sort of advice to their patients in antiquity and their modern counterparts continue the tradition in our own day.

But if this is all there is, it constitutes the immense tedium of a sub-human existence. G. K. Chesterton underscores the inadequacy of this health mania:

The mistake of all that medical talk lies in the very fact that it connects the idea of health with the idea of care. What has health to do with care? Health has to do with carelessness. In special and abnormal cases it is necessary to have care; when we are peculiarly unhealthy it may be necessary to be careful in order to be healthy. But even then we are only trying to be healthy in order to be careless. If we are doctors we are speaking to exceptionally sick men, and they ought to be told to be careful. But when we are sociologists we are addressing the normal man, we are addressing humanity. And humanity ought to be told to be recklessness itself. For all the fundamental functions of a healthy man ought emphatically to be performed with pleasure and for pleasure; they emphatically ought not to be performed with precaution or for precaution. A man ought to eat because he has a good appetite to satisfy, and emphatically not because he has a body to sustain. A man ought to take exercise not because he is too fat, but because he loves foils or horses or high mountains, and loves them for their own sake. And a man ought to marry because he has fallen in love and emphatically not because the world requires to be populated. The food will really renovate his tissues as long as he is not thinking about his tissues. The exercise will really get him into training so long as he is thinking about something else. And the marriage will really stand some chance of producing a generous-blooded generation if it had its origin in its own natural and generous excitement (1).

This presupposes that there is more to human life than preserving the body and mind. It presupposes that the dignity of man lies in his enjoyment of the world, his mastering of it, his glorying in it. But this definition of his dignity will need more than biology or psychology. It will need theology. But before we leave the realm of physical causality, we will consider another possible basis upon which to rest the dignity of human beings: employment.

6.3. Dignity and Employment

We are often told by politicians that employment gives human beings dignity and there is an extent to which that may be true. When we are introduced to people, they often want to know what we *do*. Our answer gives us a certain status in their eyes, especially if what we do is particularly skilful, or has required great training, or is highly paid, or gives us power over others. If it does none of these things we might feel that it is undignified to disclose it, for fear that they will think less of us. Of course, what we do can dignify us, but not because we are employed to do it, but because it is worth doing and requires from us the exercise of our human powers. Employment, *per se*, is not necessarily dignifying.

In fact, employment shares common features with slavery, and is not so very different from it. One could almost go as far as to say that slavery has not been abolished, but merely renamed. In the Ancient World, slavery was a way of being and occupied by vast numbers of people, but most slaves had a better time of it than the free poor. Westermann writes:

At the bottom of the pyramid one might be tempted to place the slave population. In Italy it was enormous, possibly a quarter of the whole. In the provinces the proportion may have been closer to a tenth. But a high proportion of slaves worked as domestic servants in substantial households, enjoying the certainty of three meals a day, a roof over their heads, and a good chance to build up a little savings and gain their liberty when they had passed middle age. Their children they might have to leave in their master's house to endure in turn some decades of servitude - a fair exchange, since many slaves came into their condition as the price for life itself, having been found abandoned by their parents at birth and reared by their finders for later sale. The exposing of children points to the very pinched circumstances of the free poor. Certainly they looked forward to a shorter adult life than the luckiest slaves of all, those that belonged to the emperor. Servi Caesaris sometimes owned their own slaves, travelled in pomp and luxury on the emperor's business, commanded deference from all but the highest aristocracy, and after manumission vaulted to monied prominence among the freeborn. They did not typify life in servitude, of course any more than those very different others who died in mines of Dacia. But both extremes of fortune show the impossibility of lumping all slaves together (2).

This suggests that the range of experience of slaves in Ancient Rome was similar, except in most extreme cases, to the range of experience of employed people in our own day. Some employed people are very wealthy, but large numbers are not and stay that way. Employment might be considered a very poor deal: the employee uses up his life-force for the employer, becomes weary every day for him, using up a vast proportion of his waking hours, all for a few tens of thousands of pounds per year which will only keep a roof over his head and food on his table, only the things which the slaveowner provides anyway for the slave. It can only be said to be dignified to be employed because it may be so much less dignified to be unemployed.

6.4. Dignity and Taxation

Taxation is also a form of slavery, because it requires everyone with taxed earnings to work some fraction of the year for the government without pay. Tax freedom day is the date in each year when the average taxpayer has earned the tax he pays for that year and then begins to earn money for himself. In the USA in 2016 it was on April 24th, or 114 days into the year. Americans paid $3.3 trillion in federal taxes and $1.6 trillion in state and local taxes, for a total bill of almost $5.0 trillion, or 31 percent of the nation's income. In the UK Tax freedom day was June 3rd for 2016, meaning that for the first 154 days of the year the average tax-payer was earning just the tax he paid. Income tax was first introduced in Great Britain by William Pitt the Younger in 1798 at a rate of 0.83% on incomes over £60 per year. The first collection of income tax in the USA was in 1861 and was levied at 3% of all income over $800. In both Britain and the USA, its introduction was opposed as an infringement of the right of private property which is another element which asserts human dignity and which we address below.

6.5. Dignity and Private Property

We have to resort to the realm of metaphysical causality to give an adequate account of another principle of human dignity which is the principle of private property. There is no basis for this in the natural world. The nearest we come to it in nature is the territorial instinct or the unwillingness for a lion to give up its prey to a challenger. But what is at stake in the latter case is not private property but merely lunch. No animal owns anything and there is no legal system to defend its right to do so. Private property is a uniquely human phenomenon and is not found to be entirely universal. Among native Americans, as among many settled animist cultures, exhibit a territorial instinct: areas of ground could be used and occupied by families, and even inherited by their children, but exclusive ownership of land by an individual was considered impossible. Land did not belong to the man, but the man to land. (3)

It was the Judaeo-Christian tradition which really established the prevalent private tenure of land in Israel, the Near East, in Europe and beyond. The general principle of private possessions is established by the eighth commandment, *You shall not steal*. This stands behind Samuel Adams' assertion that *What a man has honestly acquired is absolutely his own, which he may freely give, but cannot be taken from him without his consent.* (4) The possession of things and of land is founded upon the fact that God gave gifts to his people: *Thus the Lord gave to Israel all the land that he swore to give to their fathers. And they took possession of it, and they settled there* (Joshua 21:43). The absolute right to a possession is thus founded on the nature of God's grace. Particularly this is true in respect of the land of Israel, which was given in perpetuity to his people - not just corporately, but as tribes, clans, families and individuals who were inheritors of the Promised Land. They received land which was absolutely and incontrovertibly theirs and their title was so secure that they could not lose the land permanently even if they fell into debt and had to lease it to another. It returned to them in the year of the Jubilee after a maximum of 49 years. So possession of property is a sign of human dignity because it signifies the trust God places in human beings. It is part of their sharing in the divine image, that they can own things and hold land and be masters of it. It is equally a matter of human dignity that they can decide and rule over their possessions with absolute discretion and with a regnant authority.

6.5.1. Ownership of Land

From the point of view of human origins, land is not absolutely owned, and in practically all cases can be traced back to conquest, treaty, or some other form of adverse acquisition. So-called landowners do not have an absolute ownership of their land, but have a title to it and their enjoyment of it depends upon the terms of the deed by which they acquired it. Generally, title to land improves with time: land holding becomes more secure and its tenure becomes more accepted as it becomes ancient. In the case of the land of Israel, the present occupants at the time of the Israelite conquest enjoyed a title to the land which was derived from a series of previous invasions by ancient empires. The tiny Land of Israel was situated at a point over which successive imperial armies tramped in their efforts to expand their empires. This largely explains why so many different ethnicities occupied such a small space. They each were small enclaves of people left behind as successive empires retreated in the face of the advance of others. Their claim to the land, in common with most of the world, rested upon the history of the endless shifting of civilisations through war and conquest. From an Israelite point of view, the title to the land of these residual populations was thus founded on principles of physical causality while Israelites understood their own claim as rooted in the the promise of God. Israelite title was thus believed to be superior.

6.5.2 Private Property in Ancient Israel

We see very clearly, not only the exercise of a God-given right to the land, but also the defence of it in the face of a pagan tyranny in the famous case of Naboth's vineyard, the story of which is told in 1 Kings 21:

Now Naboth the Jezreelite had a vineyard in Jezreel, beside the palace of Ahab king of Samaria. And after this Ahab said to Naboth, "Give me your vineyard, that I may have it for a vegetable garden, because it is near my house, and I will give you a better vineyard for it; or, if it seems good to you, I will give you its value in money." But Naboth said to Ahab, "The Lord forbid that I should give you the inheritance of my fathers." And Ahab went into his house vexed and sullen because of what Naboth the Jezreelite had said to him, for he had said, "I will not give you the inheritance of my fathers." And he lay down on his bed and turned away his face and would eat no food.

But Jezebel his wife came to him and said to him, "Why is your spirit so vexed that you eat no food?" And he said to her, "Because I spoke to Naboth the Jezreelite and said to him, 'Give me your vineyard for money, or else, if it please you, I will give you another vineyard for it.' And he answered, 'I will not give you my vineyard.'

" And Jezebel his wife said to him, "Do you now govern Israel? Arise and eat bread and let your heart be cheerful; I will give you the vineyard of Naboth the Jezreelite."

So she wrote letters in Ahab's name and sealed them with his seal, and she sent the letters to the elders and the leaders who lived with Naboth in his city. And she wrote in the letters, "Proclaim a fast, and set Naboth at the head of the people. And set two worthless men opposite him, and let them bring a charge against him, saying, 'You have cursed? God and the king.' Then take him out and stone him to death." And the men of his city, the elders and the leaders who lived in his city, did as Jezebel had sent word to them. As it was written in the letters that she had sent to them, they proclaimed a fast and set Naboth at the head of the people. And the two worthless men came in and sat opposite him. And the worthless men brought a charge against Naboth in the presence of the people, saying, "Naboth cursed God and the king." So they took him outside the city and stoned him to death with stones. Then they sent to Jezebel, saying, "Naboth has been stoned; he is dead."

As soon as Jezebel heard that Naboth had been stoned and was dead, Jezebel said to Ahab, "Arise, take possession of the vineyard of Naboth the Jezreelite, which he refused to give you for money, for Naboth is not alive, but dead." And as soon as Ahab heard that Naboth was dead, Ahab arose to go down to the vineyard of Naboth the Jezreelite, to take possession of it.

Then the word of the Lord came to Elijah the Tishbite, saying, "Arise, go down to meet Ahab king of Israel, who is in Samaria; behold, he is in the vineyard of Naboth, where he has gone to take possession. And you shall say to him, 'Thus says the Lord, "Have you killed and also taken possession?" ' And you shall say to him, 'Thus says the Lord: "In the place where dogs licked up the blood of Naboth shall dogs lick your own blood." ' "

Ahab said to Elijah, "Have you found me, O my enemy?" He answered, "I have found you, because you have sold yourself to do what is evil in the sight of the Lord. Behold, I will bring disaster upon you. I will utterly burn you up, and will cut off from Ahab every male, bond or free, in Israel. And I will make your house like the house of Jeroboam the son of Nebat, and like the house of Baasha the son of Ahijah, for the anger to which you have provoked me, and because you have made Israel to sin. And of Jezebel the

Lord also said, 'The dogs shall eat Jezebel within the walls of Jezreel.' Anyone belonging to Ahab who dies in the city the dogs shall eat, and anyone of his who dies in the open country the birds of the heavens shall eat."

(There was none who sold himself to do what was evil in the sight of the Lord like Ahab, whom Jezebel his wife incited. He acted very abominably in going after idols, as the Amorites had done, whom the Lord cast out before the people of Israel.)

And when Ahab heard those words, he tore his clothes and put sackcloth on his flesh and fasted and lay in sackcloth and went about dejectedly. And the word of the Lord came to Elijah the Tishbite, saying, "Have you seen how Ahab has humbled himself before me? Because he has humbled himself before me, I will not bring the disaster in his days; but in his son's days I will bring the disaster upon his house."

Naboth knew what his land signified: it was his inheritance, the land that signified his place in Israel, his office as a child of God's promise, his dignity as a recipient of God's grace, authorised and empowered to govern and decide over his land, to exercise his discretion as God exercises his. Ahab knew this too - even as the king of Israel he did not have the power to displace Naboth from his inheritance and he accepts Naboth's refusal. Not so Jezebel, his wife. She was not an Israelite, she knew nothing of the divine covenant, of the promise of God and status of every Israelite. All she knew was pagan tyranny, of arbitrary power, and of a kingship which could seize anything, slay anyone, in the satisfaction of its appetites, and which knew nothing of the human dignity enjoyed by every Israelite under the covenant with the living God. So she went ahead and destroyed Naboth and seized the vineyard for her husband. She showed Ahab how to reign. But the Word of the Lord came to Elijah and thence to Ahab and summoned him to the recollection of the covenant, of the integrity of every Israelite and the wrong that he had done to Naboth.

This story exhibits a number of features of interest in our present line of enquiry. It is notable that Naboth's entire attitude is derived from his self-understanding as an inheritor of God's promise. We have seen that he did not regard himself as simply a landowner, but as a recipient of divine promise and thus he thought of his existence as metaphysically caused. This was not just theoretical idea but informed his praxis as an Israelite. Jezebel thought in terms of physical causality: in which kings are powerful, they can have what they want and do what they like. The story is typical of what happens when the simple calculation of physical causality runs up against the realm of metaphysical causality. The former prevails in terms of violence and material outcome, but the latter is morally stronger, better founded and more fundamentally persuasive. All down the ages the argument from physical causality has challenged and confronted the argument from metaphysical causality, and has often prevailed by force in the short term, but has failed to dent the resolve of its opponent which exhibits a durability long into the future. There are strengths there which the tyrant under-estimates and cannot understand.

The dignity of Naboth is revealed by the fact that his place as an inheritor of the divine promise makes him able to resist the clear advantage of rank and power exhibited by the king. But in order to make that resistance, he has to *know* of his place as an inheritor, *believe* the promise of God and *remember* from where he has come. When he does so, he can resist the power of a monarch, even one propelled by all the forces of a pagan instinct. The real life of Naboth lies in his being the object of divine promise and he prepared to face any consequence rather than give it up.

6.6. Dignity and Martyrdom

In this Old Testament story we find a template for many similar examples of the witness of martyrs to be found throughout the history of the Christian Church. The pattern is of pressure applied by the logic from the realm of physical causality, being resisted by a resolve derived from knowledge from a metaphysical causality. The resistance usually results in death of the witness, but a triumph for the metaphysical argument. We recall here two instances from the life of the early Church.

6.6.1. The Dignity of the Martyrs I - Perpetua and her Companions

It was in March, AD 203, that several young Christians were martyred in the persecution under Septimius Severus. We have parts of the diary of one of these martyrs, a woman called Perpetua, whose writings show that in dying for their faith in Christ, Christians were convinced not only of their own salvation and vindication, but that they were also instruments in the victory of Christ over unbelief in the world. Perpetua has a dream in which she is engaged in a wrestling match with an enormous Egyptian who, if he prevailed, was to kill her, while if she prevailed against him, she was to receive an olive branch. In the dream she did prevail and received the reward. When she awoke she interpreted the dream as indicating she would be fighting the devil when she faced the wild beasts and through her death she would be victorious.

The eye-witness account of the martyrdom itself suggests that the whole exercise was both horrific and chaotic. One of the intended victims, Secundulus, had already died in the prison. Another, a companion of Perpetua, eight months pregnant, gave birth just before the day of sacrifice arrived. A wild boar was brought to gore Saturus, but the animal suddenly got the better of the huntsman who brought him and gored him instead. Then Saturus was thrown to a bear, but again was unharmed, because the animal could not be roused or goaded into attacking him. Finally, he was thrown to an enraged leopard which killed him with a single bite.

Perpetua and Felicity, who had just given birth, were brought to be gored by a very fierce cow which obliged but did not kill them, and a young soldier had to be persuaded by Perpetua herself to run them through with the sword. The soldiers seemed to have been moved both by the faith of the martyrs and by their confident sense of victory despite the cruelty and squalor of their fate. Sometimes the persecutors themselves were converted to Christ by what they saw.

6.6.2 The Dignity of the Martyrs II - The Holy Obstinacy of Pionius

In AD 249 the government changed in Rome. Partly by popular acclaim, partly because he murdered his predecessor, Gaius Messius Quintus Trajan Decius Augustus became emperor of

Rome. Like all new leaders he wanted to establish his authority, and like all leaders who ascend by their crimes, he wished to legitimise his reign and make it appear as proper and lawful and right as he could. He commissioned a team of 15 special advisors and spin doctors to make sure the perceptions of his reign were as positive as he felt they should be. Manilius Fuscus, one of his most fervent spin doctors advised him that nothing would legitimise his reign as much as the widespread support of all the pagan gods and their shrines. So the public investment in the shrines and temple celebrations began. Manilius' wife Flavia Politta led the procession of loyal First Ladies to the Shrine of Juno for lavish sacrifices and spectacular ceremonies. Gladiatorial games were authorised throughout the Empire and the Masters of the Amphitheatres were on the lookout for new, ever more gory spectacles with which to quench the blood-lust of the circus audiences. The reign of Decius was to be perceived as a great new era of enjoyment, and plenty, and everyone had to be loyal to the Great Initiative!

One of the spin doctors was rummaging among the papers of Decius' predecessors and he came across what he instantly recognised as a handy little edict passed by Valerian a few years before. This could be just what they were looking for. By enforcing an edict of a previous government he would give the impression of continuity, and at the same time cement together the essential elements of the new Empire. The edict simply required everyone to sacrifice to any of the state-authorised pagan gods. The Jews were excluded - no Roman law could be enforced against their religious sensitivities. Successive governments had learned that - but everyone else would be required to make the offering. If they did, they would be declaring their loyalty to the new Empire. If they didn't, well, the games would have fresh supplies of material for entertainment.

The first sign that there would be a number of refusniks showed up in Manilius' own household. His wife Politta had a slavegirl called Sabina who turned out to be a Christian, and, likely as not, would cause trouble when the day for sacrifice came. Politta attempted to shake her out of her faith by tying her up and leaving her out in the hills. She managed to escape her bonds and make her way southwards to Smyrna where she found Pionius, a Christian philosopher who gave her shelter in the Smyrnaean Church.

But soon Decius' edict began to take effect. Polemo, the pagan temple steward of Smyrna came to arrest Pionius and Sabina and bring them to the temple to offer sacrifice as the law required. Pionius struggled so much that it required six soldiers to carry him and when he arrived he found they had hired a philosopher and rhetorician called Rufinus to persuade him to offer sacrifice. He also found to his distress that his bishop had already denied Christ by offering the sacrifice to the idol. But Pionius and his companions resisted and were thrown back into jail.

Finally, the Governor Quintilianus was due to arrive in Smyrna to hear the cases at the Assize. Calculations have shown that the year 250 AD was a busy one for Quintilianus: he heard thousands of cases, many of them capital and many against Christians, and he completed each one in an average time of about one and a half minutes. In Pionius' case, the governor made some enquires of him, ascertaining that he was a Christian and a teacher among Christians. He then had Pionius hung up by his fingers as he went on questioning him. 'Change your mind,' he said, 'and offer sacrifice.' 'No,' came the reply. Quintilianus had him subjected to torture by the removal of his fingernails and put the same question. 'I will not sacrifice,' came the answer.

The sentence was read in Latin: *Whereas Pionius has admitted that he is a Christian, we hereby sentence him to be burnt alive.* They nailed him to a gibbet and piled up wood and burnt him to death. The author of the record of his martyrdom writes: *Such was the innocent, blameless, and incorruptible life which blessed Pionius brought to an end with his mind ever fixed on almighty God and on Jesus Christ our Lord, the Mediator between God and man.*

Irenaeus asserts with good reason that the *blood of the martyrs is the seed of the Church.* The martyrdom of Christians often led to an increase in their number, a consequence which may seem, at first sight, somewhat counter-intuitive. However, the reason for this can be expressed as follows: as we have already considered, Christian faith is supported both by evidence from physical causality, as in the history of Israel, and in particular the historical occurrence of Jesus of Nazareth, and by evidence from a metaphysical causality which testifies to divine presence and working behind these occurrences. But a primary witness to Christians is the metaphysical encounter with the risen Christ through the work of the Holy Spirit. As powerful as this may be to the individual Christian, it is not easily exportable evidence, because Christians find it difficult to describe or explain, let alone, prove. They may say that it is like being admitted to the Upper Room to meet with the Risen Christ, but it is only possible to understand what that is like, by being admitted oneself. This sets a sharp limit to the degree that Christianity can comprehended by an outside observer. This would not be so significant if the inward testimony of the Holy Spirit was not of the essence of what being a Christian involves, but it *is* of the essence, and is the driving force behind Christian living and sacrificial conduct. Martyrdom, like nothing else, reveals the inward divine power of Christianity, and those who witnessed martyrdoms were often so impressed by the revelation of this inner power, they were eager to embrace the Christian faith even if it meant sharing in the mortal consequences of it.

6.7. Dignity and Faith

The martyrs impressed observers of their deaths and, indeed, their persecutors, with the dignity of their faith, meeting their end with equanimity, even joy and with an unswerving adherence to their convictions. Their demeanour and confidence rest entirely on evidence from the realm of metaphysical causality: their reliance on the reality of God's trustworthiness was exclusive - there was nothing else. This prompts us to examine

159

further the relation between faith and dignity across the range of Judaeo-Christian witness.

Our first encounter with the question of dignity and shame in this range comes in Genesis 2:25. *And the man and his wife were both naked and were not ashamed.* Then comes the story of the Fall: *Now the serpent was more crafty than any other beast of the field that the Lord God had made. He said to the woman, "Did God actually say, 'You? shall not eat of any tree in the garden'?" And the woman said to the serpent, "We may eat of the fruit of the trees in the garden, but God said, 'You shall not eat of the fruit of the tree that is in the midst of the garden, neither shall you touch it, lest you die.'" But the serpent said to the woman, "You will not surely die. For God knows that when you eat of it your eyes will be opened, and you will be like God, knowing good and evil." So when the woman saw that the tree was good for food, and that it was a delight to the eyes, and that the tree was to be desired to make one wise, she took of its fruit and ate, and she also gave some to her husband who was with her, and he ate. Then the eyes of both were opened, and they knew that they were naked. And they sewed fig leaves together and made themselves loincloths.*

The text makes a point of contrasting their lack of shame while naked before the Fall, with shame in being naked after it and their need for clothing to restore their dignity. Originally they were naked and unashamed. This, as John Paul II points out, is not merely that they were unclothed, but that they shared an interior vision as God has. God's perceptions are very deep and

160

penetrating and in the original prelapsarian condition of man, that interior vision was shared by man (5). It was substantially lost through the fall, and generally man now only has an exterior vision. As part of the redemption of man by God, however, this exterior vision is supplemented by the beginning of a redeemed interior vision in the form of insight. They were naked in the sense that they were fully known to each other and to the God who created them, and there were no grounds upon which this interior knowledge could give rise to any embarrassment.

When Adam fell, he and Eve experienced the shame of nakedness. Before, nakedness identified man as the vicegerent of the created order. It was demonstrative of the fact that he was not like the other animals. It was a sign that he could stand before the world confident of his authority as God's regent on earth and as such in his authenticity as holder of that office. There was no shame in being visible as what he was. When he fell, all that changed: his nakedness became a sign of his disgrace, that he had lost that authority and authenticity whereby he once ruled the cosmos. He became cosmically naked. And the whole cosmos began to disobey him. Before, his nakedness revealed his honour, now it betrays his dishonour. After the Fall, his nakedness revealed that he was no longer equal to the office to which God had appointed him, so he covers this up in an attempt to maintain his dignity. In fact, he is assisted in this by God himself who clothes him more effectively. He is not, therefore, dismissed from that office, but maintained in it and helped by God to hold it as well as possible.

But if we take the nakedness literally, there is another level of meaning which can be drawn from this narrative. John Paul II distinguishes between two very different ways of viewing the body: the *spousal* view and the *concupiscent* view (6). The spousal view was that perspective which Adam has of his wife when she is brought to him in their unfallen state: *Here at last*, he says, *is flesh of my flesh and bone of my bone!* He delighted in her as the inestimable gift of God that she was. After the Fall, he began to see her as an object of his desire, and a means of his gratification, and so his view of her degenerated to a concupiscent one. John Paul II points out that the spousal body is a gift from God the Father, a gift to the other, an instrument of communion, a gift for procreation, a gift for obedience, and a gift to be delighted in. Conversely, a concupiscent body is worldly, an object for self, an object for satisfaction, a self-serving object, a vessel of disobedience, and an object to be made use of. The spousal body is a gift which dignifies, the concupiscent body is an object which bears and brings shame.

In the marriage service, husband and wife are to honour one another and their marriage is to be honoured in the community (7). To honour is to acknowledge and adorn the dignity of another. Throughout the Old Testament, God is to be honoured as are those who live in conformity with their status as God's people. Parents are to be honoured by children because of their divine appointment to the parental office. The fifth commandment insists, *Honour your father and your mother, that your days may be long in the land that the*

162

Lord your God is giving you. (Exodus 20:5) and Proverbs 31:10ff extols the grounds upon which a wife must be honoured. Similarly according to the book of Proverbs, the righteous, wise, humble and generous are worthy of honour, because these characteristics are exhibited by God himself, and thus are proper to the man made in his image.

6.8. Dignity and Jesus Christ

These characteristics are thus all the more proper to Jesus Christ, who is the express image of God's glory. We must now consider this dignity of Jesus Christ, who is the exemplar and archetype of the redeemed humanity which he came to establish, and exhibits the dignity proper to human beings in the new order of which he is the author. We have already referred to the high rank to which human beings have been appointed (section 3.5.), the exercise of which has been seriously compromised by their refusal of God, but which is restored to them by the redemptive action of the Son of God. This high rank is manifest in every action and circumstance of Jesus' ministry, from the very beginning in Galilee to his passion in Jerusalem, and his resurrection victory and ascension. In all of this he does not cease to be the man of God, the genuine human being exercising a proper human office while being in the world as the only-begotten of the Father. The dignity he had was not separable into a divine component and human one. It was all divine and all human. His humanity was the recreated, redeemed humanity restored to its intimacy with the living God.

From the beginning, then, Jesus exercises this office. *And immediately he left the synagogue, and entered the house of Simon and Andrew, with James and John. Now Simon's mother-in-law lay sick with a fever, and immediately they told him of her. And he came and took her by the hand and lifted her up, and the fever left her; and she served them. That evening, at sundown, they brought to him all who were sick or possessed with demons. And the whole city was gathered together about the door. And he healed many who were sick with various diseases, and cast out many demons; and he would not permit the demons to speak, because they knew him.* (Mark 1:29-31) It is evident that Jesus was compassionate towards those to whom he came. And he was compassionate as no other person could ever be. Only he could see the depth of man's plight, the true horror of his circumstances - even of the most healthy and advantaged individual, let alone the maimed, blind, paralysed and possessed. The mercy of God which had been, under the old covenant, one of the mainstays of Israelite confidence in God, was now visibly manifested before their eyes. On several occasions, we read that Jesus was moved with pity when confronted with abject human need. But here again, the differences between Jesus' exercise of the human office and that of all others is evident. For us, pity is an unspectacular virtue, and often a very powerless one. We feel helpless in the face of the anguished desperation of the paralysed or deranged. But for Jesus pity was powerful because he had not come merely on some fact-finding mission as some politician might in visiting a disaster area. Jesus had come on a saving mission, so the pity directed him to act to relieve the suffering before him.

Of a piece with this, is Jesus' confrontation of, and victory over, evil. His deliverance of the Gadarene demoniac and his forty-day repudiation of Satan were essentially of the same order: he was reversing the Fall of Adam and its concomitant indignities and re-establishing the dignity of the human office which refuses and resists all lies and temptations and which uses its proper, God-given authority to dismiss and vanquish the devil. We recall that in the Fall, man lost the respect of the created order, which then started to misbehave. Jesus re-establishes that respect and begins to haul the whole of the cosmos into a restored obedience.

Again, Jesus turns the tables on things which we have come to regard as having the initiative, like contagious disease and death itself. When he touches a leper, his health is contracted by the diseased person who is then healed. Disease meets its match in him. In the same way, he contradicts the death of Lazarus. There is an unmistakeable un-stopability about Jesus Christ in his ministry of setting things right, reversing errors, remitting sins, curing woes and, overwhelmingly, restoring the dignity of human beings. And that restoration of dignity was already taking place around him in the lives of his disciples. When he is confronted, in a remote place, with 5000 people who need a meal, he says to Philip, *You give them something to eat.* Jesus was not jesting with Philip. If Philip had taken the five loaves and two fish, and blessed and broken them and distributed them to the people, he, Philip, would have fed the 5000. He did not manage to rise to the occasion, however, and Jesus did it instead. The point of this is that the dignity that Jesus was restoring to the human race, he was eager to share with his disciples - he did not keep it to himself. When he is preparing his disciples for his departures, he says to them, *Greater works than these will you do, because I am going to the Father.* We might pause briefly to ask what these greater works might be. At first sight it is a tall order to expect his disciples to greater works than he did. But what makes a work greater? Is it not that it glorifies Jesus more? And they did go on to glorify him more: it is a greater work that Jesus so commanded their trust and confidence that they went on to win the whole world for him, bringing him yet greater glory even than his opening of blind men's eyes and raising the dead to life. The point, with respect to our current discussion, is that Jesus did not keep this dignity to himself. Rather he deliberately passed it on to his disciples and expected that, with it, they would do even greater things than he did.

6.9. Jesus' Ministry in Re-establishing Human Dignity

St Athanasius understands Jesus' ministry as essentially the execution of the task to restore and maintain the Father's just claim upon man. He sees that man's being is founded by, and inseparable from, God's creation of him and God's authorisation of him to his office as God's vicegerent in the world. *For even in their misdeeds men had not stopped short at any set limits;*

166

*but gradually pressing forward, have passed on beyond
all measure.... For there were adulteries everywhere
and thefts, and the whole earth was full of murders and
plunderings. And as to corruption and wrong, no heed
was paid to law, but all crimes were being practised
everywhere, both individually and jointly. Cities were
at war with cities, and nations were rising up against
nations......[But] it were not worthy of God's goodness
that the things he had made should waste away, because
of the deceit practised on men by the devil.... So what
was God in his goodness to do?.... For his it was once
more both to bring the corruptible to incorruption and
to maintain intact the just claim of the Father upon all*
(8). One of the primary truths we hear from all the
witnesses to the Judaeo-Christian tradition is that God
is utterly unwilling to forsake the man he has made and
abandon his claim upon him as the object of his love
and as his companion in his endeavours. Here
Athanasius underscores that as the fundamental reason
for the Incarnation. The dignity of man resides in God's
success in sending his Son and the completion of the
Son's task.

Athanasius goes on to explain that the residence of the
Proper Man among all the others brings order,
civilisation and dignity to the whole: *And like as when
a great king has entered into to some large city and
taken up his abode in one of the houses there, such city
is at all events held worthy of high honour, nor does any
enemy or bandit any longer descend upon it and subject
it; but on the contrary it is thought entitled to all care,
because of the king's having taken up his residence in*

167

a single house there: so too has it been with the Monarch of all. For now that he has come to our realm, and taken up his abode in one body among His peers, henceforth the whole conspiracy of the enemy against mankind is checked, and the corruption of death which before was prevailing against them is done away. For the race of men had gone to ruin, had not the Lord and Saviour of all, the Son of God, come among us to meet the end of death (9). Related to this, is Athanasius' second reason for the Incarnation which was to restore rationality to a race that had lost it: *A portrait once effaced must be restored from the original. Thus the Son of the Father came to seek, save, and regenerate. No other way was possible. Blinded himself, man could not see to heal. The witness of creation had failed to preserve him, and could not bring him back. The Word alone could do so. But how? Only by revealing Himself as man* (10).

Thus Athanasius sees that both dignity and reason are founded upon the relationship of God and man, are restored by the advent of God in Jesus Christ, and are maintained by his continual presence. All the individual actions and words of Jesus Christ are exponents of this single act and purpose, and are illustrative of it.

6.9.1. The civilising effect of Christian faith on human conduct

J. I. Packer writes: *We are familiar with the thought that our bodies are like machines, needing the right routine of food, rest, and exercise if they are to run efficiently, and liable, if filled up with the wrong fuel - alcohol, drugs, poison - to lose their power of healthy functioning and ultimately to seize up entirely in physical death. What we are, perhaps, slower to grasp is that God wishes*

168

us to think of our souls in a similar way. As rational persons, we were made to bear God's moral image - that is, our souls were made to run on the practice of worship, law keeping, truthfulness, honesty, discipline, self-control, and service to God and our fellows. If we abandon these practices, not only do we incur guilt before God; we also progressively destroy our own souls. Conscience atrophies, the sense of shame dries up, one's capacity for truthfulness, loyalty, and honesty is eaten away, one's character disintegrates. One not only becomes desperately miserable; one is steadily being dehumanised. This is one aspect of spiritual death. Richard Baxter was right to formulate the alternatives as a saint or a brute: that, ultimately, is the only choice, and everyone, sooner or later, consciously or unconsciously, opts for one or the other (11).*

The evidence for this is all in the field of metaphysical causality, as it rests principally on the witness of the Apostles concerning the person and works of Jesus Christ and it leads to a much deeper and more nuanced estimation of the nature of human beings and the grounds for an exalted reading of human dignity. If human beings are foundationally what they are by virtue of their relationship to God in both his creative and redemptive power, they must be regarded in some way as *sacred*. Human beings are holy ground which is not to be trampled upon, as by thoughtless tyrants, but regarded and addressed with the greatest respect and with a holy reverence for the God who defends their interests and their honour.

The incarnate life of the Son of God retrieves the human race from the manifold indignities of the Fall and from its profanity, restoring both the dignity and holiness proper to human beings. Although this was achieved by Jesus Christ in the totality of his Incarnation, what the

Church Fathers called his "sojourn" amongst us, the various components of his earthly ministry give particular insights into the nature of the project. We have already referred to his healing ministry and his requisitioning and inclusion of his disciples into his works among the people, but chiefly, the restoration of the human race that he achieved was most decisively accomplished by the suffering he bore, and we must at this stage examine how human dignity was most restored through Jesus' suffering of apparent indignity - his wilderness temptations, his arrest, trial and condemnation, and his suffering and death.

6.9.2. The high view of God's love.

P.T. Forsyth writes: *We put too little into Fatherhood then if we treat it simply as boundless patient, waiting, willing love. It is more than the love which accepts either beneficence as repentance or repentance as atonement and eagerly cuts repentance short thus- 'Let's say no more about it. Pray do not mention it. Let bygones be bygones.' Forgiveness, Fatherhood for the race does not mean, with all its simplicity, just a clean page and a fresh start and a sympathetic allowance for things. God does not forgive, 'everything considered.' To understand all is not to forgive all. There was more fatherhood in the cross (where holiness met guilt) than in the prodigal's father (where love met shame). There was more fatherhood for our souls in the desertion of the cross than in that which melts our hearts in the prodigal's embrace. It is not a father's sensitive love only which we have wounded, but His holy law. Man is not a mere runaway, but a rebel; not a pitiful coward, but a bold and bitter mutineer. . . . . Forgiving is not just forgetting. It is not cancelling the past. It is not mere amnesty and restoration. There is something broken in which a soul's sin shatters a world. Such is a soul's grandeur, and so great is the fall thereof; so seamless is the robe of righteousness, so ubiquitous and indefectible the moral order which makes man, man. Account must be had, somewhere and by somebody, of that holiness of God which is the dignity of fatherhood, and the soul of manhood* (12).

170

6..9.3. The difference between divine grace and benediction

P.T. Forsyth writes: *To dwell on the passive obedience of Christ is but the theological way of expressing the tendency to dwell on God's sympathy and to ignore his salvation. There is little doubt that the sympathetic tendency is the more popular today, and to press salvation in a real sense is to be accused of a reactionary bias to theology. But the God who is merely or mainly sympathetic is not the Christian God. The Father of an infinite benediction is not the Father of an infinite grace. . . . . What we need. . . is a caution against anthropopathism, or a conception of God which thinks of him as the divine consummation of all our human pity and tenderness to man's mischance, bewilderment, sorrow and sin. A being of infinite pity would not rise to the height of the Christian God. . . . If God could not sympathise, he would be less than God. . . But all the same, if God were all sympathy, if his divine power lay chiefly in His ability to infuse Himself with super-human intimacy of feeling into the most unspeakable tangles and crises of human life, then also he would be less than God. Even a loving God is not really God because he loves, but because he has the power to subdue all things to the holiness of his love, and even sin itself to His love as redeeming grace.. . . He not only perfectly understands our case and our problem, but he has morally, actively and finally solved it. . . All the jars, collisions, contradictions, crises, pities, tragedies, and terrors of life are in Him for ever adjusted in a peace which is not resigned and quietist, but triumphant and exultant.* (13)

6.10. Suffering & Human Dignity

The relationship between human dignity and suffering has a certain subtlety and depth to it. The Judaeo-Christian tradition holds that in his primordial perfection, man does not suffer, but suffering entered the world through the Fall and has become a ubiquitous feature of human existence ever since. We can say, therefore, that according to the divinely-intended nature of man, recalling his original perfection, suffering is foreign to him and therefore intrinsically undignified. It only became his lot after the Fall, when sin and death and the concomitant curse fell upon the whole world in general and upon human beings in particular. But we do have a primordial recollection of our perfection, certainly through Jesus Christ who, as we have seen, recalls us to it, and this causes us to estimate suffering as an alien principle against which we rail and struggle and exert our powers to resist and vanquish. And we do so, not merely because suffering is unpleasant, but also because we think of it as undignified and degrading. So often, we conceal it as much as possible, minimising it to avoid the sympathy and pity of others. At least until recently, we have striven to deny it any validity: as authentic human beings, to whom belongs a God-created perfection, we have refused to normalise suffering, disability and degeneration, even as we have sought vigorously to relieve, reduce and prevent such contradictions to our nature. They are realities with which we struggle to cope, but we tend to refuse to validate them as truly proper to us.

According to the Judaeo-Christian tradition, sin is an irruption, an inconceivable, unimaginable disaster, a cosmic catastrophe, an abyss into which we have plummeted, and from which we can never retrieve ourselves. Suffering, in all its forms, is what we experience in this cataclysm. Even though we remember that we do not really belong in the abyss and that therefore we ought not to be there, nor suffer there, we have to accept that we are there and thus are not surprised that we experience suffering as a consequence. We thus live with suffering and struggle to relieve it, while accepting that, for the present at least, it is consistent with our fallen status.

Our attitude to suffering is thus controlled by our acceptance of the fact that our present state is paradoxical: we are still the objects of God's grace, still appointed by him to our office, but at the same time are catastrophically interdicted by our fall. Suffering is still undignified, still improper, still to be resisted, but nevertheless an inevitable consequence of our existence in the abyss. We learn to minimise it, resist it, endure it, but we refuse to normalise or glorify it.

This is possible because we have learned, from the Judaeo-Christian witness, that God is not content to leave us in the abyss and has taken steps to redeem us from this predicament. This news gives us heart to continue to believe in our authentic humanity which is being restored to us, and courage in adversity because we know that, in the successful completion of God's deliverance of us, suffering will come to an end.

It is in the manner in which God rescues us from the abyss, which introduces a further subtlety in our understanding of dignity and suffering, because God sent his Son into the abyss to suffer in order to redeem his people from it. Suffering, absolutely inappropriate to the Son of God in his perfection, and therefore inappropriate to his *person*, was nevertheless given him to endure for the purposes of his *mission*. So, to the astonishment of our eyes and to the mystifying of our minds, we see the Son of God suffer, and we have to accept that, despite all its impropriety as far as his person is concerned, God has authorised that suffering to fall on him. It is therefore *proper* to him in the execution of his mission.

As we have noted, when the disciples saw Jesus touch a leper, they found that, far from Jesus catching leprosy, the lepers contracted Jesus' health. Similarly here, when Jesus, for the sake of his mission, submits himself to suffering, he is not undignified by bearing it, but suffering itself is dignified by his appropriation of it. Suffering itself suffered a change of status. Jesus' suffering became a badge of honour because it signified, not the refusal of God as it did as a result of the Fall, but obedience and self-offering to God which was proper to original humanity. Again, suffering which was the product of the Fall was thus the great sign of the defeat of the human race, but as Jesus bears it to redeem mankind it becomes a sign of victory.

Both these transformations of suffering from being a sign of disgrace to a badge of honour, and from a sign of defeat to an emblem of victory are expressly exhibited in the Gospels. The forty days in the wilderness brought both physical deprivation and psychic pressure upon Jesus, but his bearing of them and his refusal to give way to their persuasive enchantments brought him everlasting honour as the first human being not to succumb to Satan's temptations mediated through them. Again, those forty days represent a complete victory over all the persuasive suggestions from the devil which defeated Adam and Eve and all their descendants ever since. We see a more acute version of the same battle in the Garden of Gethsemane, where Jesus, confronted with the enormity of the suffering which lay ahead, needed to summon forth his faith, dismiss the possibility of evasion and defeat, and see the task through to the very end. Then come the trial and the Cross, both utterly shaming and redolent with abject defeat, and yet transformed by his resurrection into icons of dignity and victory.

6.11. Dignity and Recollection

There is strong evidence that the recollection of the passion of Christ and its dignifying of suffering and its transformation from a sign of defeat to a sign of victory was one of the most profound factors which characterised the attitudes and conduct of the Christian community. We have already seen how it transformed the Christian attitude to martyrdom, how it instilled courage and even joy in those who were slain for their faith. It was the greatest factor which made Christianity indefeasible in the face of pagan opposition and it still has that power.

The transforming power of Jesus' incarnation does not extend to all suffering, however. Only suffering of the type suffered by Jesus in his redemptive task is dignified. St Peter writes: *But let none of you suffer as a murderer or a thief or an evildoer or as a meddler. Yet if anyone suffers as a Christian, let him not be ashamed, but let him glorify God in that name* (1 Peter 4:15). But

175

it does extend to the vast range of afflictions that come, either ordinarily to Christians by virtue of their sharing the common human lot, or specifically because they are Christians and suffer a penalty for their faith. St Paul sets this out comprehensively at the end of Romans chapter 8: *Who shall separate us from the love of Christ? Shall tribulation, or distress, or persecution, or famine, or nakedness, or danger, or sword? As it is written, 'For your sake we are being killed all the day long; we are regarded as sheep to be slaughtered.' No, in all these things we are more than conquerors through him who loved us* (Romans 8:35ff ESV). Paul is reminding the Roman Christians of the transformation of suffering which Jesus achieved and it is significant that he believes that this should change their attitude to suffering however extreme it is: they are never to regard themselves as *victims*, but only as *victors* - indeed, says St Paul as *super-victors*. In this present climate of the glorifying of victim-hood, this comes as a welcome and vitally needed correction.

Similarly, the recollection of the dignifying of suffering and its transformation to victory by Jesus Christ is urgently needed to correct current attitudes to our mortality. As we have seen in section 3.6., St Athanasius found it necessary to remind his congregations of the momentous impact of Jesus Christ upon our understanding and attitude towards death, that it has been disarmed of its power and is now defeated so that Christians need fear its tyranny no longer. To live in the fear of death is undignified - Christians should face it like the martyrs of old, with courage and even with joy, knowing that it has been robbed of its power. It is not the will of God that any should die, but it is his good order and the manner in which his redemption is completed.

REFERENCES FOR CHAPTER 6

(1) G. K. Chesterton, *Heretics*, p76

(2) S. W. L. Westermann, *The Slave Systems of Greece and Roman Antiquity,* p26-27

(3) Andro Linklater, *Owning the Earth*, p25-27

(4) Samuel Adams, *Massachusetts Circular Letter* (11th February 1768)

(5) John Paul II, *A Theology of the Body*, p177

(6) John Paul II, *Ibid*, p178

(7) Church of England, *Alternative Service Book* 1980

(8) St Athanasius, *De Incarnatione Verbi Dei*, 1.5.3

(9) St Athanasius, *De Incarnatione Verbi Dei*, 1.9.3

(10) St Athanasius, *De Incarnatione Verbi Dei*, 1.14.1

(11) J. Packer, *Knowing God,* p124-125

(12) P.T. Forsyth, *God the Holy Father*, p9

(13) P.T. Forsyth, *The Cruciality of the Cross*, p32

CHAPTER 7
HUMAN INTERIORITY

We turn now to examine the stature of human beings, the office they occupy, the responsibilities they carry, the liberty they enjoy and the authority they bear, all under the heading of human interiority. By interiority we mean the inner life of the human being in which he cogitates, reasons, exerts his decision making power, wrestles with his conscience and evaluates himself and his existence. The question arises immediately as to the reality of these, whether they actually exist as universal human properties and if so from whence do they arise. As before we will consider them from the point of view of the socially constructed reality, from the point of view of physical causality, of metaphysical causality and from historical recollection.

7.1. The Stature of the Socially-Constructed Human Being.

The world of human beings is very conscious of *status*, but perhaps less so of *stature*. The factors associated with the former are obvious: aristocratic inheritance, political ascendency, professional seniority, academic or sporting prowess, commercial success, wealth or simply being well-known all can determine an individual's perceived place in the hierarchy. But stature is something different: it is an interior quality having to do with our real nature irrespective of where we find ourselves in the socio-economic scheme. And we are not merely considering here the moral condition of men and women. To be sure, stature is a term applied to moral qualities, but it is not principally what is meant here. By *stature* we mean what a human being amounts to, what he universally is, how he should regard himself, and this inevitably will lead us to consider his interior life, his inward nature, not merely his outward aspect and appearance but his inward moral and spiritual constitution.

The status of human beings is a matter of perpetual fascination for the world at large and the basis of endless strivings and continual re-shuffling of the lists. Conversely, *stature* as we have defined it is not seemingly a matter of great interest. People think of themselves as somehow having "rights" but are usually very uncertain as to the basis of their claim. There does not seem to be any great explicit consciousness of the stature of the human being, but perhaps an implicit awareness of it might be diagnosed from human behaviour and, more specifically, what human beings will refuse to do "on principle". That "on principle" amounts to a guide as to their exercise of their human interiority.

At the lowest level, if people are found to agree to do practically anything that is pleasurable without a second thought, then they betray themselves as mere collections of appetites which must be satisfied as the occasion arises. This is an animal existence to which the idea of human office, responsibility, and human exercise of authority really do not apply at all. Even human liberty is absent because in this animal existence, all are enslaved to their appetites. But once we begin to refuse to do things which would be pleasurable on the grounds that doing them would impugn our humanity, we find ourselves defending our human stature. We may refuse to steal other people's property or their marriage partners. We may refrain from expressing our anger or contempt for another. We may decline to participate in the destruction of another's character. In all these cases and in many others we are making an inward calculation of our own human stature and that of others.

On the positive side, we may take steps to assist, rescue and sustain the lives of others. We may risk ourselves for others and put ourselves at a disadvantage for them. These actions are very commonplace and betray an understanding of the human office and of human responsibility. Furthermore, we may do these things against the advice of others not to risk ourselves, or against imposed rules which we are meant to abide by, and in doing so, we assert our human liberty and authority. Much of this may be instinctive and not subject to any philosophical or moral analysis of our own, but these actions give voice to what we really think about ourselves and our purpose in the world. At least in part they disclose something of our interior nature. Much of what constitutes our unspoken understanding of our humanity may well arise from centuries of Christianity which have shaped our collective conscience, but we usually do not analyse it that far. We do one thing and refrain from another because we just think that our humanity so requires us.

The weakness of this socially constructed estimation is twofold: (i) if it rests upon a partially remembered Christian moral reasoning, it is currently unstable as Christian belief declines, and, as we have noted earlier, it is thus subject to arbitrary drift, and (ii) because its foundation is not explicitly defined, it cannot be refreshed and strengthened by returning to first principles. So, in practice, we are finding a generally weakening confidence that we know how to respond rightly to any circumstance which may arise amongst us.

7.2. The Decay of Human Stature

Until relatively recently, part of the accepted stature of the human being was the principle that we must take responsibility for ourselves and a good deal of the task of raising children was to instil this principle so that they grew up with a self-reliance, a capacity for self-determination and an ability for self-control; that is, with an active and correctly informed inner life. This was all part of the socially constructed moral environment which prevailed certainly up to the end of the 1950s. Thereafter it is possible to trace a shift in which human responsibility was progressively lifted from individuals and absorbed into various organs of the state and other institutions. Something as seemingly benign as a cheque guarantee card marked an early stage in this process. Before their introduction in the early

1970s, a cheque was accepted for payment on the presumed honesty of the one who signed it. The presumption was of the honesty of the bank account holder and he was taken at his word. The introduction of the cheque guarantee card meant that a cheque could be offered which the bank would guarantee to honour irrespective of the state of the holder's account. Thus there was an imperceptible shift: no longer was it necessary to trust the individual offering the cheque; trust was transferred to the bank.

This minor shift was a beginning of the erosion of all trust in the inner integrity of individuals and the progressive centralisation of trust into organisations, banks and government institutions. Ordinary transactions are now conducted with no dependence on the integrity of individuals whose word now counts for nothing. Perhaps this reduces fraud although that in itself is questionable. What it certainly does do is to diminish the stature of the individual human beings involved. To live in a world in which one is never officially believed, in which one's word is never good enough for even the most basic transaction, is deeply demeaning. It makes us think less of ourselves, and worse, it makes us think that trustworthiness is less important than it is, and perhaps less worth maintaining for its own sake. In a world where our word does not count for very much, we are more likely to abandon the effort to maintain truthfulness, to give way to dishonesty, and to learn progressively to distrust others.

Of a piece with this, is the tendency, which has arisen in the same period, to make almost everything of which the political class disapproves, illegal, and make everything of which it approves, compulsory. Less and less is left to the inward judgement of individuals and the inevitable consequence is that the capacity for making wise judgements becomes atrophied, larger and larger constituencies of people are criminalised and an ever-increasing host of enforcers are required to exact compliance. Quite apart from the psychic pressure imposed on the population (which we have considered in section 2.2.), this diminishes the stature of the persons to whom it is applied. From people who are continually making moral calculations and taking decisions in consequence of those calculations, we become those who simply act or refrain from acting, through fear of reprisals. We become lessened in stature, mere automatons, conditioned as though lab rats subjected to a long-term psychological experiment. Our interior life is thus progressively short-circuited.

The obsession with health, safety and security has provided a major driving force for this de-humanising trend. The British Petroleum laboratories at Sunbury on Thames fifty years ago, were humming with energetic scientific research. Now, new recruits to the company are lectured on the necessity of always holding the hand rail when mounting the stairs and always fitting a lid to a coffee cup when carrying it. The humming has ceased, the scientific energy has abated, but professional advancement can still be made by alerting the company authorities of any fellow employee who transgresses the rules using a special telephone number for the purpose. This small example illustrates a wider change which has taken place in the nature of employment. We have already suggested that employment in general is a poor match to the intrinsic nature of the human being, but for all the attention given to employment conditions in recent years, this already poor match appears to have deteriorated further. If the employee is given a definite range of responsibility in which he is trusted to operate to achieve a defined result, certain aspects of his stature as a human being are preserved. His inward transactions and cogitations matter. He occupies an office in which his wise decisions and actions result in the desired outcome. Confidence is placed in him and this is a proper respect for the stature of his humanity. When he delivers a result, he is justly congratulated. But employment is increasingly unlike this. The employee now is supplied with protocols and policies which describe exactly how everything is to be done; the discretion of the employee is not needed and even actively discouraged. He becomes a functionary in a sterile world of mindless obedience.

It really is not surprising that recent studies in the United States suggest that part of the cause of high unemployment is that people just do not want to work in this dehumanising environment (1). The loss of humanity is just not worth the money. It may be that human beings are not quite so malleable as the designers of the cybernetic world expect them to be. Maybe there is a recollection from somewhere that this abstraction of the human being into mere functionality attempts to deny an essential undeniable reality about that human being. There are elements of humanity which human beings will not easily give up, elements belonging to their interiority, which have to do with their stature, liberty, responsibility, integrity, and wisdom. But it remains to ask how can these elements be securely maintained under the pressure to abandon them?

There is a further area of human life which does betray the interiority of human beings and that is the capacity to love. Courtship, marriage, the conceiving, bearing and raising of children, family life and the welter of affections, sacrifices, generosities to which they give rise, testify to the inner qualities of which human beings are capable. And in the context of a socially constructed reality, these can be encouraged by good example and discouraged by bad. The question is whether purely socially constructed reality can sustain the institution of marriage and family life on its own, and it appears from recent history that this may be doubtful. The decline of marriage and its durability, and the concomitant harm that its disintegration does to large numbers of children suggest that neither a socially constructed reality nor the otherwise uninformed conscience and interior life of human beings are capable of sustaining it. There evidently needs to be some other external impetus to provoke cogent moral reasoning to sustain wholesome family life.

7.3. Human Interiority from Physical Causality

Is it possible to explain man's interiority from purely physical causality? Has it arisen simply from the natural processes of evolution? If so, there is certainly a great deal to explain. The interiority of human beings is actually a vast space with a seemingly unplumbable depth. The inward life of man has been recognised as an incomprehensible mystery by Descartes and by many since Darwin himself recognised the problem and made some attempt to explain conscience from the gregarious and social nature of some species. He observed that there was some sympathy and affection between individuals of some species and he conjectured that this might evolve into conscience, but he could not explain how. Perhaps, he said, some tribes exhibited more sympathy and support for tribe members than another tribe and so perhaps this first tribe might be more successful than the other, but the governing principle of the survival of the fittest applies strictly to the advantage gained by an individual and there is no suggestion that a sympathetic member of the tribe would gain an advantage over one which did not display this characteristic. One might go as far as to say the inverse might be true. The fundamental principle of Darwinism is that every individual of a species competes with all the others. Only in this way can advantages emerge and disadvantages fall away. Sympathy, self-sacrifice, the surrendering of advantage must operate to some extent at least, against the principle of survival of the fittest.

This problem troubled a contemporary of Charles Darwin and a fellow advocate of the idea of evolution. Alfred Russel Wallace, argued: *It will, therefore, probably excite some surprise among my readers, to find that I do not consider that all nature can be explained on the principles of which I am so ardent an advocate; and that I am now myself going to state objections, and to place limits, to the power of 'natural selection.' I believe, however, that there are such limits; and that just as surely as we can trace the action of natural laws in the development of organic forms, and can clearly conceive that fuller knowledge would enable us to follow step by step the whole process of that development, so surely can we trace the action of some unknown higher law, beyond and independent of all those laws of which we have any knowledge. We can trace this action more or less distinctly in many phenomena, the two most important of which are the origin of sensation or consciousness, and the development of man from the lower animals* (2).

As far as Wallace is concerned, he has come to the limit of the theory of natural selection in explaining human nature. In our terms he has reached the boundary between physical causality and metaphysical causality when it comes to morality and conscience. For him there is no evolutionary explanation for much of the interiority of human beings. There are, of course, relatively simple instincts of survival which are perfectly explicable from a physical cause, but the complexity arises when inwardly, an individual decides against following their direction and acts in a way which increases the risk to himself for a higher purpose. Even the fact that human beings stop to make these calculations, to engage in inward debate is beyond the scope of purely evolutionary processes, because often the clear path to survival is obvious, but the alternative which might involve personal sacrifice is a much more complex and subtle matter.

7.4. The Nature and Content of the Human Interior

As complex as the physiology of the human body is, it is dwarfed by the complexity and depth of man's inner life. He is much, much more inwardly that he is outwardly, and his interior life is more important to him than his physical existence. Human beings seek an inward reconciliation, a self-possession, a happiness which they cannot achieve merely by making their external reality as perfect as they can. Often they try in this direction, they seek to become rich and beautiful and accomplished, but following the careers of people who have to a considerable degree been successful in this endeavour, frequently reveals that inner transcendence which they seek has all but eluded them.

It may be useful to map out at least some of the content of this interiority. There is, of course, intellectual capacity: enabling human reasoning, logic and argument. This is supplied and assisted by memory, a capacity to retain information, to recall and process it. Then there is the quality which rather seems to have stumped Charles Darwin, human conscience and the power of moral evaluation and capacity for the differentiation between good and evil. In human interiority there are also complex powers for making decisions and resolving between possibilities, with an ability for inward debate and cogitation. Added to this is the capacity for coping with adversity, setbacks, and the powers of courage, determination and persistence.

There is a powerful ability for self-criticism and even self-correction, for grief and regret, for guilt and penitence, and for forgiveness. The human interior can regroup, re-evaluate, and can change its mind. It contains a capacity for understanding others and placing itself in their shoes. It exhibits a capacity for pity and sympathy and can resolve to make a sacrifice for others.

This does seem to add up to a very great deal more than human physiology, complex as the latter may be. And it is seemingly much more powerful than merely the physical attributes of the creature. One can see why the pen is much more mighty than the sword. David's inner life slew the physical giant, Goliath. Nor is all of the interiority of human beings beyond the analysis from physical causality. Given its existence, and for the moment setting aside the problem of its origin, transactions within it are often highly intelligible. The way human beings respond to external stimuli can be complex and sometimes counter-intuitive, but many can be understood readily. The well-developed science of psychology is devoted to these analyses.

7.5. The Education of the Human Interior

On the other hand, the human interior has to be educated. It learns from its environment. On the negative side St Paul, in his first letter to the Corinthians, quotes a line from Menander, that *bad company ruins good morals*. More accurately it means *evil associations corrupt excellent morals* (1 Corinthians 15:33), and St Paul uses it to dissuade his hearers from following the despairing idea that Christ had not been raised from the dead, so they might as well *eat and drink for tomorrow [they] die*. He is guarding them against a false education of their minds and hearts. This susceptibility to propaganda of all kinds continues to our own day. Cynical politicians know that if they keep repeating something, especially in the form of a memorable slogan or catch-phrase, however untrue it is, or however insufficient it is to describe a complex situation, it will, nevertheless catch on, and be believed by at least a fraction of the people. The BBC in its desperate effort to re-educate our consciences with respect to homosexual conduct, confronts us continually with examples of it in plays and documentaries, usually portrayed in a good light, with the clear aim of normalising it.

On the other hand, St Paul, in his second letter to Timothy, urges his young associate to learn from the scriptures, which, he says, are *God-breathed and profitable for teaching, for reproof, for correction, and for training in righteousness, that the man of God may be competent, equipped for every good work*. In the

191

context of our present discussion, the expression 'God-breathed' (*theopneustos*) means that the instruction the Scriptures provide which informs our interiority, actually ultimately originates in God's interiority.

But the point we make at present is that the interior life of human beings needs to be educated and, as we considered in chapter 2, this education, according to the Judaeo-Christian tradition takes place from a point external to the human being, rather, than, as Kant suggested, being generated by it. With the scope of the map of human interiority in mind, it is clear that this education will have a very wide range. The intellect needs to be well-informed, the capacity for calculation and deduction needs to be developed, the conscience needs to be educated and moral and spiritual capacities must be enabled. This is primarily the task of parents who themselves need to recall the substance of this inward wholeness and help their children to grasp and receive it for themselves. According to the Judaeo-Christian tradition, parents will need the help of God to effect it fully. It is to be noted that children cannot be left to fill their initial interior vacuum on their own.

Finally, in this section it is worth noting that the interior world of the human being, if well informed and fully developed is a pleasant place to dwell. This is particularly the case if the Judaeo-Christian worldview is the determining principle of it. A well-developed interiority makes an individual well-equipped to live a full human life, to take good advantage of opportunities, to surmount obstacles, to live a self-reliant life and to be at ease in the world and before God. As aptly put by Austin Farrer, the human task is to *make of your life what your life was made for*, and that task primarily takes place in the human interior.

7.6. Metaphysically Informed Interiority

The Incarnation represented a great discovery (or, more properly, divine disclosure) of the inner relatedness of the life of God. St Paul's oft usage of the expression *in Christ* signifies that the Christian life is lived within the compass of Christ's reign with the Father and the Holy Spirit. At the same time St Paul prays for the Ephesians that *according to the riches of his glory [God the Father] may grant you to be strengthened with power through his Spirit in your inner being, so that Christ may dwell in your hearts through faith.* (Ephesians 3:16) In common with the whole of the Judaeo-Christian witness on this matter, there is an intimacy between God and man which is properly and fully realised in the faithful. We encountered this in section 5.7. in considering St Irenaeus' description of the Christian life as a "habituation" to the life of God.

The nature of this divine engagement with human interiority has to be carefully expressed. First, God is not integral with the life of thought as Plato considered. The Judaeo-Christian tradition maintains that God is absolutely differentiated from his creation and is not in any way a constituent part of it. Nonetheless the witnesses of Scripture and generations of the faithful testify to their knowledge of God and his closeness to them. Isaiah 57:15 expresses the position exactly: *For thus says the One who is high and lifted up, who inhabits eternity, whose name is Holy: I dwell in the high and holy place, and also with him who is of a contrite and lowly spirit.*

Secondly, as we have also previously considered in section 2.7., God gives space to human beings to exercise their proper office. God's mind does not eclipse theirs, his will does not smother theirs. There is a dialogue between God and man in which their respective persons remain distinct and fully differentiated. This has to be held alongside the intimacy between God and his people to which the Judaeo-Christian tradition testifies. If we take as a foundation for this evidence, the witness of the four gospels, we find that the person of Jesus exhibits an abiding and deep relationship with God his Father, but in every relationship with his fellow human beings, Jesus behaves and thinks and speaks as an autonomous man. Similarly, when St Paul is addressing the Corinthian Church, he adjures them to be children when it comes to evil, but to be mature in their thinking. It is clear that the intellectual stature of God's people is not in the least to be qualified by the spiritual intimacy they experience with God. When St Paul encourages the Corinthian Church to seek the higher spiritual gifts, the context clearly signifies that he means those which engage the mind fully in a rational manner.

However, this principle was not always recognised in the early Church nor has it been universally respected since. There has always been the temptation for the faithful to disengage the mind and believe that they are more or less passive conduits for the word of God. The Church had to rule against the Phrygian heresy, or Montanism in the second century AD, partly at least because in their enthusiasm and apocalyptic expectations, its prophets used to fall senseless to the ground while uttering their oracles. The very intellectual disengagement which this epitomises, was recognised by the Church to be discordant with Christ's own rational and intelligible witness.

7.7. Interiority and the Desert Fathers

A discussion of the inward fellowship of God with his people by his Holy Spirit would not be complete without hearing the witness of the Eastern Desert Fathers. During the 3rd and 4th centuries, or possibly earlier, a number of eastern Christians, abandoned their wealth, and selling their possessions and giving to the poor, they went out into the inhospitable desert regions around Egypt and Sinai and lived in absolute destitution in caves and in hermitages which they constructed for themselves. The act of doing this, was understood by them to be a radical obedience to Jesus Christ, who exhorted a wealthy would-be follower to go and sell all that he had and give to the poor and then become a disciple. (Luke 18:22) St Anthony of Egypt, following this to the letter and beginning his ascetic life in the desert, has come be recognised as the father of Christian monasticism.

What attracted Christians to this ascetic way of life was the inhospitable nature of the desert, which forced a much greater reliance on the interior life, and specifically, the interior life with God. Living in deprivation with little external stimulus, the Desert Fathers were forced back on their inner resources and a genuine dependence on God. In the rather sparse records of the lives of these Hermits, we find little theology of the carefully argued and well thought out sort, rather we find an immediate Christianity, kept true by a careful reading of the Gospels, but energised by a continual conversation with God through prayer. Here were lives led on the basis of an interiority informed by the presence and witness of the Holy Spirit. The essence of Desert Christianity is summed up in an ancient recollection that when an old man was questioned as to what manner of man a monk should be, responded, *So far as in me is, alone to the Alone* (*solus ad solum*). *Except a man shall say in his heart, I alone and God are in this world, he shall not find peace*, said the abbot Allois. (3) This is not the sum of the matter, because Desert Christians were intensely aware of the debt of love they owed to their neighbour, but it is a major component of what it was to be a Christian hermit. It gives expression to the observation of John Paul II, which we came across in section 5.3., that man being alone in the world (as absolutely differentiable for the animals) was a reflection of God's own solitude. The Desert Fathers demonstrated in practice that our true humanity is finally revealed when we are alone before God. It is striking that it required such a radical abandonment of the whole world to achieve it, and perhaps still more striking that so many people took this path.

The solitude of the Desert Fathers bears witness to another important truth concerning Christianity. It shows that Christianity is not merely a social construct, a self-reinforcing social movement which will need a certain critical mass of members in order to continue in the world. It shows that, potentially at least, every individual Christian is fully equipped to continue to follow Christ, and that the power of Christianity arises not from a bulk membership but from the inward spiritual processes by which the individual is engaged by the reality of God. This means that the Church need not fear diminution in its numbers because every individual member carries with him the sum of the Church's strength, nor do individual Christians have to fear that their continuance depends upon the numerical success of the Church. The testimony of the centuries of the Church's life bears this out: the Church has proved indestructible even in the face of extreme persecution and sustained worldly contempt.

7.8. The Relationship Between God and the Human Interior

We might ask, what is the relationship between God and human interiority? We recall the map of the interior to which we referred in section 7.4. Under the heading of intellectual understanding, particularly of the saving history of God's action, Jesus tells his disciples, *When the Spirit of truth comes, he will guide you into all the truth* (John 6:13). Evidently, the Holy Spirit instructs Christians. He will also prompt their memories: Jesus said, *But the Counsellor, the Holy Spirit, whom the Father will send in my name, he will teach you all things and bring to your remembrance all that I have said to you* (John 14:26). The Holy Spirit is also said to convict human consciences. Again Jesus says, *and when [the Holy Spirit] comes, he will convict the world concerning sin and righteousness and judgement* (John 16:8). The Holy Spirit is also said to participate in the Church's decisions (or at least some of them). When the Apostles write to the new gentile Christians they say, *...for it has seemed good to the Holy Spirit and to us to lay on you no greater burden than these requirements.....* (Acts 15:28) There is evidently some awareness of a consultation having taken place on the matter. A main function of the witness of the Holy Spirit is to assure Christians of their membership of God's adopted family in Christ. St Paul testifies: *For you did not receive the spirit of slavery to fall back into fear, but you have received the Spirit of adoption as sons, by whom we cry, "Abba! Father!" The Spirit himself bears witness with our spirit that we are children of God* (Romans 8:15). The Holy Spirit does, according to St Paul, claim the Christian for God, but this is not a claim of force, but of love. Similarly, there may be wise counsel, information, reminders, advice and encouragement offered by God to the inward mind of the Christian and to the Church, but there is little sign of compulsion and no sign of threat. Rather there is extra-ordinary restraint. In many cases, the decision is left to the Church and to the individual Christian. The inward cogitations of the Christian may be offered counsel but the decision is not taken for him. His position as a companion and partner of God is respected. The relationship as outlined in section 5.3. is upheld. The cost of this liberty is that misunderstandings can arise, errors can be made and the Christian may prove disobedient, but his sovereignty as the vicegerent of God is maintained.

7.9. Prayer as Interior Fellowship

This takes the discussion on to the subject of prayer, and while we will not deal in detail with all aspects of Christian prayer, the foregoing might permit us to regard prayer as an exercise of an inward fellowship between the Christian and God the Father, through the Holy Spirit's ministration. Some of the prayers in the Old Testament demonstrate conversation, even a debate, which, although not between equals, is certainly not a one-sided affair. We might think of the prayer in which Abraham engages in pleading for the lives of the inhabitants of Sodom and Gomorrah in Genesis 18:23ff. Abraham negotiates and God apparently enters into the negotiation and actually does concede some ground to Abraham who persists in driving a hard bargain. The will of God does not smother Abraham, whose petition is taken seriously. It is not surprising that Jesus' own prayers have this character. In that very serious and anguished moment in the Garden of Gethsemane, Jesus' prayer takes the form of an urgent and desperate conversation with God the Father in which Jesus redoubles his resolve to do the Father's will. There is, as it were, a joint decision to carry it through. Prayer is, therefore, the place where, with the assistance of God himself, assets are marshalled, courage is gathered, decisions are taken and victory is secured. It it reminiscent of that moment we considered in section 5.3., that pause, in which God enters back into himself to make the decision to create man. In Gethsemane, Jesus pauses to go back into himself and into the counsel of the Father, to make the decision to redeem man.

7.10. Human Interiority and the Mystery of Iniquity

The phrase "mystery of iniquity" is used by St Paul to refer to the progressive advance of evil the world, which he envisaged coming to some final showdown between God and some cosmic archenemy. But the phrase is useful in a more general sense because there is a certain incomprehensibility about evil. From a perspective of natural causality, it is possible to see that selfishness and gluttony and contempt for the welfare of others might be explained from an evolutionary standpoint and some efforts have been made along this line (4). On the other hand, it is more difficult to see how the species is improved by an instinct of its members to murder one another. A community of mass murderers can hardly be expected to grow numerically. Again, adultery has been suggested to be evolutionarily advantageous because it continually offers opportunities to extend the gene pool. On the other hand, it is destructive to family life and the welfare of the young generated by these liaisons. Virtue exhibits the same ambiguity: self-sacrifice and care of the weak could be destructive to the advance of the species through the weakening of the gene pool, although nurturing the young is obviously advantageous.

Thus, in looking for a natural explanation of evil, we resort to tracing it to economic disadvantage, poor diet, exposure to drugs and poisons, or especially to bad parenting or even legitimate political protest. Whatever effect these factors have, they do not penetrate the mystery of iniquity - they usually merely push the problem back to a prior evil which cannot be explained either. The more we consider it, the more baffled we may be by the incipient self-destructive instinct we see manifest in all human beings and even in ourselves. This brings us once again to the portals of metaphysical causality to account for the extreme moral ambiguity exhibited by human beings.

Richard Holloway sums up the position from the point of view of the Judaeo-Christian tradition:
What we are to understand here is that there has been some sort of rebellion at the heart of reality, there has been war in heaven, and it has been partly successful. The agents of that rebellion have taken over and, to a great extent, still control part of the great empire. They are holding out in one of the colonies. There is a de facto *ruler of this world. The words come from the New Testament, which describes the devil as 'the ruler of the world'. 'And the devil took him up, and showed him all*

the kingdoms of the world in a moment of time, and said to him, "To you I will give all this authority and their glory; for it has been delivered to me, and I give it to whom I will"' (Luke 4:5-6) Here, Satan makes not only a usurper's claim, he makes a legal claim to the world: 'it has been delivered to me, and I give it to whom I will'. There has, apparently, been discord, rebellion in the universe before us. There is some kind of civil war going on and we are taking sides all our life. The story of Adam's fall and expulsion from Eden, presupposes this earlier conflict, for it is the serpent who tempts Eve. ? he story of our first parents, is, of course, our story. We co-operate, collaborate with the ruler of this world. In some mysterious but true sense, we choose against our own family, we commit spiritual and moral treason, we conspire against our own happiness, by siding with what we hate, against what we love. Suicide, anorexia, addiction, self-destructive behaviour, self- neglect, child and parent abuse, predatory sexuality, anger, that mysterious resentment we retain almost exclusively for those to whom we are most closely bonded, what are all these and many more besides, if they are not evidence of some kind of self-hypnosis that leads us to destroy our own happiness? And all this in spite of ourselves! We get in our own way. Now, however you lay this out, whether in terms of rebellious spirits who seduce human beings into joining their own self-destructive revolt, or in terms of the historic sum of all free human choices for evil, the fact remains that there is a massive and

*deadening contagion of evil in the universe that bears
down upon us all* (5).

We cannot resolve the ambiguity of the existence of
evil and virtue in the same human being, but the
Judaeo-Christian witnesses give us a way of analysing
it. In the letter to the Hebrews 13:8, Jesus Christ is
described as being the same *yesterday, today and
forever*. Taking Jesus' Incarnation as the reference point,
the *man of yesterday* is the treasonable man, Jesus came
to save. He is the man viewed from the perspective of
his disobedience. As we saw in section 5.5., Jesus took
the humanity and bore the sin of this man, without
committing sin himself, in order to redeem him.
Consequently, the *man of today,* is the man of
righteousness, viewed from the point of view of his
restoration to the good order of God, and therefore fit
to be the *man of forever* who shares the glory of God.
We will call him the *man of glory*.

The Judaeo-Christian witnesses all insist that the virtue
and the evil have very different status. If we employ
Existentialist language to describe this, as Karl Barth
does, we would say that the virtue of human beings
arises from their authenticity as God's creatures, that
their nobility as his right-hand people, their dignity as
those authorised to administer his created order, render
them as truly *existent*. As hideously real as human
disobedience to God and treachery against him are,
those things are not in the least authorised and therefore
cannot enjoy the same existent status as the people of

God. To describe a human being as God's man, as his companion and ally, as his vicegerent of all creation, as the recipient of his grace and his ordinand to salvation, the *man of righteousness* and the *man of glory*, is thus to say infinitely more than to say that that same human being is the ruined reprobate, the law-breaker, the refusenik of God, the *man of yesterday*. But both things are true. This is because the whole Judaeo-Christian narrative describes God's action, not to give up on the man he has created, even though the man himself gave up on God, instead to redeem that man and perfect him and bring him to glory. Although this work has been achieved by Jesus Christ, in each person it is currently unfinished business. Therefore, in the inner life of human beings, two principles are at work: sadly enough, we are still the people of yesterday, exhibiting the characteristics of disobedience and disorder from which we have been delivered, but also exhibiting the signs of God's grace which restores us to the divine likeness.

This is the Judaeo-Christian account of the ambiguity in the inner life of everyone. Consider first, the inner life of the *man of yesterday*. The prophet Jeremiah comments on his inward cogitations: *The heart is deceitful above all things, and desperately sick; who can understand it?* (Jeremiah 17:9) The *heart* in Scripture is the centre of intellect, decision making and will. It thus represents the interiority of the human being, which, in terms of the *man of yesterday* under present consideration, exercises the human capacity for evil intent and action. Thus Jesus affirms that *out of the heart come evil thoughts, murder, adultery, sexual*

204

immorality, theft, false witness, slander. (Matthew 15:19) The whole world bears witness to the reality of this and its history in this respect represents an enormous catalogue of vice and evil. We might, however, note two points in passing:

(i) We observed in section 2.3. that in Judaeo-Christian understanding, knowledge came to human beings from outside it; was not generated within as the Greeks and Kant suggested. But we find here that evil does seem to be concocted within the interiority of human beings and issues forth from them. They are not originators of knowledge, but they are, to some extent, originators of evil.

(ii) Secondly, this is not to say there is no external evil suggestion made to them. According to St John, the devil put into the mind of Judas Iscariot to betray Jesus (John 13:2) and we have already referred to the influence of human company on moral conduct (section 7.5. above). Clearly it matters what voice we listen to. Jesus tells his disciples that his sheep hear his voice and do not listen to another (John 10:27).

The Judaeo-Christian witnesses are equally insistent on the unassailable virtue of the *man of righteousness,* the human being whom God acquits and exonerates: *Who shall bring any charge against God's elect? It is God who justifies. Who is to condemn?* asks St Paul in Romans 8:33. There is a striking confidence in the psalmist of this righteousness: *Judge me, O Lord, according to my righteousness and according to the integrity that is in me* (Psalm 7:8). The upshot of this is that although man under God has to live a life of radical penitence because he is still the *man of yesterday*, nevertheless he is, by the virtue of Christ, the *man of today*, of righteousness, against whom no accusation can be brought. And not only that, all his capacities as the vicegerent of God's reign on earth are restored to him, so that he already anticipates his future destiny as the *man of glory*.

This Judaeo-Christian understanding of the interiority of human beings accounts for the observed realities: it accounts for the extremes observed in the nature of the human heart. Its capacity for terrible evil and for exemplary virtue, for its destructive instincts and creative brilliance. It accounts for the depths of depravity and its aspiration and ascent to glory. And all this potentially in the same human being. It is still a mystery in the sense that the human interior remains incomprehensible in the strict meaning of the term, but the Judaeo-Christian reading of its reality has been continually subjected to intellectual scrutiny over thousands of years and remains the most cogent explanation of the observed nature of the human heart.

Throughout this discussion, we have not made any distinction between the human race as a whole and the Judaeo-Christian faithful. The New Testament does represent the Incarnation of Jesus Christ as an act of God for the entire world, but it also expresses the full redemptive power of that act to be manifest most chiefly in the followers of Jesus Christ. Both readings of the range of God's action have to be acknowledged, but it is made clear by the various authors of the New

Testament that the knowledge of these things presents a great advantage to the Christian, and the cooperation of Christians, as best they can, is urged to give effect to the divine purpose.

REFERENCES FOR CHAPTER 7

(1) Mike Rowe, *Fox News Video* March 1st 2017

(2) Alfred Russel Wallace,*The Limits of Natural Selection as Applied to Man*, (1869/1870)

(3) Helen Waddell, *The Desert Fathers,* Paperback Edition 1987, p18

(4) Richard Dawkins, *River Out of Eden*

(5) Richard Holloway, *Paradoxes of Christian Faith and Life*, p33-34

CHAPTER 8
HUMAN LIBERTY

8.1. Definitions

Once again, we begin with definitions. F. A. Hayek defines liberty as *independence [from] the arbitrary will of another* but it says nothing about the *authorised* will of another and since most incursions into the freedom of human beings are in some sense or other authorised, this does not take us very far (1). We have to imagine a plane upon which exist all the possibilities open to any and all human beings. Without any constraints thereto, life on this plane would be infinitely free. But there are many different boundaries of constraint marked out on this plane which would limit the freedom of people upon it.

It might be worthwhile to review the types of such boundaries of constraint. The outside one is clearly an ontological boundary: man cannot do things which are absolutely impossible for him. But within this outside envelope there are two sorts of further boundaries of constraint: those that are external to human beings and those that are internal. The external limits are those of law: of constitutional law, of common law, of statutory law, of criminal penalty. There are restraints applied to trades and professions, there are the restraints which

209

accompany employment and restraints applied by convention through social acceptability and political correctness. There are boundaries of constraint which arise from an individual's personal circumstances, his wealth, his health, his location and family circumstances. All these external boundaries of constraint set a limit to a human being and his freedom consists of his potential for existence and action within them. They may be quite relaxed and afford him considerable liberty, or they might be tightly drawn around him, greatly restricting his actions and potential. There will be further boundaries of constraint which are internal to him: his moral conscience will restrain him from activities which he proscribes, his education will set a definite limit to his thought, activity and creative potential. His capacity for imagination and rational thought will have a similar impact.

This is an objective definition of freedom as the space left in which an individual can live within the boundaries set about him. But there is a subjective definition also. This is the space that an individual believes himself to require in order to fulfil his personal vision and the realisation of his aims in life. This may be a wide and grand vision and require a correspondingly large freedom space. Or his vision may be more modest and require a smaller one. Either way, for his individual satisfaction and self-fulfilment his subjective freedom space must fit comfortably within the objective freedom space which determine his outward circumstances. If the objective space is too small, the individual will experience oppression, if it is much larger than his subjective freedom space, he may experience fear: he may not trust himself with the external scope and possibilities with which he is presented, and prefer a smaller scope of possibilities.

In what follows, we will trace necessary objective freedom space which will be required to accommodate, without oppression, human beings with increasingly large visions of their humanity and its scope.

8.2. Liberty and Power-Constructed and Socially-Constructed Realities

We begin with those political structures in which liberty is most confined: totalitarian worlds which derive their rationale directly or indirectly from Karl Marx. Marx's understanding of the nature of a human being was as an advanced animal which has a capacity for making things, for production, and not only for production, but a capacity for conceiving of a product and then making it. For Marx a human being was *homo faber*, the making man. Although this was far less in status than the Judaeo-Christian view of man we considered in section 5.4., the man that rules at God's right hand, it did acknowledge the intellectual creativity which stood behind his capacity to make things and this would have required a certain objective freedom space to accommodate it. Unhappily, by the time Marx's thought had evolved into Stalinism and other forms of left-wing totalitarian government, the already diminished understanding of humanity of Marx, became the low view of a human being as a unit of production, a unit of labour, essentially identical with every other individual. This unit of production needed very little objective freedom space and therefore was given little. A tiny place to eat and sleep, and a place to fulfil the requirement of production was all that was really needed. Perhaps an opportunity for a little entertainment and of course, opportunities to express loyalty and gratitude to their leaders, were the only items needing a little extra space. There was no need for the unit of labour to own land, and those who historically did so were often regarded as enemies of the state and were oppressed because, in owning land, their subjective freedom space exceeded that which was to be made available. Wherever possible that land was collected up into large state-owned farms and its erstwhile owners reduced to the status of units of agrarian production. A very low view of human beings was matched with the provision of very little freedom space.

The view of the National Socialists of the Third Reich in Germany bore some similarities to the totalitarian structure described above, but with some important differences. The chief of these was the doctrine of racial superiority of the Teutonic races and the abject inferiority of practically all others. Thus there was an exaggerated emphasis on the qualities and capacities of the teutons and the dismissal of the capacities of others. Consequently, people who were considered racially pure had very large freedom-spaces allocated to them, while others were reduced to servitude, forbidden to practice professions, subjected to property confiscation, imprisonment and enslavement. All this involved a total rejection of the Judaeo-Christian understanding of humanity, although serious attempts were made to recruit the German Protestant Church to serve its ideals. Even the space it generated for the favoured was not really freedom-space. It could not be as it was sustained by the suffocating false doctrines of an unjustifiable racial theory. So free thought within it was impossible, so that even those who had an ostensibly large freedom space, actually had no such thing. Everyone was enslaved in one way or another.

8.3. Liberty and Islam

In our review of structures of civilisation which have a low view of human beings and a correspondingly small freedom space allocated to them, we must include Islam. Islam is a distorted derivation from the Judaeo-Christian tradition and, among many other things, it appears to have misunderstood the status of human beings. In section 2.7. we observed that, in Genesis, man was given the responsibility of naming (i.e. characterising) the animals and that his characterisation was final and God did not interfere with Adam's judgement. In the Muslim version of this, it is God who names the animals. Here is the English text of the second Sura which describes this:

And when your Lord said to the angels, I am going to place in the earth a khalif, they said: What! wilt Thou place in it such as shall make mischief in it and shed blood, and we celebrate Thy praise and extol Thy holiness? He said: Surely I know what you do not know.

213

*And He taught Adam all the names, then presented them
to the angels; then He said: Tell me the names of those
if you are right.*

*They said: Glory be to Thee! we have no knowledge but
that which Thou hast taught us; surely Thou art the
Knowing, the Wise.*

*He said: O Adam! inform them of their names. Then
when he had informed them of their names, He said:
Did I not say to you that I surely know what is ghaib in
the heavens and the earth and (that) I know what you
manifest and what you hide?* (2)

The main difference is that in the Judaeo-Christian
tradition, man gains his knowledge of the animals *from
the animals*. As we have seen scientific research is just
this kind of conversation between the natural order and
man, and it is something in which God does not
interfere. In Islam, Allah drives and controls it all. This
inevitably reduces man to a lower status. This, of
course, means that he needs less freedom space and that
is what he gets in Islamic culture. Since Allah has to be
the author of everything, Islam has a difficult
relationship with books and has always been somewhat
suspicious of them. Even in its intellectual heyday,
Muslims translated books from Greece and Rome, but
did not write very many. To originate a book might
prove dangerous as religious totalitarianism is a
prevalent feature of Muslim culture.

8.4. Liberty in Modern Western Europe

The tradition of liberty in Western Europe was derived
from two sources: Roman Law and English Common

Law. Under Roman Law there were four rights which were conferred upon manumission of a slave: (i) legal status as a protected member of the community; (ii),immunity from arbitrary arrest; (iii) the rights to work at whatever he desires to do; and, (iv) freedom of movement (3). He was also free to own property but slaves already had that right before manumission. The first two of these rights essentially allowed him to live without interference. The second two liberties gave him the right to go anywhere and do anything. Essentially, people including the government, had to leave him alone to get on with anything he wanted to do. Add to these rights his freedom to own his own land, and the sum total is the basis by which a country could be said to be free. These rights, also perhaps originally derived from Roman Law, were the remembered rights of the yeomen (freemen) of Saxon England. In England they were supported by an ancient Christian polity strengthened and established largely during the reign of Alfred the Great in the eighth century (4). They survived the Norman invasion of 1066, and the subsequent imposition of the feudal system, which was ultimately thrown off by the creation of the Court of Common Pleas and the rise of Common Lawyers in the London Inns of Court (5).

Blackstone enumerated three absolute rights of persons under English Law:
I *The right of personal security consists in a person's legal and uninterrupted enjoyment of his life, his limbs, his body, his health and his reputation.*

II *The law of England regards, asserts, and preserves the personal liberty of individuals. This personal liberty consists in the power of loco-motion, of changing situation, or removing one's person to whatsoever place one's own inclination may direct, without imprisonment or restraint, unless by due course of law. It is a right strictly natural, the laws of England have never abridged it without sufficient cause, and in this kingdom, it can never be abridged at the mere discretion of the magistrate, without the explicit permission of the laws.*

III *The third absolute right, inherent in every Englishman, is that of property: which consists in the free use, enjoyment, and disposal of all his acquisitions, without any control or diminution, save only by the laws of the land* (6).

It was a principle of English law that these liberties should be abridged only with the utmost reluctance and the role of Parliament was to defend them rather than progressively eclipse them. They form the framework which defines the objective freedom space within which the Crown's subjects were to live and clearly that space is an ample one. Such a large space will accommodate a life of great scope. It envisages the English subject exercising a high degree of self-determination, self-reliance and creativity, able to dispose as he wills over his own affairs, in his own way and on his own land, and preserves him from undue interference as he does so. The presupposition is that he is to be trusted and his enterprises honoured.

It cannot be doubted that since Blackstone published his first edition in 1765, there has been an erosion of liberty, the closing down of much of the freedom space which these principles presuppose, and consequent reduction in the estimate of human status, potential and trustworthiness. Most of this erosion has taken place in the last seventy years. Just part of the first absolute right according to Blackstone, has been exaggerated at the expense of the enjoyment of life and all other rights. An enthusiasm for human health and safety has reached manic proportions under the encouragement of terrorist threats and every other right of human beings has been made subservient to it. Ever increasingly intrusive security checks at airports, increasing obstruction of the purchases of chemicals, road closures, the absurd habit of "lockdown", preventing movement after some incident, and many other restrictions have largely been accepted by people who think that the preservation of their lives is worth the cost of their liberty.

At the same time, people's vision for the potential of their lives appears to have diminished. Their own subjective freedom space has shrunk to match the available objective space. They expect to do less, to be less free, to be more controlled, to be more governed than ever before. They have moved from being self-determining, self-reliant, independent and creative persons to being the clients of a protecting, need-supplying and controlling system. To be sure, this process is far from complete and it is possible still to break out from underneath it and retrieve a good fraction of self-governance but generally this has to be done with some degree of cunning. The system frowns on such ingenuity and generally requires rather a dull and dutiful compliance. These changes are, to some extent, welcomed by the client body. There is an increasingly widespread opinion that the government's responsibility is to prevent everything which could be dangerous, harmful, unpleasant or even inconvenient to the client-individual, and to provide everything, needful, desirable, and pleasant. At the same time, the subjective freedom space shrinks, the desire for liberty fades and the towering majesty of what it is to be a human being crumbles to subservience.

8.5. Liberty and the United States Constitution

Homer Simpson is outside his house with his family. He glances up at the starry heavens, spreads out his hands, and declares: *We're free! we can go anywhere we like!* - pause - *I'm cold and frightened, let's go back inside.* American society is now showing this ambivalence towards its own liberties, which won't go away so easily as those in Britain, because they are enshrined in the written text of the United States Constitution.

The Constitution of the United States is a masterpiece of finely crafted principles which have as their chief design, the defence of the liberty of individuals against the tyranny of government, tyranny of the majority and the tyranny of the powerful. But it rests on the recollection of ancient principles of liberty and of what it was to be a human being which stretch back into Saxon England and further back into the inheritance of the Judaeo-Christian tradition. It is from these sources that have arisen the basic liberties referred to by Blackstone in 1765.

Hayek makes the point that these liberties were not invented but remembered: *It might be also said that it was because England retained more of the common mediaeval idea of the supremacy of law, which was destroyed elsewhere by the rise of absolutism, that she was able to initiate the modern growth of liberty. This medieval view, which is profoundly important as background for modern developments, though completely accepted perhaps only during the early Middle Ages, was that, 'the state cannot itself create or make a law, and of course as little abolish or violate law, because this would mean to abolish justice itself, it would be absurd, as would rebellion against God who alone creates law.' For centuries it was recognised doctrine that kings or any other human authority could only declare or find the existing law, or modify abuses that had crept in, and not create law. Only gradually, during the later Middle Ages, does the conception of deliberate creation of new law - legislation as we know it - come to be accepted. In England, Parliament thus developed from what had been mainly a law-finding body to a law-creating one* (7).

This principle of the recollection of law rather that its creation, was indeed substantially forgotten by the English Parliament, but it was still alive and operative until the 1760s. It was preserved by the party known as the Old Whigs who were the last real Liberals. They remembered that people could not be arbitrarily obliterated by incarceration or execution, that under God, they were to be regarded as indestructible. They remembered that they could go anywhere they chose without hindrance and each one had the right to own property over which he had the right of disposal and every other right as to its use. In remembering this, the Old Whigs were recalling the days of King Alfred and the land holding of the yeoman farmers for whom even the modest plot under their feet, afforded them a dignity and sense of freedom inaccessible in any other way.

The English Parliament may have forgotten this, but its memory was alive and well in the export which became the US Constitution. That memory of the law is important to the framers of the Constitution is demonstrated by the Ninth Amendment: *The enumeration in the Constitution of certain rights, shall not be construed to deny or disparage others retained by the people.* The Constitution does not aim to set down all the rights of the people, but only some principal rights, leaving the courts to recollect the other rights of the people in specific cases. This presupposes that there is a basis of law more profound than even the US Constitution, and the function of the latter is to express at least part of that more basic law.

The liberty described but not fully circumscribed by the US Constitution and before it by English Common Law, amounts to a very large freedom space only minimally encroached upon by some necessary limitations. But this very large space anticipates a high view of human office, capacity and responsibility. A great field of freedom needs a high order of human responsibility to fill it. It needs robustness, strength of character, a confident and thoughtful capacity to make moral decisions, a well educated conscience and the courage to act on its resolutions. This great space needs a truly great humanity to fill it, a humanity at the top of its game, a humanity of the exalted kind anticipated by the Judaeo-Christian tradition.

The space afforded to human beings by the American Constitution is thus one that takes the highest human aspiration to fill and to fill it is the American Dream. It is not surprising that it is hard to live up to, so much so, that many Americans appear to have presently lost sight of it. They are behaving more and more as the clients of the overweening, providential state instead of pioneers of their own regnant freedom in making their own life and future. The vast freedom space granted them by the Constitution now frightens them - they have not the stature to fill it - so they try to reduce the space to make it less demanding and so they can feel more secure.

This has a parallel with the political developments in Europe and other parts of the world, where dependency on government provision generates a sense of entitlement, reduces aspiration, diminishes self-reliance and lowers human expectation. The corresponding impact on individuals is a lowering of the view of the stature of human beings and the shrinking of the desired freedom space to match the reduced space available. This change is very clearly observable on American and European university campuses with the rise of the so-called Snowflake Generation (8). Through a variety of influences through childhood, Snowflakes have learned that all kinds of things are toxic and dangerous to them, including certain speech and ideas. They believe that they have the right to be protected from these things because as children they were grossly over-protected from influences which their parents did not like and thought unsuitable for them. They become terrified of the world they live in and especially if the freedom-space in which they find themselves is very wide and open. In it they may find beliefs, ideas and even words and phrases which they evaluate as hostile and dangerous to themselves and so they seek 'safe-spaces' where such ideas, beliefs and words are never uttered. In terms of the American Constitution they find the First Amendment which guarantees freedom of speech creates a space much too great for them, so they desire a space in which it does not apply. This makes the Snowflake quintessentially un-American.

When Elmer Davis, the Director of War Information during World War II said, *This nation will remain the land of the free only so long as it is the home of the brave*, he was considering primarily the threat to American liberty from an external source, but now it is equally applicable to an internal, psychologically induced loss of nerve.

8.6. Human Liberty from Physical Causality

In our review of liberty in the sections above we have contrasted the tightly circumscribed limits to the freedom space offered in totalitarian regimes with the wide space which the Judaeo-Christian tradition has historically envisaged for human beings. But could there be a theory of human liberty exclusively derived solely from the perspective of physical causality? We investigate this in this section.

There is, of course, a need for physical space. John Calhoun carried out research on the effects of overcrowding in rats and showed that beyond a particular population density, the females' pregnancy rate fell, they failed more frequently to reach full term, there was a rise of sexual deviation and cannibalism, a tendency both towards hyperactivity and towards a kind of autistic withdrawal.(9) Lewis Mumford described human overpopulation as exhibiting a wide range of defects and disease in overcrowded cities (10). The freedom space we have referred to in previous sections is not primarily a physical space, but there must be a spatial component to it. Many people will testify to the fact that they need space to think, i.e. to be a whole person and it may be that our vision of our human potential and our capacity to grasp an idea, form a plan, conceive of an invention, depends strongly on the magnitude of the physical space in which we live. The exigencies of high population density and the price of land has meant that homes in Britain have diminished in size markedly in the last 50 years. This, in turn, may have reduced our vision of what it is to be human. We expect less of ourselves and less is expected of us perhaps because we live in more confined accommodation. According to the RIBA, the average floor area of domestic homes has fallen from over 140 square metres in 1850 to less than 100 square metres in 1980 and the figure was 76 square metres in 2013.

We speak of being 'as free as a bird', but just how free is a bird? Apart from the obvious capacity to move in 3 dimensions, none of the limitations to freedom space we considered in section 8.1., apply to a bird, nor does it have a subjective freedom space which is variable according to its view of itself. It has no view of itself-it is a bird in a bird's space. Similarly, we can say that human beings viewed only from the point of view of physical causality are animals like all others, so they are merely humans in human space. To be sure they experience restrictions when overpopulation occurs and perhaps exhibit some of the pathological symptoms observed in rats, but in general, as far as liberty is concerned there are no variables, and hence liberty has little meaning.

8.7. Human Liberty from Metaphysical Causality

The whole of the Judaeo-Christian reading of history has the idea of redemption at its centre. Redemption is the act by which a slave is bought back from bondage and brought into freedom. This introduces a refinement to our definition of liberty: the freedom space is now a God-given space, and the scope of our lives is God-enabled to fill it. This transcends, of course, merely geometric space, but the story begins with the redemption of a real slave people, in bondage to Egyptian masters, brought out from that slavery into a liberty in the Promised Land, a liberty unequalled anywhere in the world at any time. The slavery itself was long, about four hundred years, but during it, a somewhat disparate and nomadic people, actually flourished numerically and began to take on a definite identity. It is to these people that a redemptive event took place. This did involve Moses' entreaties to Pharaoh, and some bad things happening to Egyptians in an ascending order of seriousness until Pharaoh ordered the Israelites' release. But the conclusion reached by the Israelites was that it was a divine act of rescue performed by a God of whom they had hardly heard, to whom they scarcely considered themselves to belong, and whose interest in them came to them as a complete surprise. They did not engineer their own redemption, rather they were overtaken by it: it happened to them and they had to then hasten to keep up with it. Often they did not cooperate with it very well, even resisting it, doubting it, perhaps even despising it, but nevertheless this redemption had them in its grasp and did not them let go. Instead, everything else which had a hold on them had to release them - the Egyptian masters themselves found themselves unable to retain them, their own inertia, that lack of the will for self-determination which often besets the downtrodden, could not hold them back. The Egyptians even plied them with gold on their departure: money which was always considered by the rabbis as back-pay, could not be withheld from the people to whom it was owed. Even these smaller elements of the Exodus story betrayed to them the action of a power which they hardly knew or recognised, of a God of whom they did not even know his name. These many smaller elements, together with the great acts of parting the waters of the Red Sea, and the people's remarkable preservation throughout their wilderness wanderings, became the emblems of a redemption the recollection of which resonates down the ages and forms the foundation of all that is known and believed about God in the great Judaeo-Christian tradition.

In the New Testament, the theme of redemption remains central and takes on a universal character: no longer is it merely a question of the emancipation of a people held in physical servitude and the granting to them of land and sovereignty. Rather, the Old Testament story becomes a metaphor for a much more profound liberation from a servitude arising from that primordial catastrophe in which man fell from his high office held by divine appointment, and enjoying a liberty of a kind only possessed by God, to the depths of an unimaginable lostness and ruin. The freedom space which he enjoyed as God's right hand man was one of vast possibility and potential in which he would have disposed and governed the whole creation as he willed. But the Fall meant that his freedom-space has now been closed down and reduced to scarcely a toe-hold with no standing before God at all. He is hemmed in by his sins, by his truculent refusal of God, by his own headstrong folly. John Paul II points out that, falling, man became ashamed, meaning that the creation would no longer accept his rule - his authority had collapsed and no longer could he exercise his office (11). The Judaeo-Christian tradition, while accepting the reality of the restraints to human freedom discussed in section 8.1. above, sees the enslavement of fallen man in a much more profound light. It is not merely a question of legal and moral restriction, the Fall eclipsed man's freedom in an existential way: it closed him down as a being and shut him off from exercising his true rôle and nature.

8.8. Liberty and Jesus Christ

There is an important moment, early in the ministry of Jesus, when he enters a synagogue and is handed the scroll of the prophet Isaiah and he reads from chapter 61:

The Spirit of the Lord is upon me,
  because he has anointed me
  to proclaim good news to the poor.
 He has sent me to proclaim liberty to the captives
  and recovering of sight to the blind,
  to set at liberty those who are oppressed,
to proclaim the year of the Lord's favour.

After completing the reading, he declares to the assembled company: *Today this Scripture has been fulfilled in your hearing*, and all eyes in the synagogue were fixed on him. They understood what that meant: not merely casting off the domination of a gentile overlordship, but a reversal of that slavery binding much more deeply the souls of men. Jesus says, in John 8:34, *Truly, truly, I say to you, everyone who commits sin is a slave to sin. The slave does not remain in the house forever; the son remains forever. So if the Son sets you free, you will be free indeed.* We have seen that the liberty of human beings consists in the freedom space in which they exist and the capacity they have in filling it. Both of these are seriously restricted by the fall of man into sin. The most direct way to observe that these two elements are restored in Jesus Christ, is first to see the vast expanse of the freedom space he enjoyed and his capacity to use it all, and to see how he opened his own freedom to those whom he called to be his disciples.

First, his own freedom: this is one of the most striking features of Jesus' own life: how utterly free he was. We often associate human freedom with wealth and privilege, but Jesus had neither of these in human terms, and yet he was the freest man on earth. Moreover, this freedom was not simply due to a large freedom space that somehow he found himself in. His freedom was ontologically his own, he bore it in himself and exercised it as he willed. The boundaries which might otherwise have set a limit to the liberty he exercised, were, instead, found to be under his own regnant disposition. When challenged about his Sabbath observance, he declared *the Son of Man is Lord of the Sabbath.* Perhaps we thought this signified his divinity, and maybe it does, but most of all it signifies his true humanity, in exercising the rank, office and authority which was proper to man in the first place. Even the limitations of the natural world, the restrictions of which we have long since been accustomed to, are found to be entirely under his direction. In answer to the disciples' question, *Who is this, that the even the wind and waves obey him?* the answer is not just that he is divine, although he is, but rather more interestingly, he is one who has a humanity as it was originally intended. To recall John Paul II, here was the natural order restored to obedience to its earthly master. In his healing of the sick, in his repudiation of the false claims of the devil, in his rescue of those held in the constraints of evil power, his ministry was divine but it was also human - truly and freely and properly human - and it is here that we find the ultimate definition of human liberty in the way the Son of Man rules and disposes as he wills, overcoming an obstacle here, righting a wrong there, teaching the truth to one, administering grace to another, and all without the slightest impression that there would ever arise anything to which he would not be more than equal.

8.9. Liberty and the Church

But as we saw in section 6.8., Jesus does not keep his humanity to himself. He came to share our humanity, so we could share his. And this is a very generous exchange! A blighted and degenerated, feeble and enslaved humanity for this unblemished, exalted, powerful and truly free restoration of the divine image. Although this exchange has been made, the fulness of it has not yet been realised (see section 8.11. below). However, the people of God have an anticipation of it, inspired by the Holy Spirit. Paul says, *Now the Lord is the Spirit, and where the Spirit of the Lord is, there is freedom* (2 Corinthians 3:17). The expectation of the

Apostle is that the liberty exercised by Jesus would be reflected, at least in an anticipatory way, in the life of Christians and in the life of the Church as a whole.

There are signs in the New Testament that the freedom which Christianity brought to the followers of Jesus Christ was occasionally misunderstood as a licence for evil or used as an excuse for civil disobedience or even criminality. St Peter warns his hearers: *Live as people who are free, not using your freedom as a cover-up for evil, but living as servants of God.*(1 Peter 2:16) and St Paul similarly urges the Galatians: *For you were called to freedom, brothers. Only do not use your freedom as an opportunity for the flesh, but through love serve one another* (Galatians 5:13). On the other hand, those same Galatians are warned not to move in the opposite direction and sacrifice their new liberty for a bondage of religious observance which was improper to them: *For freedom Christ has set us free; stand firm therefore, and do not submit again to a yoke of slavery* (Galatians 5:1).

Christian liberty is a hard thing to exercise. On the one hand, because of the temptation to wrong-doing always seems very close at hand, liberty can easily be transmuted to licentiousness and St Paul is insistent that the Christian communities guard against that fatal transition. On the other hand he does not want them to be neglectful of their freedom and lapse into a sub-christian mode of existence in which they never seek to exercise the new humanity into which they have been brought. St Paul himself charts his own progress in this exercise. He tells the Corinthians that he and the other apostles have no competence of their own, but they have been made competent by God for the office they hold. Then, in Philippians 4, St Paul declares that he *can do all things through him who strengthens [him].*

Just as Jesus himself did not use miracles or mighty works merely to impress people, and was, if fact, rather reluctant to do such works in public, so also much exercise of the new humanity which has been given to the Christians does not have a very public provenance. But there is an expectation among Christians that they can achieve things which they themselves might regard as ordinarily beyond them. Christianity raises their expectations, while a more worldly assessment might lower them. In the first millennium, Cistercian monks began to build an Abbey near the Thames in what is now south Oxford, cutting through the boggy turf with wooden spades, from which they erected a towering cathedral-like building with stone pillars eight feet across. It took them more than 100 years to build. It was not miraculous in the normal sense of the term but it required a high view of human capability to achieve.

8.10. Liberty, the Created Order and Eschatology

In Romans 8:20, St Paul writes, *for the creation was subjected to futility, not of its own will but by the will of him who subjected it in hope; because the creation itself will be set free from its bondage to decay and obtain the glorious liberty of the children of God.* This suggests three main elements of St Paul's thought: (i) the divine subjection of the whole of the natural order to decay was deliberate and temporary, (ii) that the destiny of the natural order was to freedom from decay and followed the liberation of God's people from the restrictions of the Fall, and (iii) the full liberty of the people of God was glorious and therefore eschatological: it was a future event to be anticipated in the present time, but only fully realised when the new heaven and earth took their shape.? e have already seen in section 6.7., that at the Fall man lost his commanding authority over the created order. He became disobedient to God, and the created order became disobedient to him. Both, then, fell into futility and became subject to decay. St Paul understands that the incipient futility of the created order was allowed to occur because it would be inevitably reversed when its master (i.e. man himself) was restored to his full dignity and liberty. But this has not yet been fully realised. One of the most powerful aspects of the Christian understanding of reality is that it continually anticipates its glorious future. In its best moments, the Church risks itself in leaning forward as much as it dares. It trusts its unseen future more than it does its visible present. It is at that point where it experiences the best manifestation of its liberty. It gets a hint of its future powers. This is the perspective that informed the ministry of Gregory Thaumaturgus of Nicomedia: he leant forward and put his weight on the future he was promised, and he was not disappointed.

8.10.1. Anticipating the Human Liberty of the New Order

When Gregory the Wonderworker (or *Thaumaturgus*) first went to Pontus in northern Asia Minor in the mid-third century AD, there were, apparently, only seventeen Christians in the midst of a large population of pagans. It is a tribute to Gregory's vigorous Christian witness and his diligent teaching and pastoral care that when he died there were only seventeen pagans who had not been persuaded to forsake their idolatries and follow Christ. St Gregory the Wonderworker is the patron saint who specialises in impossible, desperate, forgotten and lost causes as well as earthquakes, floods and other natural disasters. It is quite a portfolio! But taking a look at the story of his Christian ministry seventeen hundred years ago in what is now northern Turkey, we can see why he might have been the appropriate candidate for such a brief.

Travelling, normally dangerous in the Ancient World, even in areas of the Roman Empire moderately well-policed by Legions, was doubly hazardous in northern reaches of Asia Minor. It was, in the first place, immensely hard-going. Steep mountain passes, poor roads, torrential rivers, avalanches, flash floods would test the resolve of even the hardiest travellers. But they also had to watch out for brigands and desperadoes who made a living by robbing and sometimes enslaving those taking the risk of a journey.

Gregory did not merely have to escape these dangers but his task was to persuade the population, already securely devoted to the idols of paganism, to abandon these and embrace the Christian faith. And the evidence is that the paganism was thriving when Gregory arrived. At Zela there was a busy shrine to the Persian deity Anahita where oaths were sworn in the conduct of commercial transactions - an idol with the profession of notary public! At Comana there was a thriving cult of Isis with 6000 temple slaves - a great centre of luxury and licence. When the goddess had one of her 'exoduses,' visitors from as far as Armenia would swarm in for her religious fair. Comana, as Strabo knew it, housed temple prostitutes, and on the days of 'exodus,' the goddess expected them to serve the crowds. Few cities could offer such a mixture of trade and religious worship, processions, sex and a drinkable local wine.

233

Everywhere he turned Gregory would have encountered attitudes and actions which were completely contrary to the Gospel of Jesus Christ. Not only that, but those attitudes and actions made important people very wealthy and Gregory found that persuasive Christian preaching aroused serious opposition as well as engendering new faith. He confronted these things both with a preaching ministry in which he explained and taught the Christian Faith and with a ministry of mighty works in which he appeared to stake his whole life and reputation on the dependability of God to back him up. He stopped the river Lycus flooding by setting a limit to the water's advance with his staff. He resolved a quarrel over a lake between two neighbouring landowners by drying it up. He protected his Church in a time of plague and even had the insight to appoint a seemingly unsuitable candidate as a bishop who was subsequently found to be a man of great faith and learning who had disguised himself as a charcoal burner.

What Gregory discovered in his robust witness was that Christ was faithful to His Church. We often think of faith, not wrongly, as the confidence we have in God, but it is also the loyalty God shows to his Church. At the end of Mark's Gospel it is said of the Apostles, that 'they went forth and preached everywhere, while the Lord worked with them and confirmed the message by the signs that attended it' (Mark 16:20). This must have been Gregory's experience as he ministered in those adverse conditions. And it gives heart to the modern Church faced with the challenge of secularism as she is reminded of her indestructibility and the inevitable triumph of her ministry.

8.11. Liberty and Memory

It is extraordinary how rapidly we can forget our liberties, how quickly we can adapt to a reduction in our freedom space, how readily we prefer safety to freedom. From a Judaeo-Christian standpoint it is equally remarkable how quickly we can forget the liberty of our humanity in Jesus Christ and resort to a low perspective of our potential and accept enslavement of various kinds. It is striking, in this connection to observe how readily we accepted the intrusions of airport searches, the confiscation of our property, and more than that, how we accepted that we should all be considered a public risk to others. We became supine before all this in our desire to be safe: and we were hardly cognisant of the great loss of liberty for the very marginal advantage in safety. While the western world was making this very poor deal in the public arena, the Church was also making its exchange of freedom for safety in the spiritual sphere under even worse terms. We have seen that to exercise its proper office and to anticipate its own liberty it must lean forward towards its destiny in the Kingdom of God. There are considerable risks in so doing. It has to trust itself to a divinely ordained future, so it must exercise faith that it will be able to do the things that it has the liberty to do and not fall flat on its face. But quite often, all this is too much for the worldly churchman or the cautious parish council. It might be safer not to lean forward and rock back on to one's heels to feel surer ground underfoot. In order to do this, the church must forget its forward leaning vector, its future calling, its destiny in glory and its appointment to the rendezvous with the God who made it for himself. It must abandon the future for the sake of the present just like the man at the airport who gives up his liberty to save himself anxiety. We end up in a static, safe, unfree present, instead of a dynamic, risky, free future, because we have forgotten what we are, from where we have come, and the kingdom to which we are moving.

In section 8.4. we recalled the reign of Alfred the Great which did much to establish a Judaeo-Christian understanding of human liberty, which, in Britain, we often forget, but from time to time recall as if it is somehow buried in our bones and re-emerges at key moments. In the Church we find the Scriptures and the Holy Spirit prompting us to remember and exercise the liberty won for us through the Incarnation. We must shed our aversion to risk, our instinct to shelter in the comfort of a familiar present, the reassuring limits of a servile existence and draw again on the memory of our redemption, recalling the words of Jesus Christ: *All things are possible for one who believes* (Mark 9:23).

REFERENCES FOR CHAPTER 8

(1) F. A. Hayek, *The Constitution of Liberty*, p11? 2) *The Koran*, Translation of Muhammad Taqi-ud-Din Al-Hilali, and Muhammad Muhsin Khan

(3) F .A. Hayek, *Ibid*, pp19-20

(4) John L Hancock, *Liberty & Prosperity, How the Saxons created the modern world.*

(5) William Blackstone, Commentaries on the Laws of England, 1st Edition, Volume 1, p22.

(6) William Blackstone, *Ibid*, pp125, 130, 134

(7) F. A. Hayek, *Ibid*, p163

(8) Claire Fox, *Generation Snowflake: how we train our kids to be censorious cry-babies*, *The Spectator*, 4 June 2016

(9)J. B. Calhoun, *The ecology and sociology of the Norway Rat*, p238.

(10) Lewis Mumford, *The City on History*, p224, 466ff

(11) John Paul II, *Man and Woman He created them: A Theology of the Body,* p242

CHAPTER 9
HUMAN ENDEAVOUR

9.1. The Reign of Man

Human endeavour is a mystery. Not so much in its outward manifestation: many animals show a certain energy and diligence in being what they are. The honey bee, in conjunction with her companions, constructs a great and intricate edifice of architectural and geometric beauty and the task consumes her energies, but there is no sign that she plans it, envisages it or conceives it. She just builds it because that is what bees do, just as nest-building is what birds do. As we have already seen, it is the interior life of cogitation, of imagination, of creativity which marks out the human being as unique and it is this capacity to resolve, to plan, design and execute which forms the foundation of what we call human endeavour. It is a powerful drive which transcends merely the satisfaction of biological appetites and it is to a very great extent that which makes a human truly what he is.

Behind human endeavour stands an immense capacity for persistence and the expenditure of energy, a powerful commitment and an internally generated resolve which in many cases, so grips an individual that it may be pursued and prosecuted to the point of endangerment or even loss of life itself. Human endeavour demonstrates as nothing else, the regnant will of a human being; it demonstrates that he reigns in the world. An individual can be said to reign if he has the power to effect his will. In this sense, craftsmen reign in their chosen trades. The joiner can make the raw timber he begins with to conform to the design he intends. He reigns over the wood with his saw and chisel. It is not easy to establish this sovereignty: much practice and training may be required to make the saw-cuts straight, and the dovetails close-fitting. But every apprentice endeavours to acquire it because it belongs to him to impose his rule upon the wood. On occasion, he puts up with much discomfort and inconvenience to exert that rule, and to improve his powers to do so. The famous seventeenth century chemist, Johann Becher described his relationship to the science of chemistry thus: *"Chemists are a strange class of mortals, driven by a feverish impulse to seek their pleasures amongst smoke and vapour, soot and flames, poisons and poverty, yet amongst all these evils I seem to live so sweetly that I would rather die than change places with the King of Persia"* (1). Nor is this instinct to reign confined to the trades or to the mystical enthusiasm of alchemy. In order to master the Latin, Greek, Egyptian and Persian classical writers, Friedrich Wolf (1759-1824) slept for just two nights a week for six months, so as to immerse himself in his beloved classical authors as quickly as possible, keeping himself awake by sitting with his feet in a bowl of cold water. He would bind up one eye with a bandage to rest it while he used the other (2). If Becher was something of a maniac in chemistry, Wolf was also in literature.

Macaulay, in his History of England, pauses to reflect on this phenomenon: *No ordinary misfortune, no ordinary misgovernment, will do so much to make a nation wretched, as the constant progress of physical knowledge and the constant effort of every man to better himself will do to make a nation prosperous. It has often been found that profuse expenditure, heavy taxation, absurd commercial restrictions, corrupt tribunals, disastrous wars, seditions, persecutions, conflagrations, inundations, have not been able to destroy capital so fast as the exertions of private citizens have been able to create it. It can easily be proved that, in our own land, the national wealth has, during at least six centuries, been almost uninterruptedly increasing; that it was greater under the Tudors than under the Plantagenets; that it was greater under the Stuarts than under the Tudors; that, in spite of battles, sieges and confiscations, it was greater on the day of the Restoration than on the day when the Long Parliament met; that, in spite of maladministration, of extravagance, of public bankruptcy, of two costly and unsuccessful wars, of the pestilence and of the fire, it was greater on the day of the death of Charles II than on the day of his Restoration. This progress, having continued during many ages, became at length, about the middle of the 18th-century, portentously rapid, and has proceeded, during the nineteenth, with accelerated velocity* (3).

Man steps on to the world stage with a sense that he is born to rule, and, in every age and in every place he strives to prove it. He will not rest until he has mastered everything in the entire cosmos. He went to the moon, and now he is planning to go to Mars. He wants to travel faster, build taller, see further. He wants to examine things ever more minutely, understand them ever more exactly and put them to every better use in his realm of burgeoning greatness. And all this, not merely for wealth or for greater comfort and convenience, although these thing often issue from his endeavours, but chiefly because they are there to be mastered and he is the great master of all things. This is man at the top of his game, at his best, but alas, he is not always in that place. He falls from it frequently and his sovereignty is qualified and brought into question when he does so.

9.2. The Socially Constructed Reign of Man

The great exponents of human endeavour to which we have so far alluded are perhaps more numerous than we might suppose, but they do not represent the perspective of everyone. A number of factors tend to obstruct, if not entirely obliterate, the insight that human beings have to achieve and accomplish in their sovereign power. We have already seen in section 2.2. that power-constructed realities reduce people to units of labour, functionaries whose powers of endeavour are short-circuited into mere output. When this occurs, either in totalitarian regimes, or more commonly in highly developed cyber-economies, the "functionaries" find outlets for their sense of regnant creativity and instinct to achieve. They take up sports, hobbies and pastimes in which they can strive to excel. Sometimes the corporations which have reduced their staff to functionary status, provide these outlets, perhaps cynically, so that they can more readily endure the regime of chores to which they are subject. We have already alluded to the similarity between employment and slavery in section 6.3. but perhaps it is here where the comparison is most apt. Of course, not all employment deprives the employee of a sense of endeavour but rather offers a genuine participation in a corporate accomplishment shared by the whole firm. The company may claim they do this even when the sense of participation is only slight, which is more likely to be the case in larger companies. Since companies are generally getting larger, and progressively devouring smaller ones, there is a sense that the opportunity of an employee to make a felt contribution to human endeavour is diminishing. As this takes place, human expectations tend to fall and there is an increased acceptance of a functionary role in place of a sovereign one.

Referring to education once again, it does seem that schools and universities have adapted to these changes. Schools in Britain have traditionally been of two types: those which advance academic and technical education with the sometimes express intention that the pupils will be prepared for ruling and vocational appointments, and those which aim to equip pupils for everyday living in an essentially functional role. The balance between these two types of education has tilted in recent years towards the more functionary role: language teaching has moved from the treatment of literary classics towards the simply necessities of tourists in a foreign country. Health and hygiene, cooking and dietetics have gained an importance over Latin and Greek. In science and technology there has been a corresponding shift. A hundred years ago, it was possible to make at home, practically anything which could be bought. Many people had reasonably well-equipped workshops for this purpose. Periodicals were published to support a wide range of such interests and had details within their covers for the construction of many items. But in modern times, purchased items increasingly have monolithic components which cannot be reproduced at home so easily. Many of the construction magazines have gone out of print and have been replaced by journals which mainly review commercial products. Many of these changes have been good and some people keep abreast of the technological developments on an amateur basis, but generally the pioneer has tended to become a purchaser, and the would-be creator, a consumer.

Of course, people will say that not everyone can rule, but this is only true of the rule of people. When we consider human endeavour, we are not speaking of ruling people, but ruling the natural order, the cosmos and everyone can do that: simply in growing a vegetable garden, for example, we exercise a sovereignty over the natural world. But, then again, gardens in Britain are getting smaller and employed people have much less time to cultivate them. The truth is that however common, even ubiquitous, is the instinct for the exercise of human endeavour, it is often well-eclipsed by the general desire for love, laughter, eating, drinking and making merry and people feel the loss of these latter things more than they do of the opportunity for the former. They are prepared to endure relatively dull and unproductive employment if it finances sufficiently their recreational pursuits. And yet there persists a rumour that they are worthy of much more this this.

9.3. Human Endeavour from Physical Causality

Is it possible to derive a theory of human endeavour from physical causality alone? Since human endeavour occupies principally the human consciousness (which has no physical explanation as we have seen in section 3.1.2.) and transcends immediate needs, subjugating them to a cause which does not seem to give immediate advantage to the individual, some doubt could be raised as to whether such an explanation is possible. The phenomenon of human endeavour does suggest an exceptionalism of human beings over other species which exhibit no instinct or tendency to master anything beyond their particular needs and appetites. On this basis, the idea of human exceptionalism has been challenged as something improper or dangerous to the planet. We return briefly to our consideration of Agenda 21. In section 5.2., we drew attention to the main effort of Agenda 21 to put the human race back in its conceived place as merely one species among many, to remove its pre-eminence, to confine it geographically and aspirationally to a tightly circumscribed space. This is intended to counter the human instinct to reign over the whole of the natural order, on the ground that this instinct is wrong and ill-conceived. The irony of this is that Agenda 21, despite being founded on a view of humanity from physical causality, is itself a function of the human capacity for endeavour which can only be grounded in metaphysical causality. Utilising the principle of human exceptionalism, it moves in a direction which altogether denies that exceptionalism. It is intrinsically incoherent and represents a perverse human endeavour.

Human endeavour is inherently risky. In the 14th and 15th centuries, maritime navigators lost up to eighty percent of their crews to pestilence and disease. About fifty percent of the pioneer immigrants to the Americas lost their lives within a year of arriving. Between 1818 and 1908 there were thirty five publicly funded expeditions into the Arctic by land and sea, and combined they had an average death rate of nine percent. Among astronauts the death rate is currently about 1.5%. This suggests that natural selection should have made the human race very risk averse, but it has not appeared to do so. True, the general aversion to risk has increased in western society since the second world war, but this is offset by the rapid increase in popularity of high-risk pursuits, owing, it is thought, to a reaction to the overweening concern for safety in the current emotional climate. The instinct for human endeavour seems largely undaunted by the risks involved. In fact the risks are, it seems, attractive, because surmounting fear and achieving a difficult and dangerous result appears to be part of the endeavour. Human endeavour does not seem to be abated by danger and neither is it entirely prompted by material reward. Many of the most dangerous exploits in the last 200 years have been very costly in money which has not been recouped by any significant material return.? t is a cardinal principle of evolutionary theory that any advantage accrued by chance genetic alterations must directly apply to the individual bearing the alteration. Only in this way is the advantage sustained and advanced to the next generation. Survival of the fittest does not work if the survivor is not the fittest, but merely an individual that obtained a temporary benefit from another's genetic makeup. Heroism, risk-taking in one individual thus cannot transmit a benefit via a second recipient of the heroic act. Thus evolution would predict the development of extreme caution in species and that is exactly what is observed in animals. Only the minimum risk is taken to ensure survival of an individual or its young which already have its genetic inheritance. The spirit of human endeavour seems to be contrary to the basic principles of natural selection.

9.4. Human Endeavour and Metaphysical Causality

We saw in section 3.6. that according to the Christian gospel, God achieved things which were generally considered impossible. The whole story of Judaeo-Christian tradition is one of an endeavour, not primarily a human endeavour, but a divine endeavour into which the people of Israel, and then the disciples of Jesus were drawn and made its principal agents. The story of the conquest of Canaan and the subsequent adventures of the people of God under the Judges are some of the most ancient records of this endeavour, preserved to us, at least in part, by ballads which celebrated the heroism and triumphs of Israel and attributed them to God's providence and power. Israel's first encounter with God was in the context of a risky adventure to free themselves from the tyranny of Egypt. According to the narrative, God seemed to be in his element. It was his project and his endeavour and he threw himself into it with unbridled enthusiasm and some of this seemed to rub off on the Israelites as they slowly got the hang of it. They had long moments of angst, they kept losing their nerve, but with divine encouragement and sometimes rebuke, they stayed with the project, even if a generation had to pass before the Promised Land could be entered. Even at the point of entry they are seriously daunted by the proposition - the cities seems so well fortified, their residents fierce and numerous, so they baulk at the challenge before them. It takes divine encouragement and Joshua's leadership to get them to press forward.

What is clear is that the endeavour was not derived from a particularly courageous spirit which the people of Israel were able to muster from within themselves. In fact, rather the opposite was case: from them came doubts and anxiety as to whether they would be able to pull it off. The adventure was empowered by God who tells them: *I will be with you; I will not fail you or forsake you. Be strong and of good courage; for you shall cause this people to inherit the land which I swore to their fathers to give them* (Joshua 1:5f). Only a single generation ago, they were hapless slaves in Egypt, with no prospect of self-determination or the engagement in an endeavour of their own, but suddenly they were plunged into a military expedition which would issue in their establishment as a nation. It was a steep learning curve.

But it was a learning curve by which they would recollect the qualities of their humanity which they had forgotten in centuries of slavery. They would remember the high office, dignity and liberty afforded to them by the God who created them and authorised them to represent him in the world and administer the affairs of his creation. The curious thing about this is that they were remembering something they had never formally learned. The events of the conquest of Canaan predated the book of Genesis which was probably committed to writing during the Babylonian Exile. At this stage they did not have any Hebrew text to help them. They were being reminded of a primordial truth about what they were as human beings, and from which they had been abstracted by the Fall and by their enslavement. What they learned from their redemption from Egypt and their conquest of the Promised Land gave them the language and understanding of what they were before God, primordially, and the nature of their humanity that they had lost sight of, and which was being restored to them. This was knowledge of the kind we discussed in section 2.3., which comes from a external source and informs the mind of the recipient. In the first instance, it is to be noted that it was not merely propositional, rather the Israelites discovered the God to whom they belonged though experience with him in a great endeavour. At the start, the information they had was very slight, hardly more than a rumour, but as they followed the lead they had, albeit tentatively, the rumour gained strength and their confidence grew in its reliability. Through each twist and turn of their adventure, the evidence gathered weight and they were at last able to speak confidently of the God who had saved them and of their relationship to him.

The very setting of this learning encounter, in the context of their rescue from slavery, their exodus from Egypt, the wilderness wanderings and their entry into the Promised Land, meant that they were bound to understand the world contingently. There was no framework of necessity in which to classify anything they learned. All outcomes were entirely open to possibility. They were introduced by experience to contingent thinking which as we saw in section 2.6. forms the foundational principle of all Judaeo-Christian thinking and, through it, of modern science. This unites two great pillars of thought: contingent thinking was learned from the divine endeavour of the Judaeo-Christian tradition, and the idea of human endeavour was framed and empowered by the concept of contingence.

9.5. Contingence and Human Endeavour

Rooted as it was in the experience of God by the Israelites, especially in their formative years, the idea of living in a contingent world under the rule of an active God became foundational to the Judaeo-Christian tradition. This worldview, as we have seen, could not be further away from the Greek world of necessity and static immovability. Aristotle described God as the Unmoved Mover, because to move is to change and to change is to be imperfect, and God was not imperfect. But at bottom, this was a pure assumption which arose from Aristotle's definition of God. But he had no experience of the dynamic intervention of divine help which transported him from a place of horror and misery to a place of blessedness, peace and prosperity, while fighting battles, surviving catastrophes and making miraculous escapes from impending doom. Nor did Aristotle have any experience of the dynamic holiness of God which commanded obedience and such a transparent righteousness that it made the Israelites more terrified of the God they served than the enemies they faced.

Aristotle could only imagine God in the abstract, a God fitted to the platonic realm of forms - a sphere where everything is perfect, static and predictable. If at all, Aristotle did not find God in the terror of the Red Sea, or the smoking heights of Sinai, or in the challenge and risks of Ai, but in the geometry of Pythagoras. The two academies are bound to have a very different reading of reality and a very different understanding of divinity. It is not surprising that while the philosopher walks in a garden to think and to discover divine secrets, the Christian undertakes a pilgrimage. The contrast is between a static cogitation and a dynamic engagement and advance. These two protagonists have fought for supremacy throughout the Christian era and are still engaged in battle.

It is something of a wonder that Aristotle has not been eclipsed early in this engagement. The Judaeo-Christian historical encounter engenders far more conviction that the measured postulates of Aristotle and injects far more energy and resolve into its representatives. And yet in its dignified sobriety and ruthless application of method, Aristotle's philosophy is reassuringly predictable and doesn't frighten the horses. Applied to Judaeo-Christian theology, it takes the unruly unpredictability away and reduces everything to a calming syllogism. It provides a civil service solution to every crisis, rounding off all the sharp edges so that Aristotelian Christianity (if we may so call it) melds perfectly with the vision of peaceable social order governed by unruffled statesmanship. It is not surprising that Aristotelian Christianity has appealed to the Western Church, under the Peace of Constantine, much more than to the Eastern Church which has never experienced the 'comforts' of state sponsorship to such a degree.

Nevertheless, the spirit of endeavour and and the principle of contingence have proved unquenchable since those early days of rough and ready faith in the time of Joshua and the Judges. These two principles have shaped the mind of the Judaeo-Christian tradition to such a depth that the instinct to achieve and advance in a world of possibility has become so deep rooted, that we can hardly imagine what it is like to think in any other way. The world of Greek static necessity would seem like an impossible prison of the mind and spirit compared with the radical and sometimes risky vision of open possibility. But for most who have grown accustomed to the Judaeo-Christian outlook, it cannot be imagined. What has happened is that the perspectives of endeavour and contingence have so educated our interiority that they become deep presuppositions undergirding all our reasoning.

9.6. Divine and Human Endeavour

That picturesque and bizarre story of Noah's Ark provides us with an insight into contingence and endeavour in the mind of God. Genesis 6 provides us with an insight into a moment of cogitation and a consideration of possibilities in the light of horrific developments in human behaviour. Ever since the murder of Abel by his brother Cain and the subsequent expansion of the instinct for revenge and retribution by Lamech, human conduct had been on a steep descent. This continues until God sees that *the wickedness of man was great in the earth, and that every intention of the thoughts of his heart was only evil continually. And the Lord was sorry that he had made man on the earth, and it grieved him to his heart* (Genesis 6:5f). Here again there is a moment in which God turns back into himself to make a decision. This is important because Aristotle's *Unmoved Mover,* never does such a thing. But the God of Israel does have a decision to make and he does make it. It looks as though the whole project of making man and the created order to go with him, was seriously imperilled, and God grieved over the tragedy.

He was evidently deeply committed to his endeavour and he mourned his potential loss.

There was no doubt that the host of maleficient humans would have to be destroyed, but Noah found favour in the eyes of the Lord (Genesis 6:8). The endeavour was not abandoned, but instead, a partner was found to share it. At that moment, both the vision for the enterprise and all the trouble of it, was shared with Noah, who found favour and fellowship with God. Henceforth, they were bound together in an endeavour, the free possibility of which was open before them. Hardship, contempt and derision would soon fall upon Noah, who for no reason obvious to his neighbours, began building a huge boat. It is striking that although the initiative came from God, he lets Noah into the secret of his purpose and discloses his mind to his chosen companion with whom he seals a covenant. Noah is not just a servant who does not know what his master is doing, but is a fellow companion who shares the endeavour of God and exercises responsibility within the plan.

9.7. The Endeavour of Jesus Christ

The endeavour of God shared with Noah takes its final form in Jesus Christ and his life from beginning to end is a purposeful mission with an outcome absolutely contingent on his success. His task is to epitomise the lives of human beings whom he came to restore, gather in himself all the sins and rebellions they exhibited and to bring them to an end in his own death and, at the same time to identify those very people with his own righteousness and perfection and make an offering of them in himself to God to restore them to the Father. This was the endeavour of all endeavours. The necessary conditions for its success had taken thousands of years to put in place and now at the crux of history it was engaged in by the Son in the fulfilment of the Father's plan. But the outcome was not a foregone conclusion, but rather, it was absolutely dependent upon the obedience of the Son, and his capacity to resist the temptations and wiles of the devil to which Adam had succumbed. That this was a genuine battle with an open outcome is evident from the witnesses to it. In the desert, Jesus resisted and then dismissed Satan from his office as chief heavenly prosecutor, whose post, after Jesus' success, would forever remain vacant and obsolete. In his ministry, he demonstrated his mission to free the people of Israel from the thrall of their sin, and draft in the gentiles to share in the inheritance of the faithful. But the final test came at his Passion, in the Garden of Gethsemane, in the court of the Sanhedrin, at the judgement seat of the Roman Proconsul, and on the Cross of Calvary. He endured it all and finished the task.

This is the archetype of all human endeavour. In Luke 12:50, Jesus says, *I have a baptism to be baptised with; and how I am constrained until it is accomplished!* Nothing makes clearer that Jesus was fully aware and engaged in the endeavour of his life. In St John's Gospel, he is recorded as making it clear that this 'baptism', this death or 'exodus' that he was to 'accomplish' (Luke 9:31) was not something that merely overtook him, but something he willed: *for this reason the Father loves me, because I lay down my life that I may take it up again. No one takes it from me, but I lay it down of my own accord. I have authority to lay it down, and I have authority to take it up again. This charge I have received from my Father* (John 10:17). Moreover, Jesus expected his disciples to follow him in his redemptive work in the world. They participate in the endeavour during his ministry in Galilee and Jerusalem, they are despatched on preaching missions, given various responsibilities in the fulfilment of Jesus' self-offering and finally authorised to extend his mission to all people everywhere.

The contingent atmosphere in which all this was accomplished is also clear. Everywhere he went Jesus confronted people with genuine choices, principally whether to accept him and his mission or not. Decisions were taken in both directions, some stepped forward and others drifted away. This suggests most directly an Arminian world-view that not everything which happens is God's will, that choices are genuine, and decisions meaningful. The endeavour of God to bring the world home to himself is a protracted task for this very reason: that God waits for world he redeems, but he exhibits both a patience and an urgency. Jesus' ministry continually exerts both of these qualities. We have already seen that sense of urgency in Luke 12:50 in the context of which Jesus yearns for the end-time action of God. On the other hand, he is endlessly patient with the disciples' lack of faith and understanding and is readily prepared to be sidetracked by anyone imploring his help. Blind Bartimaeus had good reason to be grateful for this patience: despite the efforts of the crowd to silence him, he cries out to Jesus at the gates of Jericho and Jesus stops and calls him. It is as if the whole plan to redeem the world is put on hold, while a single beggar takes the sole attention of the Son of Man. Bartimaeus, by his irrepressible determination to gain the attention of Jesus, changed the course and pace of history.

9.8. The Effect of Christian Endeavour on the Pursuit of Science

We now come to the impact of the Judaeo-Christian inheritance upon the progress of science. There are five strands to this impact: (i)the quality of scientific data, (ii) the direction of flow of that data, (iii) the rational unity of the universe, (iv) the independence of man from God in scientific enquiry, and (v) the establishment of contingence over necessity as the foundation of science. We can now gather together our preliminary observations on these five strands.

(i) **The quality of scientific data.** We have already seen in section 2.5. that the inheritance of Plato placed observations of the phenomenal realm at an inferior place compared with the perfections of the realm of ideas i.e. thought. The Incarnation of Christ abolished this ranking and asserted the stature of the phenomenal realm and observations in it. This led to a determination that better and better data should be gathered and a progressively greater effort to improve precision.

(ii) **Data Direction.** We saw in section 2.7. that John Philoponus established the principle that we come to a true knowledge of an object, not by interior cogitation or speculative efforts to impose our preconceived classification on it as Aristotle proposed, but by allowing the object under investigation to instruct us as to its true nature in an open-ended way so that it ends up compelling us to understand it truly as it is. In other word we learn to ask *Interrogatio* questions about it and not merely *Quaestio* questions. This moves us from an atmosphere of inevitability to one of open possibility.

(iii) **Rational Unity of the Universe.** We saw in sections 2.6. and 3.6., that the Judaeo-Christian testimony to the creation of everything by God alone signals that the same intelligence stands behind all things and knowledge in one area of science must makes sense and correlate with another. This has become a principle which is absolutely assumed by modern science, but it was not the case in the ancient world. John Gribbin in his *History of Western Science*, makes the distinction between what he calls mystics and the scientists who took their place in the task of mastering the natural order (4). In this sense, alchemists and astrologers were mystics and chemists and astronomers were scientists. Mystics, as Gribbin uses the term, were those who did not found their work on the intrinsic rational relatedness of things, but assumed the world was either polymorphic - things had no intrinsic relatedness, or that their relatedness was past finding out on a rational basis, but could be exploited by discovering techniques. The knowledge of these arcane techniques could be harnessed to gain power and wealth. The alchemical field prospered in an Islamic philosophical environment because everything was controlled by the inscrutable will of God, the meaning behind which was not necessarily discoverable, but required unquestioning submission. It was possible to have knowledge of the natural order but not necessarily an understanding of it.

(iv) **The Independence of the Scientist from God**. Again in section 2.7. we observed that the field of scientific enquiry was left to man as his province into which God did not interfere. This is of vital importance as experimental science must be an untrammelled discourse between the natural order and the scientist. From a Judaeo-Christian point of view the scientist can only carry out meaningful work if he is trusted by God and from a scientific point of view the scientist can only interpret his results meaningfully if God is not in the equation.

(v) **Contingence over Necessity**. This is, of course, a key strand. We saw in section 2.6. that the concept of contingence arose within Christianity as a result of the full impact of the Resurrection of Jesus Christ on philosophical thinking. It was a scientific revolution in itself and it moved the world from an atmosphere of static necessity to one of dynamic possibility.

These are the five strands in a cable which ties the Judaeo-Christian tradition to modern science, and modern science to the Judaeo-Christian tradition. We express this in both directions because they are both important. Whether it knows or recognises it or not, science is dependent upon these key Judaeo-Christian principles, and at least in part, the Judaeo-Christian tradition is vindicated by the integrity of modern science. But we are cautioned by authors who suggest that we must not claim too much (5). Of course, we cannot tell how the world would have fared in the absence of the Judaeo-Christian tradition - perhaps some of the progress we have witnessed would have been made in any case. On the other hand, it might be justly asked why it is where Christianity has taken the deepest root, that modern science has sprung up with those five strands exhibited so strongly. But there is a more serious danger in not claiming enough for this relationship between Judaeo-Christianity and modern science. There is an assumption in our present era, that if human beings are given the opportunity to forget their history and slowly move to a secular worldview with atheist presuppositions, they would come to some gentle, liberal, moral norm, and a ever-refined rational understanding of all things and flourish as never before. Despite the fact that all indicators of history are against this idea, it persists because both the virtue of modernity and the vices of history tend to be wildly exaggerated. So, against this reading of reality the deep connection between the Judaeo-Christian tradition and modern science must be given a just place lest it be broken, and strengths that it has engendered be dissipated.

The cable with its five strands connecting the Judaeo-Christian tradition and modern science, started with only thin strands which progressively thickened and grew stronger over the two millennia through which they have passed. But this strengthening was by no means a linear process across the centuries. We have already seen that John Philoponus recognised the major elements of the scientific revolution which Christianity engendered in the 6th century, and in fact, all philosophical necessities were in place for the immediate development of modern science at that time. But it did not happen then. There were philosophical battles to be won and it took a 1000 years to win those battles sufficiently for the five strands to gain a critical strength for them to become determinative for scientific thought and progress.

In the west, the 1000 year delay was as a result of the grip that Aristotelianism had upon all minds, and the dalliance of the church in its project to express the Christian gospel in Aristotelian terms. It is a disappointment that the church condemned John Philoponus at the Synod of Constantinople in 680 AD. The mind of the church can tend to lack the imagination and insight to comprehend the significance of its own doctrine, and it has always been that way. Usually, some churchmen at least, understand some of the far-reaching implications of the Gospel message, but others do not and when they are in a position to make decisions on behalf of the whole church, those decisions can be wrong, and can take several hundred years to reverse. It is striking, nonetheless, that the church seems as surprised as the world at large at the ramifications of its own testimony. Theology is the mind of the church reeling at the message of Jesus Christ, and there is only delay, and no real danger if that reeling continues. Only when it stops and the church tries to come to a neatly organised, systematised, and fully comprehended reading of Jesus Christ, is it apt to fail to gain the insights necessary for its continued witness.

In the East, the advance of scientific thought from the church's doctrine also was inhibited, but in this case by Islam. Islamic science and philosophy has been much vaunted in recent years, but not on very good grounds. It is true that around the eleventh and twelfth centuries, there was a flowering of intellectual activity by the Abbasid Caliphate in Baghdad, but this largely involved the translation of Greek works into Arabic, in mathematics, astronomy, medicine and philosophy. Ptolemaic astronomy, for example, received a great deal of attention from Arab celestial observers, and some new data was added to the repository, and some constants were remeasured with greater accuracy, but in 200 years no serious advance was made. The reason for this is that strands (ii), (iv) and (v) could not develop well in an Islamic environment. Islamic necessity did not spring from Greek thought, although it was readily compatible with it. Rather it sprang from the conviction that everything was the absolute will of God and this locked Islamic thought into a strict inevitability. This meant that the Arabs could stare at the epicycles of Ptolemy for two centuries and not see any other possibility for interpreting the data available (6).

Apart from these specific reasons for the slowness of European civilisation to appropriate all the philosophical assets of the Judaeo-Christian tradition, history shows that, while an individual person can become a Christian in a single day and live out that faith for a lifetime, it takes upwards of a thousand years for a whole civilisation to be converted to Christian thinking and exhibit Christian instincts. Even the fourth century error of Arianism, which was an incorrect understanding of the Person of Christ took more than two centuries to put to rest even after the Church had analysed the problem and resolved it in the Nicene settlement. In section 2.1., we borrowed a concept from Michael Polanyi, the idea of the 'philosophical wallpaper', that broad range of accepted presuppositions and conceptual framework against which any new idea is assessed by people in general. It takes a long time of Christian faith, worship and reflection in any society, to Christianise that wallpaper, to establish Judaeo-Christian criteria for the public understanding and assessment of things before it. In Britain we have had more than 1800 years of such influence (the first British king to seek to become a Christian wrote to the Pope with such a request in the year AD 125) and the product of a Christian heritage of that length, is the welter of presumptions of liberty, morals, laws and world-view, which have built up over that time, many of which we do not now recognise as specifically Christian, but nonetheless are so. Our scientific heritage has been built up specifically along these lines.

What we must now do is to trace the progress of the five strands of that cable which runs from the Judaeo-Christian tradition to the full development of modern science in the nineteenth and twentieth centuries and beyond. We cannot hope to cover any more than a tiny fraction of the material available but we will select a few critically important or significant points of advance to demonstrate the progress of the transition from ancient principle to the warp and weft of scientific research.

9.9. Nicolaus de Cusa and Thinking in a World of Possibility

Nicolaus de Cusa was born in 1401 at Cues, on the Moselle. He was educated in the school of the 'brethren of the common life' at Daventer, where he was exposed to the mystic theology of this community. He afterwards studied at Heidelberg, Bologna, and Padua and his friend Pope Pius II created him Cardinal and consecrated him to the Bishopric of Brixen in the Tyrol. His philosophical system was a mixture of Neoplatonic and Christian mysticism, which he set out in his book *De Docta Ignorantia*, or *On learned ignorance*, i.e. the inability of the mind to conceive the absolute, which is to him the same as mathematical infinity. He produced a curious argument in which he sought to prove that when a line is infinite it is at the same time a straight line, a triangle, a circle and sphere. Connected with this is his conclusion that the universe must be infinite and therefore devoid of a centre and of a circumference. Therefore the earth cannot be in the centre of the cosmos, and as he supposes motion to be natural to all bodies, the earth cannot be devoid of all motion (7). This is a strange argument which does not sit well in the ears of a modern commentator, but what it demonstrates is that in the mind of de Cusa, the hitherto practically sacred Aristotelian insistence on the earth being fixed and central to the universe, was being challenged by a somewhat quirky "proof" from geometry on an infinite scale. This is a mediaeval mind beginning to think, as we might say, 'out of the box'.

9.10. Celio Calcagnini: On the Revolution of the Earth on its Own Axis

According to Dreyer (8), there was only one man, living at that time, of whom we know for certain that he taught the daily rotation of the earth before the book of Copernicus was published. Celio Calcagnini (1479-1541) was a native of Ferrara, and served in the armies of the Emperor and Pope Julius II; he was then ordained priest and became a professor in the University of Ferrara, but took diplomatic missions in Germany, Poland and Hungary. It is likely that during his visit to the capital of Poland he heard that a certain Copernicus, canon of the Cathedral of Ermland (a province of Poland) and a Doctor of the University of Ferrara was working out a new system of the world which was founded on the idea that the earth is not at rest but in motion. This is only a conjecture, but Calcagnini (apparently before 1525) wrote an essay *Quod caelum stet, terra moveatur, uel de perenni motu terrae* in which the writer begins by announcing that the whole heavens with sun and stars are not revolving in a day and a night with incredible velocity, but it is the earth which is revolving. There was evidently a certain unmistakeable infectiousness about contingent thinking: once the idea is suggested it becomes un-ignorable and then has to prove itself or be eliminated by disproof. It is also noteworthy that these two thinkers were both clergy and thus familiar with the whole Judaeo-Christian tradition. If the concept of contingence does indeed spring from that tradition, it is not surprising that exponents of the tradition would be among the first to embrace the idea.

9.11. Copernicus and his contingent imagination

Niklas Koppernigk (1473-1543) studied at the University of Cracow, was instructed in astronomy by Albert of Brudzew and in 1497 entered the University of Bologna. There he read Plato, studied Greek and became the astronomical assistant to Domenico Maria da Novara, a reputable practical astronomer. From Bologna, Copernicus moved to Rome in 1500, a great Jubilee year, and stayed there for about a year where he gave lectures on astronomy. In the following year, Copernicus returned home and received a canonry at Frauenberg. After taking his seat in the cathedral chapter he was granted further leave of absence for study, which then included medicine. In the summer of 1501, he went back to Italy, to continue his studies in both law and medicine at Padua. In 1503 he went to Ferrara and obtained a degree of Doctor of Canon Law on 31st May, returning thence to Padua once again. It cannot be doubted that his long residence at these renowned Italian universities had put him in command of all the knowledge accessible at that time, in classics, mathematics and astronomy, and in theology. From 1506 until his death, Copernicus lived in Ermland, generally at Frauenberg, where his light duties at the cathedral gave him plenty of opportunity for his scientific work.

In his review of the Ptolemaic system, Copernicus first noticed the great divergence of opinion among learned men as to the planetary motions, and that some had attributed some motion to the earth, and finally he considered whether any assumption of that kind would help matters. As he considered the system of Ptolemy, he must have seen what scores of philosophers must have noted, that the revolution of the sun round the zodiac and the revolution of the epicycle centres of Mercury and Venus round the zodiac should take place in the same period, a year. If the Ptolemaic system were correct there would be no necessity for this to be the case - a pure coincidence. There must have been a great moment of excitement in his mind when he realised that data was telling him something hitherto unrecognised. When he also noticed that the period of the three outer planets in their epicycles was equal to the synodic period, (the time between two successive oppositions to the sun) this must have suggested that there is an alternative explanation of the facts, that perhaps each of the deferents of the two inner planets and the epicycles of the three outer ones simply represented an orbit passed over by the earth in a year, and not by the sun! This would explain why Mercury and Venus always kept near the sun, and why all the planets annually showed such strange irregularities in their motions. It must have all fitted into place and he saw it while others had not because he thought in terms of possibilities (strand (v)), and because he began to understand what he was looking at under the

266

compulsion of its independent reality as John Philoponus had prescribed.

De revolutionibus, Copernicus' great work was finally published in 1543 just before Copernicus died, but the work was done soon after 1506. In the book, Copernicus says then he kept it back not nine years but four times nine years. But rumours abounded that Copernicus had worked out an entirely new theory of planetary motion. In 1533 Pope Clement VII was given a verbal report of the new system. In 1536, Cardinal Nicolaus von Schonberg, Archbishop of Capua, a trusted adviser both of Clement and his successor Paul III, wrote to Copernicus urging him to publish his discovery and asking for a copy, with the tables of data. But Copernicus did not publish his great work, despite being urged to to do so by his many friends, among them the Bishop of Kuln.

Copernicus did not produce the Copernican system as it is understood today, but what did he do? First, he allowed the data to speak to him, to give an account of itself. He put himself in a position of a student under the instruction of the data which was his master. In doing so, he showed that the posited annual motion of the earth is round the sun would explain simply and very well, the most obvious irregularities in the motions of the planets. Secondly he was able to construct an account of cosmology capable of being further developed as soon as an indefatigable observer engaged in the task of cross-examining the heavens in a persevering manner.

There was a considerable response to Copernicus' achievement, much of it positive. Probably the earliest public support in England was made in 1551 by Robert Recorde, listing some of the ancient authors who disagreed with Ptolemy: Eraclydes Ponticus, Philolaus, Ecphantus, Nicius Syracusius, and Aristarchus. Thomas Digges (son of the first inventor of the telescope) also supported Copernicus, describing the Ptolemaic system as *a set of heads and limbs taken off different people which shows that the hypothesis is not a true one and caused Copernicus to use another.* Another German Copernican, was Christopher Rothmann, chief astronomer to Landgrave Wilhelm IV, of Hesse-Cassel. He ably defended Copernicus to Tycho Brahe who had criticised Copernicus. The Italian, Giovanni Battista Benedetti (1530-90), was a forerunner of Galileo in refuting Aristotelian errors as to motion, and centrifugal tendency. He also preferred the theory of Aristarchus, *'explained in a divine manner by Copernicus, against which the arguments of Aristotle are of no value.'*

9.12 Robert Grosseteste and Johannes Kepler

Even though these two scholars are from different centuries (Grosseteste: 1175-1253, Kepler: 1571-1630), they both made a great contribution (among many others) to the manner in which we acquire knowledge and, more than that, how we get that knowledge to reveal its truth to us. Both men thus stand in the tradition of John Philoponus but they mark the progress that that tradition made in its journey to a general mastery of science. Robert Grosseteste was a philosopher, scientist, statesman and the Bishop of Lincoln. His logical theory was fully Aristotelian, being neither a great observer or experimenter, but he did conceive of the idea that it was through mathematics that scientific observations could be understood. That is, through mathematics, things we observe would speak to us concerning their true nature. Thus he reduced what was described as the *metaphysics of light* to geometric optics thus establishing a mathematical route to intelligibility. It seems a small thing from this distance in time, but it showed in that in this individual, so committed intellectually to Aristotelianism, the contrary perspective of Philoponus was already beginning its long march to ascendency.

More than four centuries later we find that observations were being understood more and more in the language of mathematics, and the refined knowledge so generated began to have a controlling influence on scientific thought and understanding. Thanks to Tycho Brahe, new data was available and in Kepler, the mathematician to make use of it was also ready. Kepler studied from 1589 at the University of Tübingen, where he became acquainted with the doctrine of Copernicus and convinced himself that it represented the true system of the world. In 1596 Kepler published his first work in which he showed that the annual motion of the earth accounts for all the hitherto unexplained features of the Ptolemaic system. He was side-tracked, however by a Pythagorean approach to understanding the planetary orbits: he thought that there must be some theoretical basis for the size of the orbits of the planets, maybe a theological explanation or perhaps one derived from the geometry of polyhedra. He investigated this but could find no correlation, so this attempted solution of the cosmographic mystery turned out to be a failure. But the study itself, revealed his second law (actually discovered before the first) that the area swept out by the planetary radius is proportional to the time.

What is now known as Kepler's first law, actually took a great deal of time to establish. He spent a long time basing his studies on an oval shape before realising that the orbit of Mars was an ellipse. This meant that he had finally reduced the observations of planetary motion to an equation, that of an ellipse. The realisation was a consequence of contingent thinking and the equation the result of the planets giving up their secrets and instructing the mind of the observer. Once the mathematical figure of the orbit was identified, Kepler went on to make his third discovery that the square of the planetary period was proportional to the cube of the semi-major axis (the arithmetic mean radius of the orbit). In Kepler we find that the insights of John Philoponus, the concept of contingence and the third strand, that of the rationality of the universe, by which we move away from superstitious presuppositions, all highly prevalent in his work. By the mid seventeenth century, all the strands linking the Judaeo-Christian tradition with science were strengthening and becoming more robust, better applied, and able to bear progressively greater weight of scientific knowledge.

9.13. Gilbert, Galileo and Newton

William Gilbert (1544-1603), renowned for his researches into magnetism, was one of the earliest scientists who proved to be a powerful exponent of first and second strands of the cable linking the Judaeo-Christian tradition with modern science. Three years before he died, he published his great work, *De magnete* in which he asserts the vital importance of careful experimentation and accurate measurements. He says, *how very easy it is to make mistakes and errors in the absence of trustworthy experiments*, and he urges his readers, *whosoever would make the same experiments*, to, *handle the bodies carefully, skilfully and deftly, not heedlessly and bunglingly; when an experiment fails, let him not in his ignorance condemn our discoveries, for there is nought in these books that has not been investigated and again and again done and repeated under our eyes* (9).

When Galileo read Gilbert's words, they must have delighted him, for one of Galileo's great contributions to the birth of science was in emphasising the need for accurate, repeated experimentation to test hypotheses. He eschews the old Aristotelian approach of trying to understand the workings of nature merely by cogitation -the approach that had led people to believe that a heavier weight will fall faster than a lighter weight, without taking the trouble to test the hypothesis by actually dropping pairs of weights to resolve the matter.

As we saw in section 2.6., it was the revelations of the Judaeo-Christian tradition that led to the overturning of Aristotle's presuppositions and to the rise of experimentation to enable the natural world to communicate its nature to us, and across some 1500 years that impact is felt by Galileo and he responds to its prompt. His whole life represented an explicit rejection of the Aristotelian approach to science, and affirmed that of John Philoponus.

When we come to Isaac Newton (1642- 1727) the transition between the old Aristotelian approach to knowledge to that of John Philoponus was at an advanced stage and had acquired considerable momentum, at least in physics. In a letter to the French Jesuit Gaston Pardies, Newton wrote:

*The best and safest method of philosophizing seems to be, first to enquire diligently into the properties of things, and to establish those properties by experience and then to proceed more slowly to hypotheses for the explanation of them. For hypotheses should be employed only in explaining the properties of things, **but not assumed in determining them**; unless so far as they may furnish experiments* (Present author's emphasis) (10).

Here, explicitly, Newton is rehearsing John Philoponus' definition of science, that the knowledge must come from the object under study and not imposed on it by a preconceived notion of its nature. However, the fact that Newton needs to say this in a letter, suggests that it is conceived, by Newton and his contemporaries, as a new advance - it is new enough to need to be said. In the next and subsequent generations of scientists after Newton, it became second nature and needed hardly to be mentioned. It had entered the philosophical wallpaper of natural science.

The foundation of the Royal Society in 1660 coincides with the ascendency of Philoponus' definition of science over old Aristotelian concepts and this transition is marked by the motto of the Society: *Nullius in verba.* This is not to signify that the Royal Society would not receive anything by word, because the fellows spent their meeting doing just that: hearing papers from various contributors who were themselves fellows, and discussing their contents. *Nullius in verba,* specifically meant that in the conduct of scientific research, they would come to believe something about an object because of what the object disclosed to them by experiment, and explicitly not because Aristotle said so. At the heart of the motivation which brought the Royal Society into existence was the repudiation of Aristotelian preconceptions and the advancement in understanding of things informed by their true nature.

Newton applied this method of elucidating truth relentlessly, building upon the work of Robert Hooke who deserved much credit for observations which later appeared under Newton's authorship. Newton is mostly renowned for his work on classical mechanics, optics and, in parallel to Leibnitz, the invention of calculus. Mathematics proved to be the means which effected a translation of the observations into an understanding and precise description of the phenomenon under study. Just as Kepler had derived the elliptical paths of the planets from astronomical observations using mathematics, so Newton applied it to gravity and was able to provide a theoretical proof for Kepler's laws. Newton's task was made much easier by the application of his method of calculus and his success signalled a major tradition, which emanated subsequently especially from Cambridge University, of developing what are called analytic solutions to physical phenomena using mathematics to interpret the data gathered experimentally. This was a fulfilment of Robert Grosseteste's insight in the twelfth century that mathematics was the key to opening the true significance of observed data and it is noteworthy that it took 500 years for Grosseteste's idea to come to full fruition in the conduct of experimental science. From Newton's time onwards, textbooks on physics would increasingly be filled with mathematics. Chemistry was perhaps about 100 years behind in this process, probably because it was more difficult to reduce chemical observations to mathematical analytic forms. Chemistry textbooks did finally fill up with mathematics, but there was longer period before alchemy gave way to the mature science of chemistry.

9.14. The 18th and 19th Centuries: Michael Faraday and Lord Kelvin

As classical science matured into the 18th & 19th centuries, the scientific method founded upon John Philoponus' definition of science (section 2.7.) became the warp and weft of scientific research. The art of designing an experiment which allowed a phenomenon or process to reveal its true nature by surrendering up data which could be treated mathematically became the perennial task of the scientific experimentalist. The widespread application of this and the success it brought rewarded the instinct for endeavour which drove it. The experiments generated data, data was comprehended by mathematics, the mathematics yielded understanding and the whole process prompted invention, manufacturing and the mastery of the world.

It is consistent with the origins of this great revolution, that many of its pioneers were convinced Christians. Convinced as they were of the truth of the Judaeo-Christian tradition, they were able to follow the entire argument which gave meaning to their researches, they were able to draw a motivation which empowered their endeavours, and they were able to put to good use, the products of their success.

Michael Faraday (1791-1867) was not only a devout Christian, a towering figure in the advance of science, but in his personal life, he was a quintessential exponent of human endeavour. Born the son of a blacksmith who died young and left the family in limited circumstances, Michael, nevertheless, provided himself with an education, by being appointed an apprentice to a bookbinder who was of liberal and benevolent disposition, and did not seem to mind that Faraday spent hours reading all the books that he was meant to be binding. He joined a philosophical group of young men, who were eager to improve themselves and met regularly to discuss the new discoveries in science, and taking turns to deliver lectures. Faraday began to carry out his own experiments in chemistry and electricity and kept careful notes of all the discussions he attended. These four volumes of notes so impressed a customer of the bookbinding business, that he gave Faraday tickets for four lectures to be given by Sir Humphrey Davy in the Royal Institution. Faraday attended and wrote up the lectures carefully and there became convinced that he wanted to be a scientist. But alas, there was no obvious way to go about this. He wrote to everyone he could think of, asking for a position - as lowly as need be - so he could begin to work in scientific enquiry. Through two lucky chances - the temporary blinding of Davy by an explosion, who then needed a temporary assistant while he recovered, and then the dismissal of Davy's assistant for assaulting an instrument-maker - Faraday secured a position as the replacement laboratory assistant on rather poor terms. Faraday didn't care. He took the job and became Sir Humphrey Davy's bottle washer. After a continental trip as servant to his employer, he returned to the Royal Institution where he was appointed superintendent of apparatus and slowly gained a reputation as a solid, reliable chemist. In the decade from 1821, Faraday rose to great prominence justly deserved for his contribution to electromagnetism which culminated in the invention of the electric dynamo and the electric motor, and the recognition of the electromagnetic nature of light. He gave lectures on Friday evenings which were packed to the doors, was appointed Director of the Royal Institution and then the Fullerian professor of chemistry there. He declined a knighthood, however, because it was against the principles of his Christian denomination to accept worldly aggrandisement.

What were the elements of the moral energy of Faraday's life? He clearly had a strong sense of purpose and the conviction that a path was open to him even though he came from circumstances which did not directly equip him for it. He had a powerful sense of possibility, from which he was not dissuaded by a lack of mathematical education or anything else. He also exhibited a humility in which he would take practically any job, however lowly, to reach his goal. He believed in an over-arching divine purpose which gave his own life meaning and significance.

William Thomson, Lord Kelvin (1824-1907) was born into an academic family. His father James was professor of mathematics at the Royal Academical Institution in Belfast, the family moving to Glasgow in 1832, following James Thomson's appointment to the chair of mathematics in Glasgow University. William entered the University of Cambridge in 1841 and graduated in 1845, becoming professor of natural philosophy at Glasgow in 1846 and remained in that appointment until he retired in 1899. His towering contribution was the establishment of Thermodynamics as a scientific discipline, achieving for thermal data its reduction to the discipline of mathematics. He also made extraordinary contributions to the field of electricity and magnetism, and took responsibility for the laying of telegraphic cables under the sea from Britain to America.

Like Faraday, Thomson had a secure and intelligent Christian faith: he was both at home in the Scottish Presbyterian tradition and in the Episcopal tradition and always began his lectures in physics at Glasgow University with the third collect from Anglican Mattins. The scientific method which was derived from the Judaeo-Christian tradition via John Philoponus, was by this time so deeply embedded in the worldview of Thomson and his contemporaries, that it is taken as read and we do not find it referred to directly in Thomson's writings. But we do find serious consideration of the relationship between Christian faith and the natural world, especially in the light of Charles Darwin's contribution to biological origins, work with which Thomson was very well familiar.

In the nineteenth century, there was a tendency to shift the argument on the relationship between science and the Judaeo-Christian tradition, from one basis to another. As we have seen throughout this book modern science can be seen to rest on the discoveries of the nature of knowledge and faith made in the course of the unfolding of the Judaeo-Christian narrative. This argument has been largely independent of any consideration that the character of God might be perceivable in the natural order. Although the Judaeo-Christian tradition does not dismiss this altogether, it rather deprecates it in favour of the revelation of God by the events of the Exodus, and the person of Jesus Christ. Perhaps because of the multitude of discoveries made by scientific enquiry in the eighteenth and nineteenth centuries, the popular argument shifted in favour of a natural theology by which it was thought that God was revealed by the order of the natural world and the seemingly intelligent mind behind its creation. This was the great argument of William Paley: the study of the natural order is like finding a beautifully crafted watch, and deducing therefrom, that there was in existence a skilled watchmaker. Lord Kelvin was impressed by this argument. He had been familiar with Paley's Natural Theology from his youth; he considered as solid and irrefragable the main argument of *that excellent old book.*

In May 1903, a course of lectures on Christian Apologetics was given at University College, London, by the Rev. Professor Henslow. A vote of thanks was moved by Lord Kelvin in a short speech which attracted much attention. The following is The Times' report, as corrected by Lord Kelvin's own hand:

Lord Kelvin, in moving a vote of thanks to the lecturer, said, '.... I do not say that, with regard to the origin of life, science neither affirms nor denies creative power. Science positively affirms creative power. Science makes every one feel a miracle in himself. It is not in dead matter that we live and move and have our being, but in the creating and directive Power which science compels us to accept as an article of belief. We cannot escape from that conclusion when we study the physics and dynamics of living and dead matter all around. Modern biologists are coming once more to a firm acceptance of something beyond mere gravitational, chemical, and physical forces ; and that unknown thing is a vital principle. We have an unknown object put before us in science. In thinking of that object we are all agnostics. We only know God in His works, but we are absolutely forced by science to admit and to believe with absolute confidence in a Directive Power—in an influence other than physical, or dynamical, or electrical forces. Cicero, editor of Lucretius, denied that men and plants and animals could have come into existence by a fortuitous concourse of atoms.

There is nothing between absolute scientific belief in Creative Power and the acceptance of the theory of a fortuitous concourse of atoms. Just think of a number of atoms falling together of their own accord and making a crystal, a sprig of moss, a microbe, a living animal. I admire throughout the healthy, breezy atmosphere of free-thought in Professor Henslow's lecture. Do not be afraid of being freethinkers. If you think strongly enough you will be forced by science to the belief in God, which is the foundation of all Religion. You will find science not antagonistic, but helpful to Religion (11).

Eighteen months later Lord Kelvin returned to the question in an address on presenting the prizes to students in the Medical School of St. George's Hospital, on October 23rd, 1904. The main thought is given in the following extract:—

Let it not be imagined that any hocus-pocus of electricity or viscous fluids will make a living cell. Splendid and interesting work has recently been done in what was formerly called organic chemistry, a great French chemist taking the lead. This is not the occasion for a lecture on the borderland between what is called organic and what is called inorganic; but it is interesting to know that materials belonging to the general class of food-stuffs, such as sugar, and what might also be called a food-stuff, alcohol, can be made out of the chemical elements. But let not youthful minds be dazzled by the imaginings of the daily newspapers, that because Berthelot and others have thus made food-stuffs they can make living things, or that there is any prospect of a process being found in any laboratory for making a living thing, whether the minutest germ of bacteriology or anything smaller or greater. There is an absolute distinction between crystals and cells. Anything that crystallizes may be made by the chemist. Nothing approaching to the cell of a living creature has ever yet been made. The general result of an enormous amount of exceedingly intricate and thorough-going investigation by Huxley and Hooker and others of the present age, and by some of their predecessors in both the nineteenth and eighteenth centuries, is that no artificial process whatever can make living matter out of dead. This is vastly beyond the subject of the chemical laboratory, vastly beyond my own subject of physics or of electricity—beyond it in depth of scientific significance and in human interest (12).

This, as we have explained, is a different argument to the one espoused in this book, but for the sake of completeness, we will continue with it briefly. We regard Lord Kelvin as one our many witnesses called to give evidence as in the model we outlined in section 3.2. As an observer of the natural order, with a great experimental ability, we might allow Lord Kelvin a reasonable degree of credibility: his opinion is that the natural order does betray an intelligence behind it. But the question arose because Charles Darwin's research indicated at least to some of his colleagues, that he had eliminated the place for that intelligence in demonstrating that all the complexity and wonder of the natural order could explained by a long series of natural chance occurrences. Whether Charles Darwin himself was entirely convinced of this is another question. He states: *I see no good reason why the views given in this volume should shock the religious feelings of anyone. It is satisfactory as showing how transient such impressions are, to remember that the greatest discovery ever made by man, namely the law of the attraction of gravity, was also attacked by Leibnitz, as 'subversive of natural, and inferentially of revealed religion'. A celebrated author and divine has written to me that, 'he has gradually learned to see that it is just as noble a conception of deity to believe that he created a few original forms capable of self-development into other and needful forms, as to believe that He required a fresh act of creation to supply the voids caused by the action of His laws.'* (13) Darwin's correspondent has pointed out that the discovery of evolution simply moves the boundary between physical and metaphysical causality one step back. As Lord Kelvin says, the nature and origin of life is a metaphysical matter.

REFERENCES FOR CHAPTER 9

(1) Johann Joachim Becher in *Physica subterranea*, 1669

(2) Peter Watson, *The German Genius*, p107

(3) Lord Macaulay, *The History of England, Chatto & Windus 1905 Edition, Volume 1*, p248

(4) John Gribbin, *History of Western Science*, p74

(5) David Bentley Hart, *Atheist Delusions*, p70

(6) J. L. E. Dreyer, *A History of Astronomy from Thales to Kepler,* p279

(7) Nicolaus de Cusa, *The Vision of God*

(8) J. L. E. Dreyer, *Ibid. p292*

(9) William Gilbert, *De Magnete*, translated by P. Fleury Mottelay

(10) John Gribbin, *Ibid*, p204

(11) Sylvanus P Thompson, *Life of Lord Kelvin*, p1097

(12) Sylvanus P Thompson, *Ibid*, p1102

(13) Charles Darwin, *The Origin of Species*, p658

CHAPTER 10
HUMAN ERROR

10.1. Definitions

When we speak of 'computer error' we mean that a computer fails to operate as expected and produces a result which is not desired, not proper to its normal intended function. There is a mismatch between the actual result and the intended result. The error may arise from some failure of hardware or software, or because the function of the machine was disturbed by some external influence, like a power supply irregularity or a lightning strike. This is our starting point for building an understanding of human beings when they exhibit errors. We need to know what *normal* human function is in order to recognise a human *error* which is a departure from that norm. We might also ask about the cause of the error and how it might be remedied. This model can apply across the range of human function and constitution. It can apply to physical illness: influenza might be regarded a human error, caused by a virus, yielding sickness which is abnormal physiological behaviour. In this case the *error* is disease, the *norm* is health, and the *remedy* is medical treatment. It can apply to psychiatric and psychological disorders: displacing the sufferer from normal mental function and requiring interventions of various kinds to provide a remedy. It can apply to social behaviour: dysfunction in human relationships, marriage breakup, failure in the raising of children, neglect of social responsibilities, substance abuse. It can apply to activity regarded as criminal: offences against persons or property, in which the errors are called crimes and the remedy is a legal process and penalty. And, finally it can apply to offences against divinity in which the errors are referred to as sins and the remedies are variously, sacrifice, penitence, pardon and penalty.

10.2. Human error and Socially Constructed Reality

In section 6.1., we considered what was socially regarded as dignified as a corpus of behaviour and attitudes which drifted over the landscape of human existence, validating and approving of new conduct and opinion on its leading edge and leaving behind a trail of freshly disparaged attitudes and actions in its wake. This model is exactly descriptive of what is considered the acceptable *norm* of human behaviour, departures from which are human errors of various kinds. Social media provides the most superficial and volatile environment for this shifting definition of human normality and error to be manifest. The use of such social media appears to be addictive and is the main way that some users seek validation for their actions, opinions and preferences. Human habits and dispositions do drift over time, even without serious influence from changing law, religion, or economic or national exigency, but social media, especially within the burgeoning community which uses it, accelerates this drift to a remarkable degree. This introduces a very high degree of anxiety in the mind of the avid social media user, who are usually young and are made increasingly insecure by the force of peer pressure around them. Social media might be seen as a madhouse of anxious seekers of approval, desperate for appreciation and terrified of rejection. Suicides are not an uncommon result of this massive pressure. And hardly ever does it occur to anyone to turn the whole thing off - for to do so would be to excommunicate oneself from the social validation it provides.

The rapidity with which the norm of human attitude and behaviour is shifting in the social media environment is easily discernible from statistics gathered from various social media sites. A survey conducted by the Jubilee Centre for Character and Virtues at Birmingham University showed that 55% of 1,700 people with children aged 11 to 17 strongly agreed that social media hinders or undermines moral development. BBC Newsround research in 2009 suggested that children as young as 10 have social media accounts despite being below the age limit, which is usually 13.

When questioned about traits they had observed on social media, participants were asked what human behaviours they had witnessed (*author's rough classification in italics*).

Traditional Judaeo-Christian vices:
60% said they had seen anger and hostility

51% had seen arrogance
43% observed ignorance
41% observed bad judgement
36% observed hatred
30% observed vanity
Traditional Judaeo-Christian virtues:
24% observed little forgiveness and self-control
21% observed a lack of honesty
20% observed a lack of fairness
18% observed a lack of humility.
"Greek" virtues:
52% observed humour
51% observed appreciation of beauty
44% observed creativity
39% observed love
39% observed courage

It cannot be determined what prompted these assessments, and these data are very 'soft', but they suggest that the social media norm of human attitude and behaviour may have shifted away from any Judaeo-Christian norm which might be taken as a historical reference point. The significant point is that parents had a largely negative view of the effect of social media on their children's moral welfare. The report asserted that, *whilst parents acknowledged that positive character strengths, including moral virtues such as love, courage and kindness are promoted through social networking sites, they were reluctant to agree that these sites could have a positive impact on their child's character.* This is diagnostic of a shift between the generations: what was being learned by the children was to some extent at variance with their parents' moral perspective. It is of the essence of socially constructed reality, that participants evaluate their own norms from prevailing norms which are learned from others. Social media may improve and sharpen a participant's sense of humour, and other virtues which were valued in ancient Greece and Rome, but weaken those characteristics which were prized by the Judaeo-Christian tradition.

Certain other shifts are more obvious: the displacement of marriage as the place in which sexual activity is to be confined, which was a position in general acceptance (even if to some extent in the breach rather than in the adherence) until the Second World War, to a very optional possibility in our present time even for the raising of children, is a striking example. We have already referred in section 5.1. to the very rapid rise in acceptability and practice of the destruction of the unborn child, and the legalisation of the euthanasing of the elderly is not far behind. These activities are no longer seen as regrettable human errors, but are now thought to be the results of wise decisions taken in the interests of women and families.

Modelled on a purely socially constructed basis, in which no account is taken of recollected traditions or other restraints, there does not seem any limit to the drift of human norms of this type. Once we have grown accustomed to the destruction of unborn infants and the elderly, mainly, it has to be admitted, because they are troublesome and expensive, surely the norms will drift again to permit the destruction of disabled people, the mentally ill and others, who, in a utilitarian world, cannot be assessed as useful, but only a drain on resources. Recent tendencies of the British National Health Service to restrict services to smokers or the obese, signal the progress of this drift.

Of course, we do not live in a perfectly socially constructed reality. There are other considerations which direct our estimation of what a human norm is, and what constitutes a human error. But confining ourselves, in the first instance, only to this socially constructed world, and progressively dismissing every other consideration, we find that we have no means of calculating an appropriate human norm. Rather, we just find out what everyone else is thinking and doing, and think and do that. Our politicians sometimes refer to the "moral compass" that directs them, but there are signs that the needle on this instrument has no pole to which to be attracted. Instead it rotates aimlessly around the scale, seeking, but never finding, a direction to assist its owner in plotting a course. Because they are elected, and need the votes, they tend to set their moral compass to a direction consistent with the drift of norms elicited from social media, focus groups and other centres of inspiration. By this means, government policy and statutory law is brought into conformity with the drift and lends it support and authority. In its worst moments, the Church (especially the Church of England) has joined in with the policy of endorsing the drift. Terrified of seeming critical, desperate for acceptance by the world, made acutely anxious by its perceived decline in numbers, the Church has hastened to approve many changes to the norms embraced by the socially constructed reality in our midst. It did this by endorsing divorce and being increasingly accommodating to it, it has become mutely accepting of the abolition of marriage and in places has altered its own doctrine to suit (1). The Church has said very little in opposition to abortion even though it is forbidden by its own tenets. It has presided placidly over the destruction of family life and raised a limp hand of blessing over sexual perversion. Church and State both stand and watch as a civilisation founded on solid moral norms slides into delinquency carrying with it generations of uncomprehending advocates of thoughtless hedonism.

There must be a better way of calculating the good of a civilisation and finding a norm which is secure and has an intelligible authenticity about it. The rest of this chapter offers a way to achieve this, but we consider first whether there might be a naturalistic derivation of a human norm of life and behaviour.

10.3. Human Norm and Error from Considerations of Physical Causality

We considered in section 7.3. the difficulty faced by those who sought from physical causality alone, to explain human conscience. It is similarly difficult to make a parallel derivation of a full account of human norm and error on this basis, but evolution can go some way in this direction. Physiologically, the human body has considerable powers of self-correction of errors. It can ward off and defeat the ingress of bacterial and viral infections with considerable success. It has very great powers to heal itself and has complex mechanisms to do so. It can expel foreign bodies, heal broken bones, restore damaged muscles and organs, and preserve life while these processes are given time to work. Very impressively, the human body can learn from its errors. An infection once contracted is defeated by the body's immune-system and once defeated, antibodies are left behind which often makes a further infection of the same type more easily defeated, and perhaps renders the individual entirely immune from it. It is quite conceivable that successive generations have become selectively more successful in doing this thus resulting in a highly developed capacity for resisting disease. At the same time, the bacteria and the viruses are also mutating and evolving and presenting renewed threats to each generation. This accounts for the fact that human immune-systems are only as good as they are - if the bacteria and the viruses were not continually changing, presumably human beings would be entirely immune and diseases conveyed by these species would be unknown. Psychologically, a similar argument can be followed, although mental illness is not normally caused by bacteria or viruses. Humans can and often do recover by themselves from errors of the mind. The human being can adapt to minimise anxiety and can recover from periods of depression and can subtly manage memory to efface or, at least, manage painful recollections.

The genetic disposition towards cancer, or the genetic capacity to resist it, do offer some difficulties to evolutionary theory. Cancer is a cellular error and cancerous cells are continually dealt with in the course of normal human life. If, however, they arise in sufficient number to gain a dominance in one part of the body or other, they can defeat the normal resistance of the individual and can result in illness and death. It appears that the capacity to resist these erroneous cells and their multiplication is at least in part, something which varies from individual to individual and which is also partly genetically derived. But it might be expected that the genetically derived vulnerability to cancer might be strongly recessive because cancers are usually associated with high mortality if not treated. It is therefore curious that genetically derived cancer vulnerability should still be so prevalent.

As we noted in section 7.10., there is an evolutionary explanation for what we might call, pejoratively, selfishness, because in the evolutionary model, each individual is seeking to survive at the expense of all the others. In this model, selfishness would not be a human error, but part of a healthy norm. The same could be true for various acts of violence which could serve as a means by which the stronger individuals survive to make stronger offspring. This would be offset by the maintenance of sufficient numbers to ensure the survival of the species. Some violence resulting in the deaths of some individuals would thus be normal and necessary. Thieving of food by an individual from another would also be normal by the same argument. Multiple sexual partners would also serve the optimisation of the gene pool. If we strictly exclude any non-physical causality and extrapolate to the projected state of human beings using these elements, we would certainly arrive at a state equivalent to "nature, red in tooth and claw" and we might surmise that the same destination might well be reached if the socially constructed reality outlined in section 10.2. above was allowed to drift for long enough without any external constraint.

This cuts across the popular idea that a secular state without any constraint from religion or other metaphysically derived influences, and without tacit historical recollection of such, would tend towards a generous-spirited, liberal, open society, respectful of human rights and dignity, forming a joyous multi-cultural utopia in which there was no crime or disaffection. This seems to be a prevalent assumption of determinedly secular politics and something towards which it seems to be working although there appears to be a long way to go. It is hard to see how it develops its philosophical base: the socially constructed reality does not seem to tend that way, the atheistic perspectives have nothing with which to drive it, if all metaphysical causality is specifically excluded. It will have to borrow something from somewhere or else tend to deify itself. David Novak comments: *persons who do regard their morality as without metaphysical foundation - true agnostics - inevitably fall into the ethical dead end of legalism, which is an irrational, absolute commitment to a system of secular, human-made, positive law. The question of whether that law is made by someone as a benevolent as Gandhi or as malevolent as Hitler cannot make any real difference to these agnostics. In other words, they cannot give a metaphysically cogent reason for why they obey anyone. All they can say is that they obey who ever has political authority over them because they will be either punished for their disobedience or rewarded for their obedience. How does that attitude differ, however, from the motivation of a dog to obey its master? As such, these agnostics have reduced ethics to power politics instead of regarding the political realm as the primary context for a person to act ethically according to his or her metaphysically constituted human nature* (2).

10.4. Human Norm and Error from the Perspective of Metaphysical Causality

We have already seen (in sections 6.7. and 7.10.) that according to the Judaeo-Christian witnesses human error arose from a primordial lapse from the true human norm. This primordial event is beyond history and the evidence for it lies in the perceptions of all human beings within history: that strange sense of being dislocated from the place where we should be and finding ourselves in a strange restlessness as a result of this displacement. We have the idea, probably mainly from the recollection of the Judaeo-Christian witness, that this displacement springs from a catastrophic human error which has given rise to a sense of separation from God and a kind of spiritual autism in which we become resistant to the love of God and seek to shrink from him. As we saw in section 7.10., there is something strange and incomprehensible about this phenomenon but it is rated as man's worst problem and that from which all other problems proceed.

The Judaeo-Christian tradition understands this mainly using three different models: the Dramatic, the Juridical, and the Sacral. The Dramatic, we came across in section 7.10. It understands that there has been some rebellion in heaven, some great cosmic irruption against God himself, which he has to put down, but there is a corresponding fall-out on earth, so human errors which result are collateral damage from the central struggle (3). The main strength of this model is that it accounts for the fact that we cannot understand what has overtaken us. Many of the errors we exhibit are against our own will and we find ourselves driven by instincts and tendencies which we do not like and do not think are proper to us. Temptation is an extremely strange phenomenon and it does seem like the serpent whispering in our ear. The Dramatic model seeks to do justice to the fact that the problem of human error seems to be a great deal bigger that human beings - it is a vast problem of which our errors appear as symptoms although they do contribute very significantly to the overall malaise.

The Juridical model sees human errors as wrongs of mind, heart and action which put human beings on the wrong side of God's law. Because we are raised with the idea we have to keep some rules, this model is the simplest for us to grasp. It does render intelligible at least part of the problem. Human errors are often wilful and deliberate wrongs, but sometimes inadvertent, and sometimes unavoidable. And the problem runs deeper still: even if we managed to avoid making a single error, we would still think of ourselves as on the wrong side of God's law, because we feel ourselves to be intrinsically errant. This could be merely a psychological mis-evaluation, but might arise because we sense our liability to commit errors before we've even done so.

The Sacral model is the strangest but perhaps, on this account, the deepest answer that the Judaeo-Christian tradition offers to the problem of human error. It is the hardest to understand because central to it is a property of God with which we are very unfamiliar: his holiness. Holiness is the union of purity, solitude, perfection and majesty in God. God is many other things: He is love, he is gracious, forgiving, powerful, wise, glorious, but he is *thrice* holy. In Isaiah 6, the angels call to one another, *Holy, Holy, Holy, is the Lord God almighty*. Of all God's characteristics, holiness is most foreign to us. In the ancient Near East, the holiness of God made Israel's faith unique among the nations whose gods were integrated into the human world and therefore were not holy - holiness was not a category in which they were even considered. In the main, they were divine wheelers and dealers - forming agreements with this or that nation on a *quid pro quo* basis. The God of Israel was aloof from this knock-about market of divine-human transactions. He was God, and there were times when he wrapped himself in his mantle and distanced himself from the profanities of his people Israel in a prickly defence of his own holiness.(4) He would help them, he would give himself for them, but only on his terms, the terms of his own holiness, and not on theirs.

Human errors placed human beings outside the periphery of God's holiness. They banish us because of God's holy intolerance of the profane. '*The soul that sins - it shall die*'(Ezekiel 18:4), because the holiness of God will burn it up. The people of Israel were warned to avoid all uncleanness (Leviticus 15:31) *lest they die.* Uzzah was struck down dead when he put forth his hand to steady the ark of the covenant when it was being returned to Jerusalem (2 Samuel 6:7). The author to the Hebrews reminds his hearers that worship with reverence and awe is required because their God was *a consuming fire* (Hebrews 12:28). All this is very difficult for us moderns. We would like an amiable, easy-going God who is happy to adapt himself to our profanity rather than insist that we must share his holiness. We want to be able to turn up to the eschatological feast in jeans and a tee-shirt, rather than all the bother of white tie. This is because, whatever the primeval catastrophe was that put us outside of God's holiness, it was so comprehensive that it made us forget, not only what God is like, but also our own true nature. We have already glimpsed the glorious liberty of the children of God (see sections 8.8. and 8.9.), we now need to glimpse their glorious holiness. From the periphery where we stand it is very hard to do that. God's holiness seems a frightening thing, an unknown quantity, a dangerous concept. We fear that it will require so much from us, we will feel unsuited to it, unworthy of it, that it will search us out and reveal us to be the inept, unholy people that we fear we are.

But we have to face it, because we cannot renegotiate our true nature, any more than the prodigal can renegotiate his relationship to his father: he cannot be a hired servant, because he *is* a son. When he returns from his sojourn in the far country he finds that he is still a son and his father puts the signet ring on his finger so he can resume his responsibilities as an inheritor of his father's estate. In the same way, even though we have been in the far country so long we have forgotten the rank and privileges of our inheritance, even though we have forgotten the holiness of our Father and our own holiness, there is no way we can return, but by relearning them and becoming equal to the holy office which is the human being.

10.5. Human Error and Jesus Christ

It is the testimony of the Judaeo-Christian tradition that we can only become equal to that holy office of our humanity through the intervention of Jesus Christ on behalf of the error-stricken human race and the Scriptures understand the work of Jesus in terms of all three models described in section 10.4. above. St Paul, in describing the deliverance of Christians from all their 'trespasses', tells the Colossian Church that Jesus *disarmed the rulers and authorities and put them to open shame, by triumphing over them in him* (Colossians 2:15). These were *the principalities and powers, the spiritual forces of evil in the heavenly places* (Ephesians 6:12). The New Testament sees the deliverance of human beings from evil as conducted at all levels: in the depths of Hades, on the ground in the harsh realities of Gethsemane and Golgotha, in the minds and hearts of the Christian community and in the lofty reaches of the heavenly realm. The deliverance of errant humanity was achieved at all these levels and repeatedly St Paul urges the Christians to whom he writes to dwell consciously in this victory, to take it as the foundational reality in which they find their bearings and to rely upon it absolutely in the conduct of their lives. We saw in section 6.8. that Jesus does not keep the assets of his own humanity to himself but shares them with his disciples. In the same way, Jesus shares his victory over the spiritual forces arraigned against him with his followers, to such an extent that St Paul is able to say that amid every conceivable trouble, opposition, or danger, they are *more than conquerors through him who loved [them]* (Romans 8:37).

The New Testament also sees Jesus as the means of deliverance of errant humanity via the juridical model. The Colossian passage we have just referred to, also speaks of this in juridical terms: *And you, who were dead in your trespasses and the uncircumcision of your flesh, God made alive together with him, having forgiven us all our trespasses, by cancelling the record of debt that stood against us with its legal demands.*

This he set aside, nailing it to the cross (Colossians 2:13ff). In some way the Cross was a final reckoning between a holy God and an unholy people whereby the liability for the errors was abolished by the willing self-offering of Jesus. This is apt to be understood crudely as Jesus bearing the punishment for the sins committed by the people for whom he died, that he satisfied the vengeance of God, taking the burden of it himself instead of it falling on them. This has become the main way the Cross is explained in many Protestant Churches and has some mileage to it. The New Testament passages which support it do not go quite so far in describing this mechanism. *God was in Christ reconciling the world to himself* (2 Corinthians 5:19), not against Christ in so doing. Also the New Testament writers regard Jesus as the Lamb of God who takes away the sins of the world (see below), but only a perfect animal can be offered as a sacrifice and if the sins of the world were actualised in Jesus and therefore subject to the wrath of God, the offered 'Lamb' could not be perfect and therefore could not be accepted. Some restraint needs to be applied to the juridical model of the atonement for this reason. Christ did bear our sins and win for us reconciliation with God, so that nothing stands against the penitent in legal terms, but exactly how this took place cannot be fully explained.

The third (Sacral) model of the atonement is that of sacrifice for sin. And this is properly understood in terms of the holiness of God. Just as we find the concept of holiness difficult to understand, so the idea of offering a sacrifice is equally puzzling to the modern mind. At the heart of Old Testament sacrifice is the idea of *identification*. The animal, chosen as the best of the flock or herd, would be brought by the offeror who would place his hands upon it, not to pass his sins to it, but to identify himself with its perfection. It was then sacrificed as an offering of that perfection to God and in that act, the offeror would be presented to God with the same perfection. On that basis, the offeror would be received by God and restored to him. The Eastern Church, especially, understood the Last Supper in this way. In sharing the bread and the cup, the disciples were identified with Jesus and with his perfection and then, on the following day, Jesus, the Lamb of God offered himself freely to God his Father. The disciples were thus presented to God in the perfection of Christ. The Eucharist bears the same relationship as the Last Supper to the Cross. At the celebration of the Eucharist, the participants share Jesus' perfection and are identified with him on the Cross, thereby being restored to the Father.

Which of these models appeals to the Church rather depends on the tradition. Churches which are content to live with mystery, with an open-ended understanding of atonement, will find a sufficiency in the sacral and dramatic models and be content not to push the juridical model too far. Churches which have an Enlightenment influence upon them, may find mystery more difficult and opt to emphasise the juridical model because it is more explicable in everyday terms. But all three are testified to by the various witnesses of the Judaeo-

Christian tradition and all have their place in the preaching of Christ crucified. Their view of human error, or sin, is different. In the case of the Dramatic model, sin is a collateral effect of the great battle between God and the errant spiritual powers. The liability for the fall of Adam and Eve is chiefly laid at the door of the serpent, although our first parents were also called to account for their collusion. Essentially, the Dramatic model *rescues* the sinner from the thrall of sin. The Juridical model reifies sin more than the others. The errors of human beings, on this model, have a kind of quantitative property: they can be transferred and borne by Jesus and have to be destroyed by wrath. The Juridical remedy for sin is a *purging*: the weight and burden of sin is lifted. In the Sacral model, conversely, sins are not reified: the errant human being is *transferred* out of their realm to a place where they are not permitted, i.e. to the realm of divine holiness.

In all cases, the effect of the Cross, mediated by the Sacraments, is to reconcile the Christian to God the Father, to move him from an errant to a holy status. The features of that holy status we have already seen in the human life led by Jesus Christ. In section 8.8. we saw Jesus as the exponent of a true human liberty in which he was able to rule and dispose truly as God's right hand man. It was therefore mainly to do with the exercise of his human capacities. His human holiness lay not so much in what he could do, but in the respect and obedience he was able to command from others, often almost unconsciously. When they sought, on occasion to harm him (Luke 4:29), they found themselves unable

302

to do so, and he passed unharmed through their midst. An even more striking example is presented at the time of his arrest in the Garden of Gethsemane, as recorded in John 18:6. They came asking for Jesus of Nazareth and when Jesus replied *I am he*, they drew back and fell to the ground. Even though they had come with authority to arrest him, his presence and word were enough to bring them to obeisance. What Jesus did in his coming and in his suffering was to re-instate human holiness and it is to the qualities of that holiness and its capacity to reverse human error that we must now turn.

10.6. The Basis for understanding Human Norm and Error

We could choose any of the three models outlined above to construct an understanding of human ethics. Traditionally, in the west, the juridical model has prevailed largely because it exhibited an obvious continuity with Aristotelian ethical thinking which was founded on justice (*dikaiosune*) which was the most important personal trait to encourage and reward. Thus Christian ethics tended to be founded upon the concept of *right* and *wrong*, qualities which were, in principle, determined by a law court and ultimately by the Great Assize on the Day of Judgement. This specially appealed to the many canon lawyers in the mediaeval Church and, of course, dovetailed well with civil and criminal law appropriate to the union of Church and State since the Peace of Constantine. Grounded in the practicalities of the world, having an immanence and stability, the juridical reading of ethics works well, but it suffers from that product of its predictability and prescriptive nature: *tedium*. Ethics have always suffered from being boring. If Christian obedience was reduced to the mere diligence of staying within the law, it is not surprising that it does not attract or inspire those with a pioneering spirit or imbued with an appetite for adventure.

For a bit more excitement, we might try the dramatic model in which human life is estimated as a scrap with the devil. Here the concepts of right and wrong are replaced with *good* and *evil*. In this model everything reduces to a fight to get one over on Satan and to score a victory for the Kingdom of God. St Peter advises the churches along these lines: *Be sober-minded; be watchful. Your adversary the devil prowls around like a roaring lion, seeking someone to devour. Resist him, firm in your faith, knowing that the same kinds of suffering are being experienced by your brotherhood throughout the world* (1 Peter 5:8). This was doubtless highly appropriate advice to Christians liable to persecution but is equally applicable to a church in a materially satiated age with all its seductive power. It sees human life as a frontier between the Kingdom and the devil's empire, a battlefield in which ground can be made or lost, courage or cowardice exhibited, sacrifices made or shirked. But there is always a downside: it might make each day an exciting engagement with the enemy, but maybe too much of that might lead to being a bit unhinged. Martin Luther is said to have thrown an ink-well at the devil, much, no doubt, to the horror of his landlady.

For something more mystical, perhaps the sacral model will suit. Here the antagonisms are *holiness* and *profanity*. There is a certain simplicity in this model, at least at first sight: the great question to be asked is, 'can this be offered to God?' In scripture *qadosh*, 'holy', denotes the separation of something from its ordinary use in the world for the sake of what lies beyond the world. Ethical considerations grounded in the idea of holiness therefore have this forward vector: they anticipate the future destiny of the human race, they make heavenly calculations and not merely worldly, expedient ones. The New Testament describes the Christians as *hagioi*, 'holy ones', because they are already counted as having reached their future destiny. It would be wrong to describe this approach as impracticable: it is only so when viewed from a worldly standpoint where it will have a tendency to be idealistic as opposed to exhibiting a this-world realism. But in terms of what is eternal, it is most practical: it takes its bearings from what is going to stand forever, so its constructions, here and now, can be said to be built to last. It also has a further advantage: it will, at least at first sight, be unintelligible to the worldling, but it will never fail to remind those who have to do with it, of eternal things, of the future with God, and the kingdom which is unshakeable.

10.7. Human Sanctity

It is striking to observe the degree to which the concept of sanctity, so particular to the Judaeo-Christian tradition and so foreign to secular thought, has nevertheless occupied a central place in the latter at least until recent decades. The sanctity of human life is a decaying principle in the modern world, but it is still perhaps a significant restraint against the commission of murder, and the principle standing behind the grief of bereavement and the public sorrow expressed over catastrophic loss of life. The violent death of people we do not even know still provokes grief and outrage because it just ought not to happen. A line is crossed somewhere which should never be crossed, it is not merely civil law which is offended, or human assets wasted, or even that people will be missed. Much more than that, an unspeakable violation has occurred that justice cannot efface, that grief cannot erase and for which no compensation would ever be remotely sufficient. If we go on asking why the loss of human life is so grave, we come eventually to an understanding of what sanctity is: not a human value put on human life, but rather a divine claim to it as God's inviolable territory upon which any encroachment is utterly inconceivable. When we encounter that irreconcilable affront as a response to the murder of a human being, we are remembering something, perhaps primordially, about what a human life is, not merely a biological excrescence, but something God made his own and thus holy. This recollection makes us careful and wary in our approach to human life, especially when that life is vulnerable. It must be the directing instinct behind every medical intervention and the patient is safe as long as that instinct dominates. The same recollection of the sanctity of the life of our fellows, restrains crime and even moderates warfare, the holy even thus having some sanctifying influence on these most unholy activities.

Because human sanctity has its origins in God, it can never be fully comprehensible. It has its ground in the belief that we humans are much more than we can know and have an incomprehensible beginning in God who stands by his creation and sets a precedent by honouring it. This incomprehensible beginning thus exerts a continual formative influence over our decisions and judgements, over our thought and conduct, and specifically over our attitude to one another. It may be the basis of common law which is unwritten but remembered, and remembered even though it had never been enunciated previously. It is perhaps thus being remembered at least partly, from something beyond history.

10.8 Human Sanctity and the Story of Cain & Abel

The story of Cain and Abel is such a story from beyond history, a primordial reading of the significance of murder, its unthinkability, its character as a violation of the inviolable, an act of repudiation, of rejection of the creative act of God. And not just the repudiation of the creative act of God in general, but of the special act of

God, which takes a particular divine resolve and decision: the creation of man. (see section 5.3.)

Now Adam knew Eve his wife, and she conceived and bore Cain, saying, "I have gotten a man with the help of the Lord." And again, she bore his brother Abel. Now Abel was a keeper of sheep, and Cain a tiller of the ground. In the course of time Cain brought to the Lord an offering of the fruit of the ground, and Abel brought of the firstlings of his flock and of their fat portions. And the Lord had regard for Abel and his offering, but for Cain and his offering he had no regard. So Cain was very angry, and his countenance fell. The Lord said to Cain, "Why are you angry, and why has your countenance fallen? If you do well, will you not be accepted? And if you do not do well, sin is couching at the door; its desire is for you, but you must master it."

Cain said to Abel his brother, "Let us go out to the field." And when they were in the field, Cain rose up against his brother Abel, and killed him. Then the Lord said to Cain, "Where is Abel your brother?" He said, "I do not know; am I my brother's keeper?" And the Lord said, "What have you done? The voice of your brother's blood is crying to me from the ground. And now you are cursed from the ground, which has opened its mouth to receive your brother's blood from your hand. When you till the ground, it shall no longer yield to you its strength; you shall be a fugitive and a wanderer on the earth." Cain said to the Lord, "My punishment is greater than I can bear. Behold, thou hast driven me this day away from the ground; and from thy face I shall be hidden; and I shall be a fugitive and a wanderer on the earth, and whoever finds me will slay me." Then the Lord said to him, "Not so! If any one slays Cain, vengeance shall be taken on him sevenfold." And the Lord put a mark on Cain, lest any who came upon him should kill him. Then Cain went away from the presence of the Lord, and dwelt in the land of Nod, east of Eden (Genesis 4:1ff).

What Cain did not appreciate was that in sharing the image of God, human beings have an

308

inextinguishability about them that is not shared by the animals. They cannot be slain and then regarded as if they had never existed. Cain could not shrug when asked about his brother's whereabouts. Abel's existence was unforgettable and un-ignorable; even after he had been murdered, his life attested itself to God from the ground. Man is not an eternal creature: he has a finite beginning, but as St Thomas Aquinas affirms, man has an aeviternity: he has an eternal future which is especially realised in the full revelation of the Gospel in Christ. It is thus a very different thing to kill a man than to kill an animal; for the murder of a man, his murderer is eternally liable and his victim's life is an indestructible witness before God to the flagitious crime of his destruction. It is possibly the case that at least part of the motive for making murder a capital offence, is that the crime is so profoundly serious in ways beyond merely human calculation, that account for it must be given to a higher court than can be assembled on earth. The execution of the murderer brings him before such a court.

The depth of catastrophe which Abel's murder represented is demonstrated by the consequences for Cain and evidently for the whole of the natural order. Agricultural productivity slumped and Cain was displaced from any sense of proper belonging in the earth. Nothing was ever going to be the same again - the world would not work properly, man would not be at peace in it and Abel's voice would be continually ringing through the cosmos making Cain's crime and his guilt unforgettable. In this way, written into the whole fabric of reality would be the inescapable truth that human life was sacrosanct and the taking of it would not only menace the continuance of the perpetrator, but also jeopardise the creaturely existence of the whole world. In the anticipation of the account due for this grave offence, Cain was to be preserved. The sanctity of Cain's life was still unimpeachable despite his gross transgression, no unauthorised harm was permitted to befall him, but the life he was thenceforth to lead was to be passed without the presence of God. The distancing of God from man was a lasting result of the latter's fall from holiness.

10.9. Human Sanctity and Calculating a Good

The rationality of the Judaeo-Christian tradition enables the calculation of the good of human beings. Christianity does not rely on a static, prescriptive moral code to determine what is good. Even the Ten Commandments derive themselves, even within their own text, from the nature of God and the status of his people. It is, in principle, possible to work out whether something is good or bad from what we know of the person of God and of his creative and redemptive work. And so very often as we do this, it is God's holiness and the sanctity of the objects of his creation and redemption which will prove to be the controlling factors in our calculations. It is so much more satisfactory to make this calculation *ab initio,* using all the evidence available from the Judaeo-Christian tradition, than to seek a prescriptive answer from a proof text. Even if we do the latter (and in simple cases, we can do so), we will need to trace back the argument from the nature of God and his work, to render the result of our calculation as thoroughly intelligible as possible.

Let us take as an example, one of the most prominent issues of our time which prompts us to think in terms of the sanctity of human life: the issue of abortion of unborn children. As we saw in section 5.1., this practice is now very widespread and has resulted in the termination of 1.4 billion pregnancies since 1980. The Church in the west has been relatively timid in its opposition to it, mainly because its protagonists have wrapped it in a women's rights mantle, and the Church does not want to get on the wrong side of that argument. To distinguish abortion from murder, an attempt has been made to identify a point in time when a foetus becomes a human being, before which it is morally permissible to dispose of it as an object under the control of the mother. But how is this point in time to be determined? To answer this, we might borrow from the Arian heretics of the second and third centuries. For Greek philosophical reasons, they wanted to insist that, in the Godhead, the Son could not be co-eternal with the Father, so, in the words of their syllogism, *en hoti, pote ouk en*, there was [a time], when he was not. This notion was anathematised by the Council of Nicaea in AD 325, which found it contradicted by Apostolic witness concerning Jesus Christ. The Arian syllogism, while certainly not true about the Son of God, is actually true of all other human beings. There was certainly a time when we were not. The question is, what time that was. As an existential point, it cannot be at some arbitrary stage in foetal development. It cannot be at the point of birth, because no mother could confirm that her baby had no human existence in the minutes before its birth. The only secure location for the time in question is at conception. At the point of conception, human existence and the divine claim on that new life must begin. The zygote and then the developing foetus immediately enjoy the greatest protection possible in the form of a sanctity, which through the fear of God, serves to restrain all thought or activity hostile to its continuance. This operates most immediately in the Christian-informed consciences of those closest to the unborn infant, and until relatively recently, at least, this sanctity has governed the law in Christian-informed societies.

The holiness of God challenges the main motive for most modern abortions which is expediency and convenience. (This is often dressed up as a matter of the health of the mother, but in reality this is rarely the case.) The prospect of the arrival of a child can be inconvenient, introducing a financial burden and a significant change of lifestyle, adding a great responsibility to parents and requiring long dedication to the welfare of the new child. Not for the selfish is the gift of being parents! But the holiness of God is all these things: it is inconvenient for the worldling to give time and space and resources to the acknowledgement and worship of a holy God. The holiness of God summons forth the expenditure of money, the allocation of human life-force to godly endeavours and sacred tasks. A new child is new holy ground upon which parents make their sacrifices to honour God in the raising of the child to live for God's glory. All this is very impractical. In the utilitarian world of the atheist, the raising of a child must above all be a *practical* matter. In the Judaeo-Christian tradition it is a *sacred* matter.

Of course, it is claimed, there are special cases. What about pregnancies arising from rape? It is admitted that it would be most burdensome to carry an infant to term in these circumstances, but again the holy purposes of God will come to the rescue. We considered in section 4.5., the recollection of the Israelite that his beginning and end were in God, not in the caprice of history or in the random acts of a wrong-doer. The redemption of God has a retrospective capacity - it restores a corrupt and lost past, so the offspring of an evil deed is just as much the object of God's holy purpose as one rightly conceived.

The recollection of the holiness of God and of his creation is properly the basis for all Christian moral calculations and will come to markedly different conclusions than those derived from secular utilitarianism. To the secularist, the argument from holiness will always be difficult to accept, and the results will seem unnecessarily troublesome to follow. The Church and individual Christians will find it difficult to explain well, as every moral issue will reduce to a discussion about the holiness of God. The long-term investment of the Church in sanctity will set it in good stead for such arguments. It will do well to prepare people for holy reasoning, by living a holy life itself:

maintaining its church buildings as places of worship, as sacred space, rather than making them all multifunctional venues, by maintaining daily prayers in public, by always being seen to be looking upward to God rather than to its material assets. It will serve the world well when it is other-worldly. It will be a blessing to men, when it devotes itself to blessing God.

REFERENCES FOR CHAPTER 10

(1) The Scottish Episcopal Church, *Canon 31 and the redefinition of marriage.* 2017

(2) David Novak, *The Sanctity of Human Life*, p9

(3) Gustaf Aulén, *Christus Victor*, 1965

(4) Walter Brueggemann, *Hopeful Imagination*, p77

--

CHAPTER 11
HUMAN RELATIONS

When it comes to the conjugation of verbs apparently nothing very weighty can be made of the fact that while the grammarians of many languages choose to order the verb forms in the sequence *I, you, he,* in Hebrew the order is reversed, *he, you, I.* This reversal is, they say, merely a matter of convenience because of the relative length of the verb forms for the three persons. But even if only accidentally, the reversing of the order of conjugation is consistent with the Hebrew prioritising of the "other" over the subject person, and particularly the divine "other". As much as Christianity inherited the sense of the presence of this divine other, there has been, especially in the west, a progressive forgetfulness of it, and a deliberate philosophical rejection in favour of a relocation of what we might call the *centre of gravity of person,* into the individual subject. We traced this development in chapter 4 and observed that it was Immanuel Kant's relocation of the source of knowledge within the individual which shaped much of the philosophical development until our own day. This relocation has had a profound effect on all human relationships because it is from this centre of gravity of person that we take our moral and spiritual bearings. It is the point from which we view and understand ourselves and others. In this chapter we examine some of the consequences of this relocation, some of the advantages of reversing it and some of the ways the Judaeo-Christian heritage might be recovered and its virtues exploited.

11.1. Socially Constructed Human Relationships

The present state of human relations in the modern western world is not enviable. Many commentators have described them as governed by a single factor: a dominant and pervasive *narcissism* which now largely controls our worldview, our self-understanding and our view of others. Narcissism is like a personal Ptolemaic cosmology in which the narcissistic subject views everything around him as a function of himself, the existence of which is entirely *for* himself, and which, in the fullest development of the phenomenon, is essentially under his direction and control. It represents a late stage in the development of the consequences of the Kantian reduction of meaning into the individual. It leaves the Judaeo-Christian concept of 'the other' far behind. Narcissism is the Prodigal on his great journey of self-expression, on his self-love fest, on his great spending spree, on his joyous adventure into the autonomous paradise of his self-made glory (see the parable in Luke 15:11ff). This narcissism was always latent in post-Kantian Europe, but was reinforced by Freud who, by understanding much of the human psyche to be controlled by repressed sexual instincts, legitimised those instincts and gave them a valid place in the internal schema of the individual. The Prodigal's spending spree was curtailed by the exigencies of two world wars, the dangers and deprivations of which served to restrain the advance of narcissism. But, recovering from those wars, the Western world became progressively more prosperous and the Prodigal was suddenly able to rise to his full vainglorious stature and exhibit himself with the glittering prestige which he knew all along was proper to him.

The western world is now full of people like him, and indeed, we are all a bit like him. We must examine the life of this Prodigal to see what impact his narcissism has on his humanity. Because he is self-absorbed, even self-obsessed, all his relationships, to the extent that he has them at all, are trivialised and exploitative. Deep friendships are sacrificial in character: the strength of them rests upon the knowledge that the one has that the other will go to great lengths on his behalf. But narcissists cannot go to any great lengths for anyone, or even really for themselves, so their friendships are debased. They are reduced to acquaintances or, worse, *followers* on social media, who are not friends at all, but just names of satellite personages who adorn the ego of the narcissist. There is a kind of self-serving mutuality about this, because all the Prodigal's followers are also prodigals and are using him like he uses them. However, these relationships, if they warrant the title, are very unstable. *Followers* can stop following, *likers* can stop liking, friends can be *defriended*, and attachments can be made with other prodigals at a moment's notice. In reality, our Prodigal is a very lonely person because all his connections are so volatile and weak and only continue as long as they sustain his high opinion of himself. They are mirrors placed so he can admire his reflection, but they easily shatter and so he is constantly searching for new mirrors to reflect a reassuring image of himself. As flimsy and friable as these reflections are, our Prodigal has an over-weening dependence on them. He is in constant need of their reassurance, their approval, their admiration. When he puts up a new photograph on his social media page, if he doesn't get 20 'likes' on the same day, he begins to get seriously anxious and then angry.

Anxiety and rage were prominent features of the ancient Roman world. The famous physician, *Galen had seen his mother fly into a rage and bite the servants. He describes his journey with an irascible friend who split the heads of two slaves when they muddled the luggage; anger was the man's besetting passion, as it clearly was for others in their dealings with the servile classes. 'Many friends' were reproved by Galen's father when they had bruised themselves by striking slaves in the teeth: 'They could have waited a while, he used to say, and used a rod or a whip to inflict as many blows as they wished, acting with calm reflection . .'* (1).

But in the ancient world, anxiety possibly arose more from the external dangers from pestilence or earthquake than from the internal anguishes of individuals although we know that prominent persons of the Roman empire could exhibit strongly narcissistic traits and a paranoeia which terrified those around them. Acts 12:21ff records the narcissism of Herod when, according to Josephus, *he had been three years King of all Judæa [when] he went to Cæsarea, to a festival celebrated in honour of Claudius. On the second day of these games, when a vast number of people were assembled in the theatre, Agrippa came in, clothed in a garment wholly made of silver, which reflected the rays of the morning sun with a most dazzling and awful brilliancy. Whereupon his flatterers cried out that he was a god, and offered prayer to him. The king did not rebuke them nor reject their impious flattery. He was presently seized with a violent pain in his bowels, which soon became so intense that he was carried out of the theatre to his palace, and expired after five days of excruciating pain* (2). Evidently the pestilence finally justified the anxiety of a man obsessed by his own glory.

In our own times this combination of vainglory, anxiety and rage is evident in many everyday circumstances. Our Prodigal is driving in a powerful and impressive BMW. He does so to reassure himself. Deep down he is anxious that he cannot really live up to the bright shining exterior which he projects, so he is in constant defensive mode. He is cut up at a junction by a rusty twelve year old Ford. The sheer hubris of this act exhibited by someone who is obviously infinitely inferior to our Prodigal, instantly enflames his rage, and he roars after the miscreant and seeks to visit violence upon him at the next traffic light. When he gets home he edits the incriminating sections out of his dash-cam footage and publishes it on social media so his followers can appreciate once again his superiority. If they fail to do so, he *trolls* or *defriends* them.

He does this because he is *entitled*. To be entitled is to have a claim (as far as possible, an exclusive claim) to everything around him. The Prodigal lives in his personal cosmos in which everything terrestrial and celestial rotates around him and exists for him. He is entitled to be ahead of the rusty Ford. He is entitled to make others fear him and for them to suffer pain to his advantage. He has already exercised his entitlement in demanding his share of the family estate and he continues to exert that same demand over practically everything around him. So the Prodigal should have free education at an institution which acknowledges his superiority and his right not to be exposed to any opinion which might upset his own self-image or question his own self-worth. As our Prodigal hails from the Near East, and is therefore a member of an ethnic minority, he demands a "safe space" where his delusions about himself are undisturbed and protected. Consistent with this, the voicing of certain opinions has been criminalised, but even in 1979 changes were already taking place to accommodate our Prodigal. Christopher Lasch writes, *recent developments in higher education have progressively diluted its content and reproduced, at a higher level, the conditions that prevail in the public schools. The collapse of general education; the abolition of any serious effort to instruct students in foreign languages; introduction of many programs in black studies, women's studies, and other forms of consciousness raising for no other purpose than to head off political discontent; the ubiquitous inflation of grades - all have lowered the value of a university education* (3). But a lowered standard does not matter too much to the Prodigal, because he does not derive his sense of self-worth from achievement. Again as Lasch puts it: *Today men seek the kind of approval that applauds not their actions but their personal attributes. They wish not so much to be esteemed as to be admired. They crave not fame but the glamour and excitement of celebrity. They want to be envied rather than respected* (4).

So as he roars about town in the Beemer, and swaggers around the campus in his designer sunglasses, he has no regard for the achievement of others, or for their learning or office. He does not defer to his professors, he rather regards them as functionaries to supply the excellent grades he deserves. Everything around him is for him. The State exists for him: it must supply and authorise what he wants, and restrain and even criminalise everything he doesn't like. He must be supplied with endless pork from the infinite barrel which the State must somehow produce - how he does not care. Wherever possible he must be treated as a special case for his advantage. He was always told he was special as a child and now the State must put its money where its mouth was. Everyone he meets he classifies as a component of a vast apparatus which exists to serve him. They have to do what he wants, that is what they are there for. If they fail to oblige, he will become angry, and maybe, with his fellow prodigals, he will have a tantrum in the street and burn some cars and loot some shops.

Our Prodigal devotes himself to looking and sounding good. He does so, in large part, to attract the opposite sex. And in this he is quite successful. He is actually fun to be with, he's impressive, witty, charming to his date. She finds she likes being with him and possibly as a prodigal herself, she might well find a mutuality existing between them. But increasingly, there will be little or no seriousness in their relationship. There is no courtship in their so called 'hookup'. It is for sexual gratification on both sides without any other commitment. According to a 2009 analysis, *hookups are not only uncommitted but devoid of emotional connection. Some people who hook up do not even talk to the other person. 'Hooking up is also very selfish,' says a George Washington University student. 'It is all about what you want not about what the other person wants'..... [Some young people interviewed] felt it was better to retain control by hooking up; some made it sound like a narcissistic game of dominance. Tonya, a Duke sophomore, liked to jump out of bed right after sex with a guy, which 'makes men feel feeble. It gives me such a rush.' Her friend Alicia nodded and said, 'sometimes you just want to screw them before they screw you'* (5). Modern western universities are like rabbit warrens when it comes to sexual relations - actually worse, because rabbits may be lusty but they are not narcissistic.

He also finds that all his relationships, such as they are, are potentially, or actually sexualised. Practically every relationship between adults can be lawfully sexualised and even when legal lines are crossed, if children are

323

not involved, no action is usually taken. Truth has been so subjectivised in the narcissistic utopia, that our Prodigal may indulge is some internalised psychological sex change even though his physical sexual characteristics remain the same. He may wake up one morning and decide he is female, or 'non-binary', or perhaps a sheep, or a porcupine, or perhaps he might follow the example of the doctoral student at the University of Arizona who 'self-identifies' as a hippopotamus (6), and then command the whole world to honour this decision, build new changing rooms for him at the gym and new rest-rooms in the local bars. But maybe by lunchtime he's changed his mind and is already altering his Facebook page to reflect his latest status. This is the ultimate narcissistic control escapade and with it he can have the whole world chasing after him, adjusting his environment to honour his choice.

The Prodigal may, however, refrain from these excesses and form a less short-term relationship and share a flat with a girl for some time and she may eventually become his wife and perhaps bear his children. According to data published by the Marriage Foundation, only about half of children born in 2015 will still be living in a family with both birth parents when they are 15. So the cohabitations and marriages currently being contracted have a poor prospect of durability. Looking at the character of our Prodigal (albeit something of a caricature) perhaps we would not be surprised by this statistic. Marrying couples often think that their marriage is some kind of deal which they as individuals create in a joint agreement, and do so on the basis that if it ceases to be advantageous to either one it can be terminated at will.

Our Prodigal may well be caught up in the new parenting culture which fuels another generation of narcissists. Parents have always viewed their responsibilities with a certain degree of anxiety, but this has multiplied greatly because they themselves need the approval and admiration of others, and they are desperate to get the same from their children. They become psychologically enslaved to pleasing their offspring who are very quick to appreciate the power they now have, use it with great effect and are themselves made anxious by the dependence they perceive their parents to have on their approval. This is particularly acute in the case of single parents who are without another adult to stabilise the family relationship. Then there is the "low esteem" trap. As a counter for some parents' tendency to disparage their children, they were told to bathe their infants is a continual glow of congratulation and approval. Children were told they were 'special', and therefore inevitably, entitled.

And this continues in the schools. No doubt when the little Prodigals turn up to class they are treated as special again. Their errors will not be corrected, they will all get a prize on sports day whatever their performance, and they will emerge with that exaggerated estimate of their own abilities and with that sense of entitlement exhibited by their parents.

Meanwhile our Prodigal is making his way in the world of work. Because he attends so much to his image, his outward appearance and to the impression he makes on others, he may well find himself quite a success in the modern corporate arena. After all, people like him have got there ahead of him, and have designed the interview questions to select preferentially the candidates with narcissistic tendencies. Our Prodigal will no doubt be asked to describe instances in which his capacities for accurate assessment of situations, his strength of character and personal courage, his razor sharp analytical powers have been best utilised and revealed. And, no doubt, he has produced fluent and and striking answers to these questions. So he gets the job and from henceforth he can contribute to the corporate narcissism of the institution to which he now belongs.

Many corporations are indeed now narcissistic. They guard their image with a fanaticism which directs them to make huge sacrifices to preserve it. They hire expensive consultants to hone the impression the company projects. Behind the scenes, they are ruthless in dismissing anyone who does not contribute to their image appropriately, but publicly, they present as a caring paternalistic employer with the welfare of their employee 'family' as their great concern. Our Prodigal fits in very well, receives the approbation to charm him as he uses his life-force to burnish the golden image of which has become a part. Until he does not look the part any more. Until he looks too old. Until, instead of polishing, he tarnishes the image. Then he's gone quickly and is even more quickly forgotten. And there's nothing more pathetic than a worn-out narcissist.

11.2. Human relationships from physical causality

Narcissism involves a vanity and a self-consciousness which might be argued to derive from solely physical causes. The Prodigal whom we have appointed to represent narcissism, is by his very definition in the parable, engaged in an act of disobedience, of ingratitude and of defiance against his father and against heaven itself. Similarly the act of disobedience of Adam in the primordial Fall of the human race could be regarded as a descent into narcissism. Both of these readings resort to metaphysical causality to comprehend the phenomenon of narcissism. If we are to resort only to physical causality, we can explain competition from natural selection, and we can explain efforts to attract a sexual partner, even the desire to emerge as the dominant member of the herd. These are all principal characteristics of the narcissistic personality. It might be argued that it is a normal and necessary feature of human relationships from a purely physical cause.

If we reply that we find narcissism unattractive, and in its more extreme forms we have classified it as a personality disorder, perhaps it might be said that although its features are generally condemned by the Judaeo-Christian tradition as undesirable, that condemnation is itself a repression of a behaviour which is entirely normal and proper to the human race. There is a tendency for some modern atheists to take this line. When it was suggested to Professor Peter Atkins that his insistence that his intellectual opponents were deluded could be regarded as arrogant, he replied,

What's wrong with arrogance if you're right? He later regretted saying that, but he needed not to regret it, as he was actually right: if his view of reality is true, then there nothing wrong with arrogance (7).

Actually narcissism works well with a world governed by natural selection, but it has a mutilated understanding of human love. The reason we do not like narcissism (and even narcissists do not like being accused of it) is that it is really quite hateful. It is quintessentially loveless, it has no sense of the other person; everything around the narcissist functions as a mirror to reflect the narcissist's glory. It is about as far removed as possible from exercising a sacrificial love for any other person. Quite the converse is expected of other people: they have to sacrifice themselves for the narcissist. This consistency with the argument for everything to be derived from the principle of natural selection, makes the latter a very unattractive and implausible basis for understanding human existence and the human condition.

11.3. Human Relationships from Metaphysical Causality

It is striking that the parable in Luke 15:11ff describes the behaviour of the Prodigal son as a *departure*. From a Judaeo-Christian point of view, it is a profound departure from the norm and the place and the dignity proper to an inheritor of a great estate. The model is so well established in Israelite thought, ever since those heady days of entering the Promised Land, that the meaning of the parable could not be missed by its hearers. The Prodigal was departing from his inheritance and seeking to live, quite incomprehensibly, outside the compass of the grace of God. The Prodigal takes that impossible step, and makes himself impossible with respect to the grace of God which still addresses him.

The Judaeo-Christian witness understands the Prodigal thus to be living in an astable state - displaced from where he should be as a recipient of grace, and now living a false and mutilated existence in rejection of that grace. This accounts for the misery and anxiety of the narcissist. He is maintaining an illusion that he is his own source of grace, that he has no use and no need of another. He pretends to be self-sustaining in every respect. He assumes himself to have power which he does not have - to summon what he needs, rather than to receive it. He thus exonerates himself from any obligation to another. The parable tells us that that it may be possible to sustain this false existence for a while, but it is very short-lived. There is a period in which he lives on the inheritance which he has received on his departure, but soon, this begins to run out and the Prodigal finds himself in need. The rejection of God and his grace, seems to work very much like this: there is a period of time in which the narcissistic world can manage on the unacknowledged reserves from a former time of faith, but after a generation or two, this reserve begins to run out, and the harsh and cruel realities of life without God in the far country begin to bite.

In the parable, the Prodigal, *attaches himself to a landowner.* He has had a singularly better attachment before his departure, which he sought to break and still now disregards. Still the narcissist, he summons the landowner to his own aid. To the landowner he is a pathetic beggar outside the back door, but the Prodigal imagines he is still managing his circumstances and marshalling those around him to provide his needs. He fancies himself equal to any emergency. Even when the landowner finally takes him on and sends him to feed the pigs in utter humiliation, and he finds himself eating the pig food, even then he is still the narcissist: he plans to renegotiate his status with his father. He comes up with the plan: he will cease to be a son, but instead he will become a paid servant. He may be able even to pay the money back, and thus settle his own account himself. He has not even begun to realise the deep hole he is really in. He thinks it is just a matter of a spot of misfortune, just a lack of money, requiring some reorganisation of things.

He is rehearsing this plan in his mind all the way back to his father's estate - his narcissistic outlook always seeking to manage things for his benefit - even his father to whom he is going to present the change of status plan. He has his pre-devised repentance speech ready, but he is not able to finish it because the father, who has seen him at a great distance and runs to meet him, is already embracing him warmly, and ordering his complete reinstatement including furnishing his hand with a signet ring to give him once again the authority of a son. What we see here is a powerful and complete contradiction of the Prodigal's narcissism by the generosity and sacrificial love of the father for the son. Hitherto, in his journey into the far country, the most powerful influence, the most significant, indeed, the only *pole* in the Prodigal's life has been himself - his ego, his heart, his capacity for disposing, deciding and ruling. Even in his return, this personal regnant centre of his soul is working overtime to come up with a viable solution to the crisis in which he finds himself. But it is suddenly overtaken by an infinitely greater pole: the love of the father, the greatness of whose power lies in commanding the good for the son trapped in the poverty of his own narcissism, and breaking open that trap and restoring its captive.

This is what Christianity has done for a narcissistic world. It is generally believed among psychologists that narcissism, when it reaches the critical intensity of a borderline personality disorder is all but incurable. This is even indicated in the parable in the reluctance of the Prodigal to abandon it, still looking to himself even up to the last moment before the father interrupts him. But once the father does interrupt him, the reign of his generosity again governs the life and experience of the Prodigal.

We have used the term *pole* to describe the central reference point of the Prodigal, from which, in his sojourn into the far country, he sought to determine everything. In this endeavour he was *unipolar*: there was only one reference point and it was he, the Prodigal. Even other people around him were not taken seriously as people, but only as objects to serve his unipolar needs and aspirations. Only in a very limited way could his relations with other people be described as *dipolar,* because there was really very little exchange of grace between them. The traffic was all one way.

Christianity establishes the *pole* of God's grace in the person of Jesus Christ as the governing principle of all human relationships referenced to him. This is the meaning of the *Kingdom of God.* Any two persons in that kingdom, stand in a *tripolar* relationship: their relation one to another is governed and empowered by their relationship to God himself, the third pole. The disciples in the New Testament found this to be the practical way in which they related to one another in Christ's presence. The way in which St Paul addresses the Christian churches at the beginning of his letters underscores this. He introduces himself as the Apostle of Christ and addresses them as the elect of God, the holy ones, or those who call upon the name of Jesus Christ. (see, for example, 1 Corinthian 1:1-3). St Paul could not see any of the Churches without seeing them as the Churches of Jesus Christ, nor any Christian except as one chosen by Jesus Christ. He could not even see himself apart from that same designation. It is easy to see how such sustained application of the discipline of Christian thinking could represent a powerful assault on, and defeat of, narcissism. Even if he made no such calculation himself, the Prodigal's return to the father was the very best answer to his predicament.

This *tripolar* view of all relationships which is central to Christianity does far more to redeem human relationships from narcissism than any psychological counselling or cognitive therapy ever can. The Christian must see everyone as beloved of God, whose existence and place before God is authorised and sacred. Not only that, but he is also potentially an agent of God, an *angel* of God, with a word and purpose from God himself. The Christian will also see his fellow man as a recipient of God's grace of which he, the Christian, may at that moment, be the agent. Even if he proves to be an apparent agent of evil, the Christian must see him as an object of God's retrieving purpose, a soul, as the Christian is, in need of redemption. It must be said, that this disposition to others does not always come so easily but must be a life-long ambition of the Christian. But in a world in which it is practised and efforts are continually made to practise it, healthy, respectful, kindly and wholesome relationships result.

On the other hand, the tripolar view of relationships does not dovetail smoothly into the narcissistic world of the errant Prodigal. The narcissist will generally find the Christian annoying and frustrating. His schemes to enlist the Christian as a satellite to his unipolar persona will not work so well, because the Christian serves Christ and not him. As amiable as he may try to be, the Christian will inevitably be a challenge to the Prodigal, because he will be a reminder that there is another pole with respect to which all relationships will find their meaning and fulfilment. If he is in the slightest faithful, the Christian will not be able to avoid being a witness to this other pole, testifying to Jesus Christ in the way he conducts his life and engages with others. Of course, Christians are in the flesh and are as capable as anyone else of being annoying in a thousand ways, but whether they are or not, they will, if faithful, be annoying at least in this way.

11.4. Marriage and Family Life

What we have called the tripolar nature of relationships has no better or more explicit expression than in holy matrimony. As we saw in section 4.4., whether or not the church acknowledges marriage as a sacrament, St Paul describes it in sacramental terms in Ephesians 5. The introduction to the order for the solemnisation of holy matrimony, in the Anglican 1662 Book of Common Prayer give a brief description of what marriage is: *[Holy Matrimony] is an honourable estate, instituted of God in the time of man's innocency, signifying unto us the mystical union that is betwixt Christ and his Church; which holy estate Christ adorned and beautified with his presence, and first miracle that he wrought, in Cana of Galilee; and is commended of Saint Paul to be honourable among all men: and therefore is not by any to be enterprised, nor taken in hand, unadvisedly, lightly, or wantonly, to satisfy men's carnal lusts and appetites, like brute beasts that have no understanding; but reverently, discreetly, advisedly, soberly, and in the fear of God; duly considering the causes for which Matrimony was ordained. First, It was ordained for the procreation of children, to be brought up in the fear and nurture of the*

Lord, and to the praise of his holy Name. Secondly, It was ordained for a remedy against sin, and to avoid fornication; that such persons as have not the gift of continency might marry, and keep themselves undefiled members of Christ's body. Thirdly, It was ordained for the mutual society, help, and comfort, that the one ought to have of the other, both in prosperity and adversity.

We have to go back to the Book of Common Prayer to obtain a definition of marriage which stoutly maintains the principles from the Judaeo-Christian tradition which stand behind it, because in recent years secular pressure has encouraged the Church to dilute and weaken its stance on marriage and the resolve it has to sustain it. But this definition published in 1662 expresses the tripolar nature of the marriage relationship. Marriage is a divine institution and it is to be entered in the fear of God, in the humble acknowledgement of divine authority over it and within it. This has proved to be a great asset to all married people because in this understanding, a husband and wife do not make their own marriage - they do not create it, nor is it a contract to which they sign up. It is, rather, a divine creation to which they subscribe and so is stronger and greater than they are. With divine authorisation behind it, it is capable of holding man and wife together through adversity and prosperity, through suffering and hardship, and through all the years of their lives. God's presence in it and over it sanctifies it and both husband and wife together. In it, husband and wife treasure one another as God's gift to each and in honouring each other, they honour God the giver.

The marriage service is clear that one of the purposes of marriage is to hallow sex and provide a lawful and moral environment for human sexual activity, the primary purpose of which is procreation and from which the sexual act should never be completely separated. Marriage is the way in which, according to the Judaeo-Christian tradition, the primordial divine command that man should fill the earth should be fulfilled. It is also the indissoluble union between husband and wife that they both should be able to trust in every exigency, because sacramentally marriage reflects the indissoluble union between Christ and his Church.

As we have seen in sections 6.9 and in 8.9, the Judaeo-Christian tradition has a very high view of the human being, and here we see it has an equally high view of marriage. Christian marriage expects much from both husband and wife. It expects life-long fidelity, great durability in hardship, devotion, generosity and gratitude, honour and respect from both parties to each other, and an honouring of the institution itself and of the God who gave it to them. The Church should not betray this standard through a misguided sympathy for those who fail to reach it. They should be treated with mercy but nothing of the great institution of marriage should be forfeited in so doing, otherwise all marriages are betrayed. The Church owes all married people a constancy in upholding the sanctity and inviolability of the marriage bond. In this sphere many church denominations have failed signally and increasingly and in so failing have contributed to the decay of marriage and the concomitant moral delict which been the result.

11.5. The Raising of Children

The lifelong durability of Christian marriage provides the basis for the raising of children, for educating them and equipping them to take their place in adult society. Statistics abound that show children in families with secure marriages are healthier, better educated, achieve more, are better socially and morally adjusted than children from other environments. But it is not merely a utilitarian calculation which encourages us to hold fast to Judaeo-Christian standards of marriage and family life. Just as marriage is a tripolar relationship, lived out by man and wife under God. so also is the raising of children tripolar. Parents occupy a definite office with respect to their children, and children to their parents. The child is not the property of the parent, nor the servant, nor the friend, nor the freebooting lodger in their house. Nor is the child their fashion accessory nor the one through whom they live out their dreams and unfulfilled ambitions. No, the child is the *spiritual apprentice* of the parents (8). The parents stand *in loco Dei* with respect to their offspring. This status has simplicity and depth. Its presupposition is that to know God is to be properly and truly human, to enter in to the divine appointment that all human beings are called to, and to occupy that office of representing God's reign on earth, with competency and distinction. Children need to be raised to this office and are best prepared for it by being introduced fully and correctly to the God whom they will serve in this capacity.

This introduction is the task of parents. The daunting truth for parents is that the child learns what God is like from them. They represent God to their children, so the first qualification of parents is that they know God well themselves. As far as they do, they will inevitably reflect his likeness to their children. Not perfectly, perhaps, but sufficiently. The child will learn, through the parents, the unequivocal devotion of God for his creatures; the holiness of God as the terms of his acceptance of his people; the sacrifice the love of God makes for their rescue and deliverance; his care for them as the apple of his eye; and his ready companionship with them as co-workers with him in the service of his kingdom. All these things are learned by the child, not merely in formal instruction, although that will be required, but in a thousand little ways which reveal the instincts of parents, their own sense of God, and his gentle, confident authority over their home.

A moment's thought will reveal how far this is away from the nightmarish narcissistic world we have just described in section 11.1. At the most basic level, the Christian home is not generally an over-anxious place. Consciously living under the ordered reign of God, the family accepts that divine fixed point as a reference from which to take their bearings. Even acknowledging this asset, parents can still become anxious about their task, but the tripolar relationship certainly sets a limit to their fears. Every parent takes delivery of a tiny infant whose life so far represents something of a *tabula rasa* and it is largely the parents' responsibility to write upon it wisely and well for the benefit of their child. This is a solemn responsibility, but if it be discharged under God in a Christian home, there is abundant evidence that children can be raised as wise and capable inheritors of the human office.

11.6. The Prodigal's Return

We have forgotten much of this so completely that we now think we never knew it, and so it is a reassurance that it was to a Jewish home that the Prodigal returned. He set out on his homeward journey because he *remembered* his heritage, his true belonging. And the story is a parable, so it is not just about the Prodigal remembering his own personal history, but it is about Man remembering primordially his origins and true belonging. It is, of course, Jesus Christ who, in his representative capacity of the fallen human race, made that journey into the far country to restore humanity to its proper relationship to God. So we discover that not only is the journey into the far country ours, but, in Jesus Christ, so is the return. The narcissistic enterprise of the human race has been a vexing experience to say the least: it epitomises man in his misery. The great task of the Gospel is to bring to remembrance our home life with God which we had before we embarked on this futile and vexing enterprise and to open up to us the way of return to the God who watches for us to appear on the horizon.

REFERENCES FOR CHAPTER 11

(1) Robin Lane Fox, *Pagans and Christians*, p65.

(2) Josephus, *Antiquities of the Jews*, 19.8.2.

(3) Christopher Lasch, *The Culture of Narcissism,* p145

(4) Christopher Lasch, *Ibid*, p59

(5) J. M. Twenge and W. K. Campbell, *The Narcissism Epidemic*, p224

(6) *Fox News*, June 10th 2017

(7) P.W. Atkins, *Channel 4's The Trouble with Atheism*, reported by *The Times*,December 19th 2006

(8) Karl Barth, *Church Dogmatics*, *Volume 2:4*, p243.

CHAPTER 12
HUMAN TIME

12.1. Introduction

Augustine asks *'What, then, is time? I know well enough what it is, provided no one asks me. But if I am asked what it is and try to explain, I do not know.'* Many of us will understand the sentiment behind this especially after taking some moments to think about time ourselves. Is it 'out there' as an objective reality, or is it just in my head? Does it flow? Is it itself moving? Or are we moving past it? Why does it seem to pass quickly and at other times slowly? We are, of course, inevitably always in the present, but much of our thought and a great deal of our life energy is employed recalling the past and anticipating the future. Are these mental activities really worthwhile? Most of the time we don't ask these questions - we just get on putting entries in our diaries, planning the week ahead, preparing for our summer holidays and unconsciously living in the time we're in. But in this chapter, we step up to look at time a bit more closely. Some answers to the above questions can be derived from experimental physics and from careful philosophical reflection, but our main concern here will be the answers to these questions as they bear on the issue of human recollection of the significance of the past, our human purpose in the present, its validity and that which drives it forward, and human hope, expectation for the future and sense of destiny.

12.2. Human Time as a Socially-Constructed Reality

Karl Barth has pointed out that human *sloth* takes two quite radically different forms (1). The first is what he calls the eastern version. It is the familiar manifestation of human inertia, a physical and mental laziness which possesses all of us from time to time, but is more prominent in some than in others. This eastern sloth lets the world go by, it drifts in and out of sleep, it minimises both physical and mental exertion, resting itself in either a careless negligence as to the future, or in the confident knowledge that it exists in a world of ultimate inevitability and that nothing it can do will change anything. Even when it is awake, it might as well be asleep, for it considers itself to have no influence on any outcome. There is some virtue in a bit of this. A little negligence of the world denies the latter some of its overweening insistence for our attention and servitude. The world hates being ignored but it does it some good for its pseudo-sovereignty to be challenged from time to time. This kind of sloth is also, to some extent, a repudiation of anxiety. The world feeds off the anxieties of people, pressing them and urging them with its vast and demanding agenda. For it to encounter the dumb resistance of a seriously accomplished sloth is a salutary lesson for it, as it finds that rare individual who is immune to its threats and oblivious to the anxiety it wants to instil.

Barth does not think, however, of eastern sloth as a reluctance to obey the world. If he did, he would, no doubt, champion it. But he thinks of sloth as a reluctance to come to God. The sloth does not come when he is called. If the world is calling, that may be fine, but when God calls, it is a question of our whole humanity and destiny which is at stake. So as far as Barth is concerned, sloth is not just an inertia, but an *evasion*, and a fatal evasion. We live in an age, at least in the West, in which we seem practically unrousable with respect to God and the things of God. We exhibit a combination of spiritual autism and torpor to sacred things which seem insurmountable. We live in a moral coma, from which nothing seems to wake us.

It was not always so. In the fourteenth century mediaeval preachers were able to gather large crowds to hear their proclamation of the mercy and judgement of God, and the people were frequently reduced to tears by their message. In all the towns where the famous Dominican preacher Vincent Ferrer was expected, the people, the magistrates, the lower clergy, and even bishops, set out to greet him with joyous songs. He journeyed with a numerous and ever increasing band of followers, so numerous that officials were appointed to take responsibility for lodging and feeding these multitudes. Large numbers of priests of various religious orders accompanied him everywhere, to assist him in celebrating mass and in confessing the vast numbers of the faithful. Ferrer's pulpit had to be protected by a fence against the pressure of the congregation which wanted to kiss his hand or habit. All work ceased when he was in town to preach. He rarely failed to move his congregations to tears. When he spoke of the last judgement, of hell, or of the passion, both he and his hearers wept so copiously that he had to suspend his sermon till sobbing had ceased. Malefactors threw themselves at his feet, before everyone, confessing their great sins (2).

But in our age we have become inured to such ministry, unmoved by its message and unawakened by its clarion call. But this is not because we are generally unable to make any movement or because we lack vigour. We can certainly exhibit energetic activity when we care to. This brings us to Barth's second manifestation of sloth, of the type he calls western. Again, like eastern sloth, this has to do with time and whether and how we use it. But in this western form we busy ourselves to such a degree that we have no more room left in our calendars for anything. This too is a form of evasion. We make sure we are too busy for God, certainly too busy to attend formal worship on a Sunday, but also actually so busy that we can never stand still and think a divine thought. We do need to keep moving, because God is never far away and even a temporary pause in our busy programme will be enough for a spiritual thought of our eternal destiny, or of our need for reconciliation with God, to enter our minds. The key thing for success in this is to make sure we are always at the point of rushing off to the next thing. The modern world has constructed itself to make this particularly easy. With all the adults in the family trying to hold down jobs while caring for children and transporting them everywhere so that they too can share in the totality of this hyperactive western sloth, to construct a personal timetable of unceasing activity is not so difficult. To stand still in a sacred space for a sacred moment is, we're afraid, just not on at present. Actually, we do stand still from time to time, but this is at the direction of the counsel we receive from the time management handbook we've just bought, which recommends, nay, *insists* that we have such a thing as 'personal time'. But this is not time for God. It is time to be in our own presence - to find some kind of Kantian, self-generated transcendence, which, in itself, is another evasion. Even when we retire, we have to maintain the illusion of 'busy-ness'. This is a form of what is now called 'virtue-signalling' - the construction of western sloth has become so complete and well-crafted, that we now count it to our great credit to have achieved it.

Again, this was not always so. We have to ask why so very many people in the Middle Ages entered monasteries and convents, abjuring their claim to money, sex and power and taking vows of poverty, chastity and obedience to live a life essentially of worship of God. There may have been many reasons, but a principal one was their desire to live a sanctified life in holy space and time. No doubt it is possible to evade the call of God even in a monastery, but the discipline of standing in his presence hour by hour and day by day was the principal joy of the holy life. They did not manage their time, they sanctified it. They

345

solved the problem of the meaning of their time, by living in the intersection between it and eternity. They were no more able than St Augustine to explain what time and space meant, but they found a way of living out its meaning even if they could not put it into philosophical terms.

So we do not sanctify our time, we merely organise it, but as we organise it, we really abandon it altogether. Our grasp of our own history is so poor that we cannot rate our present with respect to our past. The mediaeval period was certainly no paradise: life experience was brutal, filled with danger of violence, risk of mortal disease, and a good day was one in which it was just the toothache that had to be endured. And yet the joys were all the more intense. We have lost the intensity of pleasure from a warm coat, a good fire in the hearth and a glass of wine. Most of all we have lost the joy of the saving of our souls, of sins forgiven, of the grace of God's presence, and the promise of his glory. We have equally dismissed the soul-searching sense of divine judgement on wrongdoing, the fearful holiness and purity against which God measures his people, and the depth of our moral plight from which he raises us. The middle ages were filled with powerful contrasts such as these, reflected in the everyday experiences of ordinary people: the darkness was impenetrable and the sunshine radiant, the silence was intense, the sounds were penetrating. A single tiny light in an otherwise pitch black world would hold the fascinated eye as a single cry would capture the ear. But now, the powerful contrasts have been washed out of our lives, everything is grey, our senses are anaesthetised, our minds are numbed. We have so much but we cannot appreciate it because we expect it; we are so satiated we cannot taste anything and we are desperate to keep everything we have because we have not the moral strength to endure loss. By the same token, we have ceased to anticipate the future glory of a redeemed world. We have ceased to imagine it, far less, long for it. Instead of past, present and future, as we noted in section 4.3., we now believe only in an elastic present, hoping that next year's prosperity will equal or exceed the current one.

It is not surprising that we have a very poor grasp of the nature of time and its meaning. In general, we have little idea how we got here, a very poor idea of where we are, and no idea at all of where we are going. We need to recover some sense of our beginnings, our origins and rediscover a sense of our destiny. We will need to repudiate the idea that human beings are bland, timeless items of insignificance, who only think back as far as their youth, even if that far, and only think ahead as far as their pensions. Like the Israelite (see section 4.5) we will need to recover a sense of our beginning and end in God which will mean our place in the full span of the history and future of the cosmos, and beyond that to the inheritance which is promised as its fulfilment.

12.3. Time from Physical Causality

Despite his avowed inability to define time, Augustine does make an attempt to understand it. He says: *Nevertheless we do measure time. We cannot measure it if it is not yet in being, or if it is no longer in being, or if it has no duration, or if it has no beginning and no end. Therefore we measure neither the future nor the past nor the present nor time that is passing. Yet we do measure time* (3). This sums up the elusive character of time. You can never pin it down, because it continually escapes into the past, and you can never grasp the future because it has not yet arrived. All that remains is an infinitely thin slice of time representing the present which continually vanishes as it is replaced by its successor.

How can we get a grip on this? Studies on time over millennia and intensely in recent decades in the context of physics and cosmology, have generally resolved into four poles: *idealism* versus *realism*, and *static* versus *dynamic* understandings of time. Idealism understands time as a subjective matter: its nature is to be comprehended according to the inward perceptions of the observer. Realism considers time to be 'out there', an objective reality. Static understandings of time arise from relativistic considerations and envisage a space-time block in which all events are represented by points throughout, and the present is not absolutely defined, but is dependent upon the frame of reference of the observer. Dynamic models of time are more familiar to us as they more nearly reflect our everyday experience, and have been represented by the 'Big Bang' theory of the Universe, and more recently, by the 'Big Crunch' theory, which marks the final stage of the Universe when it collapses again after reaching a maximum expansion.

For anyone who took a course of Newtonian physics and differential calculus at school, the Idealist position seems least accessible. To reduce the passage of time to a psychological phenomenon seems implausible but it was a position taken by the 5th century BC Greek Eleatic School, but perhaps only because they rejected change in principle and then had to deal with the apparent change which seemed to take place with the passage of time. The problem was that if past and future events were real they would be in the present now. But they are not, and so can have no real existence. So we cannot describe the world temporally, because when we do so, we end up with a contradiction. Their solution was to abolish the idea of the passage of time and distil the whole problem into the mind of the observer. In common with many idealist arguments, there is something forced and artificial about this line of reasoning, because, by choosing the definitions, the outcome of the argument is inevitably determined. If you say past and future events are not real, thus defining 'real' as 'present', the predetermined outcome of the argument is that there is no change and any perception of change must be in the mind.

The Realist understanding of time became cemented into modern western consciousness by the advent of Newtonian mechanics. The movement of the planets, the flight of a projectile, the rolling of a ball on an inclined plane were all reduced to mathematical analysis which treated time as a real quantity and as a real variable. Because it was now possible to plot the trajectory of a moving object when subjected to a force, the history of its passage, its present position, and its predicted destination all took on practically identical reality. In the context of our previous argument concerning knowledge (chapter 2) as something compelled upon us by the independent reality of an object, that object can be an object in the past or in the future, not just in the present.

This brings us to the further distinction between a static understanding of time and a dynamic one. The static view arises in part from relativistic considerations. Suppose an aircraft was flying at some fraction of the speed of light, past an observer in the airport. Suppose two lightning strikes occurred at the moment of passing, equidistant from the aircraft, one behind and the other ahead. The observer in the airport would observe these two strikes as simultaneous, but the observer in the aircraft would observe them as non-simultaneous events. What this means is that simultaneity is not absolute: whether two events are simultaneous depends upon the frame of reference of the observer. Two events A, and B, could be simultaneous, A could precede B, or B could precede A, perceived by different observers in space and time, travelling at different speeds relative to one another. This means that we cannot consider time without also considering space, and what we now describe as the space-time continuum is essentially a four dimensional region in which events in it can appear to be in any order depending on the place from which they are observed.

The fact that the events are only ordered relative to one another and the frame of reference of the observer, dissolves the idea that past and future events are not real but only those in the present. There is now no absolute present, and so all events must be equally real no matter where they are in the space-time block. From the point of view of any observer, the past events are still 'there' in their positions in space-time. Similarly, future events are 'there' in their places. We now have a static understanding of space-time, and from a human point of view this has the effect of reifying our past and future as much as it does our present.

But of course, there are difficulties with this. Why does time seem to pass? There seems no such imperative when it comes to space. It is as if there is some kind of index, or pointer, moving along the time axis marking the present. We cannot describe the speed of this pointer, but it does seem to move. What makes it move? Several answers have been given to this question, none of which are fully satisfactory. According to the Second Law of Thermodynamics, the degree of disorder in the universe (the entropy) is rising to a maximum and so provides a direction for passing time. But it is hard to see how the connection between the two can be made secure. The psychological understanding of the passage of time rests on our experience that we remember the past and anticipate the future, and although there have been attempts to link thermodynamics with memory, again the suggestion lacks rigour. Attempts have also been made to derive the direction of time from causality, because causes always precede their effects, but in some photon experiments there has been a suggested detection of what is called retro-causation, in which an effect gives rise to a previous cause! The General

Theory of Relativity apparently predicts the possibility of time travel near very large masses or concentrations of energy, so the normal experienced progressive change of the position of the present in the space-time continuum (if we can describe the progress of time in such a way) is not the only possible movement. So we seem to be near the edge of the subset which contains all explicable truth (subset A in section 3.1.). As further research is carried out, that boundary will expand outwards.

A further problem of that static space-time view is that it is strongly suggestive of a thorough-going determinism. If the future events are somehow 'there', we are suddenly engulfed by a total inevitability, which is contrary to our experience and, as we have seen elsewhere, is a threat to vision and achievement. The problem of determinism represents a limit to the static model. In contrast, the dynamic model of time in which there is an acceptance of temporal progression, provides the basis for some form of beginning of the universe (maybe the 'Big Bang'), a genuine history in which the universe expands and an end in which it shrinks back to the 'Big Crunch'. This does not insist on an absolute determinism, but it does have the problem of a beginning. Adrian Bardon quotes Bruce Reichenbach: *Given the grand theory of relativity, the big bang is not an event at all. An event takes place within a space-time context. But the big bang has no space-time context; there is neither time prior to the big bang, nor a space in which the big bang occurs. Hence, the big bang cannot be considered as a physical event occurring at a moment of time. As Hawking notes, the finite universe has no space time boundaries and hence lacks singularity and a beginning. Time might be multi-dimensional or imaginary, in which case one asymptotically approaches a beginning singularity but never reaches it. And without a beginning the universe requires no cause. The best one can say is that the universe is finite with respect to the past, not that it was an event with a beginning* (4).

This is an argument which is vaguely rabbinic in character, constructed, possibly to avoid any metaphysical cause of the universe. On the whole it is right that Physics does try to avoid resorting to metaphysical causes. As we say in section 2.7., science is a conversation between man and the natural order, in which, according to the Judaeo-Christian tradition, God does not interfere. Because man has been left to get on with it, he should not invoke a supernatural cause the moment he encounters something inexplicable in his research results. He should press on with the research. This is important because science is not the means to establish whether there is or is not a Creator; it is a misuse of science to attempt to do so. Science may have developed as a result of Judaeo-Christian insights, but the process should not be reversed to attempt to prove the veracity of those insights.

12.4. Human Time from Metaphysical Causality

The metaphysical element in the argument arises when the Judaeo-Christian tradition is consulted because that tradition rests on the eternal otherness of God, that he is not integral or composite to the temporal-spatial regime of creation but rather absolutely differentiated from it, and yet, he engages with it and make himself present to it in the most intimate way he can, through the Incarnation of Jesus Christ. What Jesus Christ is, then, is the intersection between the eternal, uncontained God and the space-time continuum.

In the Incarnation of Jesus Christ, God appropriates space and time as his own. It is not part of him, but it is the field in which he exercises his regnant freedom. This must introduce contingence into a regime which from physical considerations we might regard as highly determined. The Judaeo-Christian witness also confirms at many points that past events have a present and future power and significance. In section 4.1. we considered the act of divine recollection which was to bring the truth of a past event to bear on the present. The presupposition of the Judaeo-Christian testimony is that those past events are, indeed, real, even eternal. So contrary to the Eleatic thought of Parmenides, who considered only present events real, events in the rest of the space-time continuum are taken with equal seriousness as those of the present, and indeed, some with much greater seriousness.

The space-time continuum, in this reading, becomes a library of truth, information and assets which are accessed by recollection and applied to a present circumstance. This is actually how Christianity works in so many ways. The forgiveness of present sins is accomplished by applying the past event of the Cross to the penitent. The Resurrection (about which, more later) is similarly applied to the faithful to enable them to live the Christian life. This is far more than a past illustration or example, or inspiration. It is sacramental: an act of God in the space-time continuum.

When the Christian Creed speaks of the *communion of saints*, what it refers to is living fellowship of all those who belong to Jesus Christ from everywhere in space-time. The people of God are not merely recognised as heroes and champions of the past, they are *remembered*, in the full sense of the term: brought forward and made present wherever Christ is. The Church militant is always in their company.

Similar lines of reasoning can be applied to future events. The Judaeo-Christian witnesses expect the return of Jesus Christ as the fulfilment of his reign, the Day of Judgement and the consummation of his Kingdom in a 'new heaven and new earth.' This event, albeit lying in the future, is taken as seriously as the events of Christ in the past and is even, to some extent, anticipated by the deliberate efforts of Christians to live according to the realities in Christ's Kingdom now. These efforts are limited in scope and not fully successful, but they do confirm the seriousness with which the future events are viewed.

12.5. Resurrection Time

This intersection between the space-time block and the eternity of God as it took place in the Incarnation, raises another perspective on the nature of time through the specific event of the resurrection of Jesus Christ. As we saw in section 2.6., N. T. Wright has demonstrated that the resurrection of the body of Jesus to life in an apparently new order, was absolutely discontinuous with any Greek concepts of post-death existence although it was predicted theologically by the pharisaic tradition of the Jews, but not witnessed until Jesus Christ. Thomas Torrance has astutely noted the consequences of this resurrection on our understanding of time. He writes: *The kind of time we have in this passing world is the time of an existence that crumbles away into the dust, time that runs backwards into nothingness. Hence the kind of historical happening we have in this world is happening that decays and is so far illusory, running away into the darkness and forgetfulness of the past. As happening within this kind of time, and as event within this kind of history, the resurrection, by being what it is, resists and overcomes corruption and decay, and is therefore a new kind of historical happening which instead of tumbling down into the grave and oblivion, rises out of the death of what is past into continuing being and reality. This is temporal happening that runs not backwards but forwards and overcomes all illusion or privation of being. This is fully real historical happening, so real that it remains real happening and does not slip away from us, but keeps pace with us and outruns us as we tumble down in decay and lapse into death and the dust of past history, and even comes to meet us out of the future. That is how we are to think of the risen Christ Jesus. He is not dead but alive, more real than any of*

356

us, because he does not decay or become fixed in the past. He lives on in the present as real live continuous happening, encountering us here and now in the present and waiting for us in the future (5).

What is being said here, is that although the event of the resurrection of Jesus Christ is a historical event and thus takes its place in what we have called the library of the past, nevertheless, the subject of that resurrection, Jesus Christ himself, is not merely a volume, so to speak, in that historical library, but sharing the eternity of the Father, has the run of the whole space-time continuum and is therefore able to keep pace with us, overtake us, and fill the future.

There is an interesting parallel here between the conclusions of modern physics concerning space and time, and the theological deductions which flow from the witness of the Apostles concerning Jesus' resurrection. As in other considerations about space and time, there is no exactness about the relationship between these two sets of observations, but they are of the same inclination and inference. The aspiration of time travel, distant though it may be, the ability to move around the space-time continuum and explore it as the cosmos is being progressively explored, has a consistency with the vision of Christ's liberty in exercising his reign in what Torrance calls 'resurrection time'.

12.6. Time, memory and hope

In section 12.2., above, we observed that the mediaeval period was characterised by the conscious living of people in that intersection between our space and time and the eternity of God. The constancy of divine involvement in their lives through sacramental actions, the continual reminders of God in every aspect of their lives, brought a powerful contrast between the joys and glory of divine life and the painful pilgrimage of human existence. In our own day, we have forgotten all this in our search for a universal secularism which makes no demand of faith. The result has been a bland featurelessness of life which contains so little real stimulus that we are tempted to create artificial dangers to amuse us or to take drugs which temporarily heighten our conscious perceptions or alternatively blank them out altogether as we lapse into stupor. We've given up standing in the portals of heaven and taken up meth-amphetamines or bungee-jumping instead. We can scarcely be blamed for that, because when we go to the local church or even to a cathedral, we find all the Christians seemed to have abandoned life in the heavenly realms too, and now are preoccupied with their building fund and food bank.

The devoted opponents of "substance abuse" cannot seem to understand why we are dissatisfied with the safe, moderately comfortable ordinariness which they presuppose is the optimum of human existence. Clement Freud's famous aphorism, that *you don't live longer if you don't smoke, - it only seems like it,* sums up the tedium of safe and healthy living. But we are not satisfied with it. And that fact alone is something which Peter Berger might regard as a 'rumour of angels' - it is a hint that after all we were made to live in that intersection between space-time and the eternity of God, that intersection which is the resurrection life of Jesus Christ (6).

But has time moved on and civilisation changed, even some will say 'matured,' to a point where we can only expect life to consist of an interminable wait at a drab bus stop in the drizzling twilight, as C. S. Lewis envisaged hell? (7) Or could we hope and seek for something better? Could we get back to a life with God in that transcendent intersection of time with eternity? There are two answers to that question. The first is yes, because of what we know of God's intention that we should after all inherit his kingdom. It is the intention of God that the Prodigal returns and takes up his inheritance under God's generous terms and not via his own renegotiation. If the Judaeo-Christian witnesses are sure of anything, it is that God has the will and power to save man, and that he assuredly will do so. The second answer is also yes, because, we have been granted the power of decision. We can decide where to live, and how to spend our lives. We can choose meth-amphetamines or bungee-jumping or we can seek out that intersection between space-time and God's eternity; we can retrace our steps to that intersection which is Jesus Christ himself.

REFERENCES FOR CHAPTER 12
(1) Karl Barth, *Church Dogmatics, Volume 4:2*, p473
(2) J. Huizinga, *The Waning of the Middle Ages*, p13
(3) Adrian Bardon, *A Brief History of the Philosophy of Time*, p24
(4) Adrian Bardon, *Ibid*, p165
(5) Thomas Torrance, *Space, Time and Resurrection*, p90
(6) Peter Berger, *Rumour of Angels*
(7) C. S. Lewis, *The Great Divorce*

APPENDIX 1
THE QUALITY OF EVIDENCE PROVIDED BY THE NEW TESTAMENT

In this appendix we review the basic witness of the Bible and assess its reliability and trustworthiness. Enormous effort has been expended in this direction over centuries and we cannot hope to do justice to is all, but sufficient information can be given to justify the reliance that the Church has placed on its evidence and to demonstrate its integrity. In a court of law, two qualities of witnesses are taken into account: the credibility of a witness and the reliability of his evidence. Credibility has to do with whether he is telling the truth and his evidence is trustworthy. Reliability has to do with whether he was in a good position to see well what he now testifies to in court. Both of these are important: a witness may be credible but not have seen much. Or his testimony may be reliable even though his recollection is muddled. However, the best witnesses are both credible and reliable. It will be the purpose of this short appendix to demonstrate that the canonical scriptures exhibit both of these characteristics.

A1.1. The Life and Letters of St Paul

The dating of the life, ministry and letters of St Paul has been exhaustively studied by, among others, Ramsay in the 19th Century (1), by Kummel (2) and Robinson(3) in the 20th. Robinson's dating was subject to criticism when it was first published, but since then has gained considerable respect. It is reproduced in the table below.

AD 33	Paul's conversion and visit to Damascus	Galatians 1:27
AD 35	Paul's first visit to Jerusalem	Acts 9:26
	Flight to Tarsus from whence Barnabas fetches him	Acts 11:25
AD 46	Paul's second visit to Jerusalem (famine relief)	Acts 11:29,12:25
	Paul and Barnabas return to Antioch	Acts 13:1
AD 47-48	First Missionary Journey (Cyprus, Perga, Pisidian Antioch, Iconium, Lystra.)	Acts 13
	Paul and Barnabas return to Antioch	Acts 14:19
AD 48	Council of Jerusalem	Acts 15, Galatians 2:1
AD 49-51	Second Missionary Journey (Syria, Galatia, Phrygia, Samothrace Philippi, Thessalonica, Beroea, Athens, Corinth & Ephesus)	Acts 18
AD 51	1 Thessalonians & 2 Thessalonians written at Corinth	1Thessalonians 3:1,6
AD 52-57	Third Missionary Journey. Syria, Galatia, Phrygia, Ephesus, In Ephesus for 2 -3 years, then Macedonia, Corinth, Achaia, Philippi, Miletus	Acts 20:31
AD 55	1 Corinthians and 1 Timothy written in Ephesus	
AD 56	2 Corinthians and Galatians written in Ephesus	
AD 57	Romans & Titus written in Ephesus	
AD 57	Arrival at Jerusalem	
AD 57-59	Imprisonment in Caesarea	
AD 58	Spring Philippians written and despatched via Epaphroditus to Philippi	Phil 2:25

AD 58 Summer	Philemon & Colossians written, Timothy sent to Philippi Ephesians written and despatched with two other letters via Tychicus Mark sent to Colossae	Phil. 2:19
AD 58 Autumn	2 Timothy written and despatched to Philippi	
AD 60-62	Imprisonment in Rome	

J A T Robinson's work has revealed how much precision can attend the reading of the New Testament and particularly the detail of times, people and places has shown that the presumptions of the Wredestrasse (see chapter 3) to be seriously wide of the mark. As Birger Gerhardsson has remarked, in the New Testament, we are far from any theological constructions from unidentified, anonymous groups in unknown locations. The persons we encounter in the text have names and are found in identifiable locations at known times (4). Robinson's early dating of the books of the New Testament is supported strongly by the observation that the destruction of the Jewish Temple in AD 66 is never capitalised upon in any of the arguments made by the authors. In their efforts against the Judaisers in Galatians and in Hebrews and in many other places, the fact that the Temple was no longer standing, and was longer available for the offering of atoning sacrifices would have been an irresistible argument if it had been available. But it evidently was not, thus placing the New Testament books before AD 66.

A1.2. Dating the Book of Acts

In the market place of the old city of Corinth, archaeologists found a raised stone dais, on which a Latin inscription indicated that it had been the judgement seat and this is very probably the place to which Paul was dragged by the Jews, saying, *This fellow is persuading men to worship God contrary to the law* (Acts 18:12-16). The proconsul Gallio refused to intervene and sent them all away. The date of this event was not known until in old Delphi, a letter was found from the emperor Claudius which referred to *Lucius Junius Gallio, my friend, the proconsul of Achaia.....*, and which was dated at the beginning of the year AD 52. Since proconsuls left Rome to take up their year-long appointments on June 1st each year, Gallio arrived in Achaia about July 1st AD 51. According to Acts 18:11, Paul *stayed a year and six months, teaching the word of God among them.* before Gallio arrived so we can place Paul's arrival at Corinth at the beginning of AD 50 (5).

A1.3. The Available Manuscripts

The question arises, how do we know that we now have what they originally wrote? The antiquity and number of manuscripts available to establish the best possible reading of the biblical witness are impressive and far exceed in evidential quality, the authorities for many extra-biblical texts. The following table illustrates this:

WORK,	WHEN WRITTEN	EARLIEST COPY,	TIME SPAN,	NUMBER OF COPIES
Herodotus,	488-428 BC,	AD900,	1300yrs,	8
Thucydides	c460-400BC,	cAD 900,	1300 yrs,	8
Tacitus	AD100	AD1100	1000yrs	20
Caesar's Gallic Wars	58-50BC,	AD900	950yrs	9-10
Livy Roman History	59BC-AD17	AD900	950yrs	20
New Testament	40- AD100,	AD350, fragments: AD100-130	300 years	5000+ Greek, 10,000 Latin, 9,300 other manuscripts

The oldest surviving fragment of the New Testament is the Rylands papyrus. This dates from about 100 AD and contains part of John chapter 18. It was found in Alexandria and since St John did not die until about 95 AD, it shows that copies of his gospel were circulating around the Ancient World during his lifetime.

A1.4. An Example of the Quality of the Textual Evidence of the New Testament?

e have texts and early versions of Paul's Letter to the Philippians. The text is preserved in three fragmentary papyri, eighteen parchment uncials (of which nine contain the entire text, three are fragmentary, and six are accompanied by commentary), and more than 625 minuscules . The earliest is P46, one of the three Chester Beatty papyri of the New Testament. It dates from about AD 200 and contains 1:1, 5-15, 17-28, 30-2:12, 14-27, 29-3:8,

10-21; 4:2-12, 14-23. A second early papyrus is P16, which dates from the 3rd or 4th century and contains 3:10-17 and 4:2-8. The three earliest parchment uncials that contain the entire text of Philippians are Codex Sinaiticus, Codex Vaticanus, and Codex Alexandrinus. These five manuscripts, plus three minuscules containing Philippians (33, 1739, and 2427), belong to the text critical category I, which indicates that they are of a very special quality, and should always be considered in establishing the original text. There are ten additional manuscripts of Philippians that are of generally high quality and belong to the next class, Category II. They include three 5th-century fragmentary uncials (04, 016, and 048), the bilingual codex Claromontanus (6th century), Pei (ca. AD 700) and 5 minuscules (81, 1175, 1881, 2127, and 2464). On the basis of these and other witnesses, a reliable text of Philippians which involves no major textual problems can be reconstructed (6).

A1.5. Biblical Studies in Prison during the Decian Persecution

Robin Lane Fox writes: *Dionius made his prison a rival to the city's literary Museum. Christians did not sit idly in the prisons' darkness. Confessors in Rome told Cyprian how they were studying their Bible, and then proved the point by citing proof texts on martyrdom. The evidence of prison scholarship is still written clearly on one surviving biblical manuscript. A text of the Book of Esther cites its remarkable origin: 'copied and corrected against the Hexapla of Origen', runs its subscription, 'as corrected by Origen himself. The confessor Antoninus collated. I, Pamphilus, corrected the roll in prison.' Pamphilus was a devoted pupil of Origen, and while he waited in Caesarea's prison, he had practised his master's art of biblical scholarship. Pamphilus worked on Scripture, whereas martyrs like Perpetua kept diaries. Pionius practised prison 'philology,' and among it, he recorded his speeches and the story of his own captivity (7).*

The above represent but a tiny fraction of the detailed and comprehensive studies of the quality, authenticity and dependability of the text of the New Testament. The references quoted below will open the reader to a mine of information which testifies both to the reliability and to the credibility of the witnesses within it.

REFERENCES FOR APPENDIX 1

(1) Sir William Ramsay, *St Paul the Traveller and the Roman Citizen*,1895

(2) W. G. Kummel, *Introduction to the New Testament*, 1966

(3) J. A. T. Robinson, *Redating the New Testament*, 1977.

(4) Birger Gerhardsson, *Memory and Manuscript,* 1964

(5) Werner Keller, *The Bible as History*, 1956, p363-5

(6) D. N. Freedman (Ed), *The Anchor Bible Dictionary, Volume 5* p324.

(7) Robin Lane Fox, *Pagans and Christians*, p471

INDEX

24025116R00213

Printed in Great Britain
by Amazon